Temporal Boundaries of Law and Politics

In the last decade, the changing role of time in society has once again taken centre stage in the academic debate. A prominent, but surely not the only, aspect of this debate hinges on the so-called acceleration of time and its societal consequences. Despite the fact that time is fundamental to the way in which law and politics function, the influence of the contemporary experience of time on law and politics remains underdeveloped. How, for example, does society's structural acceleration impact on justice? Does law actually offer stability and predictability in an ever changing global world? How can legal and political institutions function in the wake of ever increasing uncertainty? Both law and politics employ time to order society but they are also limited in what can be effectuated by time. It is this very tension between temporal possibilities and limitations that the contributors to this collection – drawn from different fields of law, as well as from other disciplines – examine.

Luigi Corrias is Assistant Professor of Legal Philosophy, Vrije Universiteit Amsterdam.

Lyana Francot is Associate Professor of Legal Theory, Vrije Universiteit Amsterdam.

Part of the

LAW AND POLITICS:
CONTINENTAL PERSPECTIVES

Series

Series Editors
Mariano Croce, *Sapienza University of Rome, Italy*
Marco Goldoni, *University of Glasgow, UK*

For information about the series and details of previous and forthcoming titles, see https://www.routledge.com/law/series/LPCP

A GlassHouse book

Temporal Boundaries of Law and Politics

Time Out of Joint

Edited by
Luigi Corrias and Lyana Francot

Routledge
Taylor & Francis Group
LONDON AND NEW YORK

First published 2018 by Routledge

2 Park Square, Milton Park, Abingdon, Oxfordshire OX14 4RN
52 Vanderbilt Avenue, New York, NY 10017

Routledge is an imprint of the Taylor & Francis Group, an informa business

First issued in paperback 2019

British Library Cataloguing in Publication Data
A catalogue record for this book is available from the British Library

Library of Congress Cataloging in Publication Data
Names: Corrias, Luigi, editor. | Francot, Lyana, editor.
Title: Temporal boundaries of law and politics : time out of joint / [edited by] Luigi Corrias, Lyana Francot
Description: Abingdon, Oxon ; New York, NY : Routledge, 2018. | Series: Law and politics : continental perspectives | Includes bibliographical references and index.
Identifiers: LCCN 2017051591 | ISBN 9781138693975 (hbk)
Subjects: LCSH: Time (Law)--Philosophy. | Law--History.
Classification: LCC K579.T5 T458 2018 | DDC 340/.11--dc23
LC record available at https://lccn.loc.gov/2017051591

ISBN: 978-1-138-69397-5 (hbk)
ISBN: 978-0-367-40438-3 (pbk)

Typeset in Galliard
by Taylor & Francis Books

Contents

List of contributors vii

Temporal boundaries of politics and law: time out of joint 1
LUIGI CORRIAS AND LYANA FRANCOT

PART 1
Justice 13

1 Judging the past: three ways of understanding time 15
ANTOINE GARAPON

2 Law at the right time: a plea for slow law in hasty times 33
BART VAN KLINK

3 Law, time and inhumanity: reflections on the imprescriptible 53
LUIGI CORRIAS

PART 2
Legal certainty 71

4 Airports built on shifting grounds? Social acceleration and the temporal dimension of law 73
HARTMUT ROSA

5 Suspended in Gaffa: legal slowness in the acceleration society 88
LYANA FRANCOT

6 Uncertain futures and the problem of constraining emergency powers: temporal dimensions of Carl Schmitt's theory of the state of exception 107
MARC DE WILDE

7 Constitutional preambles and the uncertain future 126
NOMI CLAIRE LAZAR

PART 3
Expediency 147

8 Collective memory, constitutional polity and differentiation of modern society 149
JIŘÍ PŘIBÁŇ

9 Informing life: temporal politics of information in the administration of pandemics 170
SVEN OPITZ

10 Immediacy, *potentia* and constraining emergency powers 192
BAS SCHOTEL

Index 204

Contributors

Luigi Corrias is Assistant Professor of Legal Philosophy, Department of Legal Theory and Legal History, Vrije Universiteit Amsterdam (The Netherlands).

Lyana Francot is Associate Professor of Legal Theory, Department of Legal Theory and Legal History, Vrije Universiteit Amsterdam (The Netherlands).

Antoine Garapon is Secretary General of the Institut des Hautes Etudes sur la Justice (France).

Bart van Klink is Professor of Legal Methodology, Department of Legal Theory and Legal History, Vrije Universiteit Amsterdam (The Netherlands).

Nomi Claire Lazar is Associate Professor, Public and International Affairs, Faculty of Social Sciences, University of Ottawa (Canada).

Sven Opitz is University Professor, Institut für Soziologie, Philipps-University Marburg (Germany).

Jiří Přibáň is Professor of Law, School of Law and Politics, Cardiff University (United Kingdom).

Hartmut Rosa is Professor of Sociology, Friedrich-Schiller-University Jena and Director of the Max-Weber-Kolleg Erfurt (Germany).

Bas Schotel is Assistant Professor of Jurisprudence, Faculty of Law, University of Amsterdam (The Netherlands).

Marc de Wilde is Professor of Jurisprudence, Faculty of Law, University of Amsterdam (The Netherlands).

Temporal boundaries of politics and law: time out of joint

Luigi Corrias and Lyana Francot

> Let us go in together,
> And still your fingers on your lips, I pray.
> The time is out of joint – O cursèd spite,
> That ever I was born to set it right!
> Nay, come, let's go together.
> *Hamlet* Act 1, scene 5, 186–190

Introduction

Our time is out of joint. The global state of affairs appears – not unlike Hamlet's Denmark – dislocated, chaotic, violent and uncertain. We live with an enduring terrorist threat, materializing in attacks such as those in New York, Madrid, Paris, Brussels and London. The threat has evoked a war on terrorism by nation-states, a war that has proved to be a game changer when it comes to fundamental rules and values, such as the rule of law, legal certainty and justice. Caught right in the middle of this war are we, the citizens. We live in an enduring 'state of exception'.[1] The rights to privacy, freedom of movement and of speech, just to name a few, are under siege now that safety and security prevail.

The experience of dislocation and uncertainty is exacerbated by the recent migration waves. These dislocate refugees to whom the world cannot but seem an increasingly inhospitable place, as they try to escape the violence in one state just to find the often harsh and violently expressed fear of citizens on the other end.[2] No less significant are the global ecological problems that put contemporary society at a juncture: how, if at all, can we bring the man-made damage to our environment to a halt or at least slow down the climate change that seems to accelerate more and more?

Unlike Hamlet, we as individuals cannot even hope to set it right and heal our time. Undoubtedly, individual contributions count and are indispensable. But the magnitude of the challenges we are facing requires a joint effort. Can we, as a

1 Giorgio Agamben, *Homo Sacer: Sovereign Power and Bare Life*, trans. Daniel Heller-Roazen (Stanford: Stanford University Press, 1998).

2 Zygmunt Bauman, *Strangers at Our Door* (Cambridge: Polity Press, 2016).

society or as a community, set it right? For solutions we turn to law and politics, the problem solvers of modernity. Law, certainly in modernity, was and still is to a certain extent, considered a solid safety net: it provides rules that seek to offer legal certainty and justice. Politics, especially in the guise of the state, claims to secure life, liberty and property. In its war on terrorism, the nation-state seeks to fortify this claim once again. Law and politics are, however, at least partially, also at the root of our contemporary problems.

The foregoing sketches a global social and spatial disjuncture. Still, there is more, since the discordance of the temporal dimension is omnipresent. The war on terrorism shows us that past experiences cannot fully anticipate, let alone prevent, new strikes. The battle against climate change necessitates rules and measures that have to deal not with one uncertain future but with multiple ones: since we need to take decisions here and now, without complete knowledge of the consequences, we need to come up with alternative scenarios for our future. The urgency of environmental problems also leaves us with less and less time to decide, in the present, how to cope with future climate problems. Finally, the mass migration waves illustrate how a violent past collides with the hope of a better future as the present is happening in a no man's land, a void in so many lives – not able to move forward nor to go back.

In this volume, authors inquire into the temporal dimension of law and politics. In itself, the relation between time, politics and law and the temporal dimensions of both systems has been addressed before.[3] It is a recurring research perspective. Nevertheless, we consider it a timely research issue for several reasons. A lot of global developments were triggered or at least facilitated by law, such as world-wide trade, internationalization on all kinds of levels, the development of a European market, functional differentiation and so on. In their turn, these developments affect law, not only at the level of national and supra/international systems but in its very essence. Hence, in a society 'obsessed' with time[4] and characterized by social developments of a global scope, a traditional question regains momentum: what is law? For a thorough analysis and a better understanding of law and its connection with politics, we consider the temporal dimension to be pivotal. How does law 'use' time? What timelines are typical of law? How do these timelines relate to those of other systems, such as politics? And how does our experience of time affect core values of law such as justice, legal certainty and expediency?

3 Examples include Jes Bjarup and Mogens Blegvad, ed., *ARSP Beiheft nr. 64: Time, Law and Society – Proceedings of a Nordic Symposium May 1994 Denmark* (Stuttgart: Steiner Verlag, 1995); François Ost, *Le temps du droit* (Paris: Odile Jacob, 1999). For the variety of conceptualizations of time see: Roberto Cipriani, 'The Many Faces of Social Time: A Sociological Approach', *Time & Society* 22 (2013): 5–30; also see Carol J. Greenhouse, 'Just in Time: Temporality and the Cultural Legitimation of Time', *The Yale Law Journal* 98 (1989): 1631–1651.

4 Elena Esposito, *The Future of Futures: The Time of Money in Financing and Society*, trans. by the author with Andrew K. Whitehead (Cheltenham: Edgar Elgar, 2011).

Justice, legal certainty, expediency

Justice, legal certainty and expediency are three values of law that are central to what both lawyers and non-lawyers seem to regard as essential to law. It is in the work of Gustav Radbruch that one may find one of the best articulations of these values and their relationships. As a short reminder, we would like to discuss these three values and how they relate to each other. Justice is, first and foremost, of a distributive nature. It postulates that – in the ancient wording – each should get his due (*suum cuique tribuere*).[5] Hence, it starts from the viewpoint of a third (e.g. the state) who distributes among different parties.[6] In this regard, it is crucial that the distribution is done equally. In other words, the idea of distributive justice boils down to the demand of formal equality. However, formal equality leaves two questions unanswered. First, who is equal to whom? Second, what constitutes an 'equal treatment'?[7] The idea of formal equality is in need of a material elaboration.[8] This is done by way of the different goals law may have. Here, Radbruch introduces the idea of expediency to answer the two questions of formal equality. Expediency, or *Zweckmäßigkeit*,[9] denotes that law always has a purpose.[10] Now, these purposes are given to law by politics, or, more precisely, by the political goals of the ruling majority.[11] Yet, political discussions are (virtually) endless and may lead to (violent) conflicts. We call upon the law to end these conflicts. Here, Radbruch argues, we find another value of law: legal certainty. At the end of the day, law should (also) procure order by providing for peaceful means to end potentially violent conflicts.[12]

5 Gustav Radbruch, 'Legal Philosophy', in *The Legal Philosophies of Lask, Radbruch, and Dabin*, trans. by Kurt Wilk, (Cambridge, Mass.: Harvard University Press, 1950), 74: 'Relative equality in treating different persons, e.g., taxation according to ability to bear the tax, or relief according to need, or reward and punishment according to merit and guilt, is the essence of "distributive" justice.'

6 Gustav Radbruch, 'Legal Philosophy', 74.

7 Gustav Radbruch, 'Legal Philosophy', 75.

8 Gustav Radbruch, 'Legal Philosophy', 75: 'In either direction, justice needs to be complemented by other principles if rules of right law are to be derived from it.'

9 Other translators make use of the term purposiveness. While this might be a better translation, we stick here to expediency for practical reasons.

10 Gustav Radbruch, 'Legal Philosophy', 91: 'Justice determines only the form of the law. In order to get the content of the law, a second idea must be added, viz., expediency.'

11 Radbruch connects expediency with the purpose of the state, cf. Gustav Radbruch, 'Legal Philosophy', 91. Here, we deviate from his views, since his emphasis on the role of the state would not do justice to the role of other actors in formulating the purposes of the law, e.g. international organizations.

12 Gustav Radbruch, 'Legal Philosophy', 108: 'the question of purpose and expediency could not be answered unequivocally but only relativistically, by the systematic development of the different views of law and the state, the views of the different parties. Yet that relativism cannot remain the last word of legal philosophy. The law as the order of living together cannot be handed over to disagreements between the views of individuals; it must be one order over all of them. So we are confronted with a third

We consider these three aspects as important now as they were in Radbruch's era. Hence, we chose to use them as the framework of this volume. Nevertheless, the world has changed considerably ever since these ideas were first introduced and this demands a reconsideration of the meaning of these values. This reconsideration should not be understood as a rejection of Radbruch's ideas. Rather, our reconsideration seeks to replenish and complement Radbruch's views. To start with justice, from the two World Wars onwards we have seen that it is not enough to think of justice as formal equality. There is a need to encapsulate the temporal dimension of justice, for example, when one is called to resolve questions concerning historical injustice or restorative justice.[13] The past thus seems to last longer and longer, spilling over in the present and in the future. The temporal dimension, especially but not solely the past, cannot be grasped by a conception of justice which takes its starting point in the situation of justice between equals living *at (roughly) the same place and at the same time*. Doing justice to past injustices thus exceeds the limits of Radbruch's theory.

In Radbruch's view, expediency seems to presuppose foreseeable purposes or goals.[14] These are ends we can and should know. The war on terrorism shows, however, that the ultimate end of fighting terror has become highly abstract, even to the extent that one may speak of a 'desirable state' rather than of an attainable goal. Indeed, besides the so-called 'known unknowns', theorists now distinguish 'unknown unknowns'.[15] While the former category seems to be still included by Radbruch, the latter goes beyond what he could have imagined. The temporal dimension of the 'unknown unknowns' involves the relation between a present which leaves less and less time to take decisions because of a future moving in faster and faster.

Legal certainty seems to demand clear-cut rules in order for citizens to know what to expect in future situations.[16] Thus, foreseeability and the possibility to adapt one's behavior according to foreseeable actions is at the very heart of legal certainty and hence of order. At times that it becomes increasingly difficult to know what to expect and when, it is nearly impossible to foresee the future. As a result, the legislator prefers framework legislation above more concrete norms. The uncertain future also requires flexibility of the law to the extent that legal certainty is limited to the existence of open norms. It is, in other words, the judge who assumes the main responsibility for taking a decision in uncertain

postulate concerning law, ranking with the other two, a third element of the idea of law: legal certainty.'

13 Wouter Veraart, 'Forgetting, Remembering, Forgiving, and the Mundane Legal Order', in *Public Forgiveness in Post-Conflict Contexts*, eds. Bas van Stokkom, Neelke Doorn and Paul van Tongeren (Cambridge-Antwerp-Portland: Intersentia, 2012): 65–89.

14 For Radbruch, the idea of law's purpose is linked to absolute values, of which he distinguishes only three. These absolute values connect with corresponding worldviews and, finally, views on law and state: individualism, transindividualism (or collectivism) and transpersonalism, cf. Gustav Radbruch, 'Legal Philosophy', 90–97.

15 Cf. Claudia Aradau and Rens van Munster, *Politics of Catastrophe: Genealogies of the Unknown* (Abingdon: Routledge, 2011).

16 Gustav Radbruch, 'Legal Philosophy', 109: 'But legal certainty (…) demands that the law be capable of being administered with certainty, that it be practicable.'

circumstances. This pertains to the fact that she has to deal with incomplete information about what a norm may entail.

When it comes to the relationship between the three values constituting the idea of law, Radbruch has famously argued that they are antinomies.[17] This entails that they both need one another and are in a relation of constant tension.[18] From what we have written earlier, it can easily be discerned that the three values need each other. Formal equality cannot answer two questions – who is equal to whom and what is an equal treatment – and we thus need expediency. The political views underlying expediency are, however, themselves in constant conflict with one another, so we need legal certainty to end this conflict. Moreover, emphasizing only one of these values without any regard to the other two might be a recipe for what Radbruch calls 'fatal one-sidedness'.[19] We cannot do without all three values. Nevertheless, tensions abound.[20] Justice asks for equality, while expediency individualizes. Both of these values may also come into conflict with the positivity of law which is required from legal certainty. The early Radbruch argues that the relationship between the three values is relative.[21] He stresses the value of legal certainty and even calls it the first task of law.[22] After the Second World War, in his formula Radbruch famously stated that in some circumstances the demands of justice may trump the value of legal certainty. Indeed, in the case of an unbearable tension with the value of equality, positive law may never have become valid.[23]

While justice doubtlessly resonates with lawyers and citizens as the first function of law and its most emblematic value, nowadays we witness the preeminence of the instrumental role of law. This has even led to a dominant instrumentalism in

17 Gustav Radbruch, 'Legal Philosophy', 111: 'So our result is this, that the three aspects of the idea of law, justice, expediency, and certainty of the law, jointly govern law in all its aspects, although they may sharply contradict one another.'
18 Gustav Radbruch, 'Legal Philosophy', 109.
19 Gustav Radbruch, 'Legal Philosophy', 111.
20 Gustav Radbruch, 'Legal Philosophy', 109–111.
21 Gustav Radbruch, 'Legal Philosophy', 109: 'Universally valid elements of the idea of the law are justice and legal certainty; a relativistic element, however, is not only expediency itself but also the rank of the three elements relative to each other.'
22 Gustav Radbruch, 'Legal Philosophy', 108.
23 Gustav Radbruch, 'Statutory Lawlessness and Supra-Statutory Law', trans. by Bonnie Litschewski Paulson and Stanley L. Paulson, *Oxford Journal of Legal Studies* 26 (2006): 1–11, 7: 'The conflict between justice and legal certainty may well be resolved in this way: The positive law, secured by legislation and power, takes precedence even when its content is unjust and fails to benefit the people, unless the conflict between statute and justice reaches such an intolerable degree that the statute, as "flawed law", must yield to justice. It is impossible to draw a sharper line between cases of statutory lawlessness and statutes that are valid despite their flaws. One line of distinction, however, can be drawn with utmost clarity: Where there is not even an attempt at justice, where equality, the core of justice, is deliberately betrayed in the issuance of positive law, then the statute is not merely 'flawed law', it lacks completely the very nature of law. For law, including positive law, cannot be otherwise defined than as a system and an institution whose very meaning is to serve justice. Measured by this standard, whole portions of National Socialist law never attained the dignity of valid law.'

the sense that law seems to be called upon to solve all kinds of societal problems and it is only (or at least primarily) evaluated by how effectively and efficiently it does this. Note that both effectiveness and efficiency are instrumental criteria. In this view, justice and legal certainty do not vanish but they have to yield to the primacy of expediency. In a society marked by all-pervasive contingency and a structural process of acceleration, justice is rapidly becoming a luxury and legal certainty becomes an untenable ideal.

The growing role of expediency may be discerned in the organizational part of adjudication and access to justice. In the Netherlands, for example, this has put a lot of pressure on the judiciary. Due to the general acceleration of society, judges are also expected to do their job faster. In evaluations, efficiency becomes increasingly important.[24] This has led to protests from the judiciary. Around the same time, access to justice was made more difficult because of cuts in the budget for legal representation. Also in other countries the political pressure on the judiciary, and thus the primacy of expediency over justice and legal certainty, becomes visible. Here, the threat does not so much come from different societal demands but from the populist challenge to the judiciary and to the *Rechtsstaat* in general. In countries like Poland and Hungary, the 'undemocratic constitutional courts' are systematically robbed of their influence by, for example, forcing the judges into early retirement, diminishing the time a person can remain judge in the court and the nomination of government-friendly judges.[25] While using the language of constitutionalism, populists often adapt constitutional democracy to fit their own narrative of a 'politics of immediacy'.[26]

24 Lyana Francot and Sophie Mommers, 'Picking up the Pace – Legal Slowness and the Authority of the Judiciary in the Acceleration Society (a Dutch Case Study)', *International Journal of the Legal Profession*, 23 (2016), 1: 'Complaints from both private and public actors about the slow delivery of justice are the rule rather than the exception. This "system overload" in terms of cases not only roots in the increased demand for justice by its "consumers" – first and foremost the autonomous and emancipated citizens – but is exacerbated by the managerial reforms imposed upon the Dutch judiciary in the last decades. These reforms are without exception presented as measures to improve and guarantee the quality of the administration of justice but bring along massive financial cutbacks and an irreversible turn from "institution" to "business".'

25 For the Hungarian situation, the judgment of the ECtHR in *Baka v. Hungary*, (Grand Chamber, 23 June 2016), (appl. no. 20261/12) is very relevant. For a commentary on the judgment, see Pieter Cannoot, 'Baka v. Hungary: judicial independence at risk in Hungary's new constitutional reality', July, 12, 2016, accessed February, 9, 2017 https://strasbourgobservers.com/2016/07/12/baka-v-hungary-judicialindependence-at-risk-in-hungarys-new-constitutional-reality/. For a critical assessment of the way in which the government managed to 'pack the court' in Poland, see Tomasz Tadeusz Koncewicz, 'Farewell to the Polish Constitutional Court', VerfassungsBlog, July, 9, 2016, accessed February, 9, 2017, http://verfassungsblog.de/farewell-to-the-polish-constitutional-court/

26 For more on this, see Luigi Corrias, 'Populism in a Constitutional Key: Constituent Power, Popular Sovereignty and Constitutional Identity', *European Constitutional Law Review* 12 (2016): 6–26.

The hegemony of expediency may also be witnessed in the instrumental use of criminal law in the above-mentioned 'war on terrorism'. The threat of terrorist attacks has led to security being conceived as the primary political goal. In this picture, security is the objective to be attained, criminal law the instrument to attain it.[27] Hence, the police may use far-reaching investigative powers more easily and earlier. In the US, the discussion on the legality of torture was reopened.[28] In the Netherlands, the Ministry of Justice was recently renamed the Ministry of Security and Justice (note the order of the two tasks). While no one denies the importance of security or the role of criminal law in 'policing society', here, too, the balance seems to be lost. For criminal law also serves the values of legal certainty and justice. These values are translated into criminal law as its core principles, such as legality, habeas corpus and the right to a fair trial, amongst others. The pursuit of these principles may save criminal law from sliding into abuse of (state) power and the Kafkaesque scenarios which this may entail.

An overview of the chapters

In line with Radbruch's theory, we have ordered the contributions to this volume under the headings of justice, legal certainty and expediency. In *Part I*, devoted to justice, there are three chapters

In his contribution, **Antoine Garapon** focuses on how judges deal with historic injustice. He argues that judging history reveals three types of temporality: a new regime of historicity, a new era for institutions, and an ability to make the past present. Transitional justice, he argues, does not mark the end of history as some have claimed; rather, it brings an end to a specific regime of historicity. This intrusion of justice into historical matters marks a transition from historical time, dominated by the future, to one that is commanded by the present and grounded in disaster, which simply will not go away. The intrusion of courts into historical matters is not a product of judicial institutions; rather, he argues it is the consequence of a more substantive shift, a new attitude towards the past that will have repercussions on the international system and its bedrock Westphalian articulation of domestic and international law, resting on the principle of equality of state sovereignty. This new role for justice, however, reveals a world order more akin to medieval Christendom, in which morality emanated from an independent, spiritual

27 For a critical evaluation of the main EU measures taken immediately after 9/11, see Jan Wouters and Frederik Naert, 'Of Arrest Warrants, Terrorist Offences and Extradition Deals: An Appraisal of the EU's Main Criminal Law Measures against Terrorism after "11 September"', *Common Market Law Review* 41 (2004): 909–935. For a human rights perspective, see Joan Fitzpatrick, 'Speaking Law to Power: The War Against Terrorism and Human Rights', *European Journal of International Law*, 14 (2003): 241–264.

28 For a defence of the absolute prohibition of torture in the wake of this discussion, see Jeremy Waldron, 'Torture and Positive Law: Jurisprudence for the White House', *Columbia Law Review* 105 (2005): 1681–1750.

Magisterium. This role is now given to some courts through the principle of complementarity. Finally, Garapon argues that a fundamental characteristic of any trial is to re-enact history, so that it may be acted upon. This singular use of time can indeed be described as a timeless moment in which historical events are staged in order to be finally overcome.

In his chapter, **Bart van Klink** holds a plea for 'slow law'. He starts from the thesis that law seems to be either too late or too soon, but never 'in time'. It is often too late, because at the very moment that a statute is promulgated, the social norms that it tries to codify may have changed. Moreover, due to rapid technological developments, regulations are doomed to be outdated as soon as they have come into force. At the same time, law sometimes appears to come too soon. People are not always ready for the norms that the law offers. Legislation with a high aspirational character often meets with resistance in society. Furthermore, the legislature is sometimes accused of issuing legislation too quickly, without having taken enough time for deliberation and reflection. Van Klink investigates whether there is a right time for the law. In particular, he focuses on modificatory legislation that aims at changing current or traditional ways of thinking and acting. He tries to identify some principles that could guide the legislature in deciding when it is the right time for making seemingly untimely law and how to do this, that is, by means of which legislative strategies. By prescribing a certain way of doing things by law, there is inherent slowness in the forms that constitute the law. In his view, law should take its time: slowness is exactly what is called for in these hasty times.

In his contribution to the volume, **Luigi Corrias** broaches the topic of imprescriptibility. His starting points are the so-called core international crimes: genocide, crimes against humanity and war crimes. These crimes are all legally imprescriptible in the sense that there are no temporal limitations on the prosecution of suspects of these crimes. The International Criminal Court is, one may argue, established in order to prosecute suspects of these imprescriptible crimes and bring them to justice. The notion of imprescriptibility triggers the question of the relationship between time and law in the face of inhuman suffering and mass atrocities. Corrias sets out to investigate this relationship by distinguishing between legal, historical and philosophical understandings of the imprescriptible. Drawing on legal theoretical sources on the one hand and continental philosophy on the other hand, he outlines the different time lines involved in imprescriptibility and what these entail for the possibilities of doing justice.

The chapters in *Part II* of this volume share a focus on legal certainty.

In his contribution, **Hartmut Rosa** argues that social acceleration has serious consequences for the temporality of law. He starts from the observation that modern societies can be interpreted as 'acceleration-societies', which is to say that the speed of life, and the speed of change, increase incessantly. In such societies, Rosa continues, law serves a double function. On the one hand, it provides for the social stability necessary for long-term investment and long-term planning. Without political and legal stability, social acceleration in the sense of technological progress and economic growth would be impossible. On the other hand, law itself needs to adapt to changing conditions, too. Modern law is no longer supposed to be the expression of 'eternal' or 'timeless' orders, or even to persist over decades or centuries. Instead, law-making, that is legislation, has become a permanent task: Law is made anew again and again. Now, interestingly, it seems that law-making itself is speeding up: The decay rates of legislation are shrinking in most areas of social life. Rosa believes that the only alternative for law to keep its functions in a dynamic social world would be to become more and more formal and 'empty of contents', such that changing social content would not require new legislation. Overall, he warns for the danger that the classic 'rule of law' and its institutions progressively become too slow for the high pace of social life, and hence new forms of mediation and legal plurality pop up.

In her chapter, **Lyana Francot** takes up the thesis of the structural acceleration of society. Complaints about legal slowness are of all times, as is the recurring observation that society is speeding up. However, now that social acceleration has become a structural feature, the experience of legal slowness may acquire central significance when it comes to the position and function of the law in contemporary society. This is due to the fact that modern law is confronted with the social demand to speed up while it is bound to always lag behind: it is a system geared to deal with past events rather than, in general, to anticipate the uncertain future. This discrepancy between the legal tempo and the accelerating tempi in society forms the background for Francot's inquiry into the state of the authority of contemporary law. Drawing upon (critical) systems theory, she maps out the different tempi of the law vis-à-vis social time and the connection between time and authority. More specifically, Francot focuses on courts as they are the core organizations of the legal system. Hence, the central problem is understood in terms of judicial slowness and the potential erosion of the authority of the judge.

The contribution of **Marc de Wilde** looks into the temporal dimensions of the state of exception, with special regard to Carl Schmitt's theory. De Wilde argues that it is characteristic of modern law that it relates to a future it aims to regulate. In times of normality, the future is believed to be largely predictable. By contrast, in times of crisis, the future may suddenly seem uncertain and unpredictable. This different experience of the future has important consequences for our understanding of law: as crises are believed to be uncertain and unpredictable, the legislator cannot determine in advance what measures will be needed to respond to it. Thus, he cannot set strict limits to governmental emergency powers, for this may cause these powers to be insufficiently flexible to cope with the crisis. Hence, emergency powers are generally formulated in wide and vague terms, which makes effective judicial and parliamentary control of these powers virtually impossible. It is thus largely left to the executive to decide whether there is a crisis at all and what measures are necessary to respond to it. De Wilde examines what temporal experiences are characteristic of present-day responses to crises, and how they affect the law's protective capacity. He takes issue with the general assumption that crises are radically uncertain and unpredictable, so that the use of emergency powers can neither be regulated *ex ante* by the legislator, nor effectively controlled *ex post* by judges and parliaments.

The chapter of **Nomi Claire Lazar** takes up the question of how constitutional preambles deal with an uncertain future. Because purposive human action is not possible in a condition of radical uncertainty, constitutions secure structures for political action, delineating rules to guide the otherwise uncertain future behavior. But, Lazar points out, constitutions are not just forward looking, but Janus-headed, bridging the past into an expected arc with the future. When explicit, it is frequently the function of preambles to do the bridging. These preambles reflect diverse conceptions of the flow of time, placing the founding event marked by the preamble in an arc suggestive of conservative progress, of renewal, of eschatological arrival or restoration, etc. These conceptions, in turn, communicate what is taken as certain or even self-evident, beyond contestation with respect to where the state is going and what one might expect the future to bring. However, Lazar argues, not all self-evident truths asserted in preambles are stated explicitly. Others are implied by the temporal frame itself. In this way, the manner in which preambles draw the past into the future can be understood to reflect a legislated balance of certainty and uncertainty which forms part of the state's political identity. What is uncertain depends, in part, on what ought to be expected and it is frequently the job of preambles to delineate precisely this. Thus, the imagined futures that guide our understanding of the law are, in turn, often guided by the law itself.

In *Part III* of the volume, contributors turn their attention to the value of expediency, i.e. the purposiveness of law.

Jiří Přibáň also takes a systems theory approach in his contribution which deals with collective memory and symbolic temporalization in constitutional law. Starting from how memories can be constructed, reconstructed and shared as a common culture in modern society, he argues that societies make up their shared symbolic universe. These symbols possess the expressive power of representing modern functionally differentiated society as a morally and culturally integrated unity. Přibáň points out that the production of social symbols is internally processed by functionally differentiated social systems, such as law and politics. In this regard, the concept of culture refers to the temporal dimension of individual systems and can be functionally and sectorally differentiated into legal cultures, political cultures, economic cultures, scientific cultures etc. Hence, with regard to the legal and political systems and their historical constitutionalization, the concept of culture does not predetermine the existence of constitutional polities and cannot guarantee their normative integration. Instead, the social systems of law and politics constitute the societal symbolic universe by internalizing the temporality of the constitutional polity.

In his chapter, **Sven Opitz** elaborates the temporal dynamics immanent to the contemporary regime of global health security. He is especially interested in the information paradox at the core of governing emergent pandemics: the need to attain information about an entity not yet fully formed. Drawing on Niklas

Luhmann's concept of *Eigenzeit* – the idea that different social logics develop different modes of referring to past, present and future – Opitz highlights the extremely tensed relationship between the temporality of liberal law and the temporality of health security interventions dealing with this information paradox. Whereas liberal law prefers to base its rulings on substantial evidence about completed facts, the government of pandemics targets a future potential of something in formation. Opitz, however, does not content himself with circumscribing the temporal inversion of liberal law in the field of security, something already to be found in the critical literature on preemption and precaution. He rather stresses the necessity to focus on how particular administrative devices imply distinct strategies of acting on processes of contagion about to happen. Making use of Gregory Bateson's concept of information, Opitz analyses both quarantine and computer simulations of pandemics as information technologies that aim at capturing the not yet fully formed. Both exhibit very particular modes of extracting 'differences that make a difference' (Bateson) from a radically uncertain future. Analysing quarantine and pandemic simulations as information technologies, Opitz exemplarily points to the varied temporalities at work in the anticipatory administration of global health security.

In his contribution to the volume, **Bas Schotel** investigates the power to perform factual actions (*potentia*) in times of emergency. His starting point is the fundamental challenge for public law: how to both enable authorities to take effective measures in times of emergency and to restrain those very same emergency powers. Schotel explores how the tendency of emergency powers becoming permanent is reinforced by the temporal dimension of immediacy. In this context, immediacy refers to the capacity of authorities to perform actions without intermediary and immediately. When authorities directly perform factual actions – do physical things – they act immediately. The notion of *potentia* represents the capacity to perform factual actions. Schotel shows how already in times of normality, factual actions and *potentia* defy the law's normal constraints and temporal categories. However, it is especially the combination of *potentia* and emergency which produces a logic of permanent immediacy, making it difficult to put legal constraints on emergency powers.

Bibliography

Agamben, Giorgio. *Homo Sacer: Sovereign Power and Bare Life*, trans. Daniel Heller-Roazen. Stanford: Stanford University Press, 1998.

Aradau, Claudia and Rens van Munster. *Politics of Catastrophe: Genealogies of the Unknown.* Abingdon: Routledge, 2011.

Bauman, Zygmunt. *Strangers at Our Door.* Cambridge: Polity Press, 2016.

Bjarup, Jes and Mogens Blegvad, ed., *ARSP Beiheft nr. 64: Time, Law and Society – Proceedings of a Nordic Symposium May 1994 Denmark.* Stuttgart: Steiner Verlag, 1995.

Cipriani, Roberto. 'The Many Faces of Social Time: A Sociological Approach', *Time & Society* 22 (2013): 5–30.

Corrias, Luigi. 'Populism in a Constitutional Key: Constituent Power, Popular Sovereignty and Constitutional Identity', *European Constitutional Law Review* 12 (2016): 6–26.

Esposito, Elena. *The Future of Futures: The Time of Money in Financing and Society*, trans. by the author with Andrew K. Whitehead. Cheltenham: Edgar Elgar, 2011.

Francot, Lyana and Sophie Mommers. 'Picking up the Pace – Legal Slowness and the Authority of the Judiciary in the Acceleration Society (a Dutch Case Study)', *International Journal of the Legal Profession*, 23 (2016): 1–19.

Greenhouse, Carol J. 'Just in Time: Temporality and the Cultural Legitimation of Time', *The Yale Law Journal* 98 (1989): 1631–1651.

Ost, François. *Le temps du droit.* Paris: Odile Jacob, 1999.

Radbruch, Gustav. 'Legal Philosophy', in *The Legal Philosophies of Lask, Radbruch, and Dabin*, trans. by Kurt Wilk. Cambridge, Mass.: Harvard University Press, 1950.

Radbruch, Gustav. 'Statutory Lawlessness and Supra-Statutory Law', trans. by Bonnie Litschewski Paulson and Stanley L. Paulson, *Oxford Journal of Legal Studies* 26 (2006), 1–11.

Veraart, Wouter. 'Forgetting, Remembering, Forgiving, and the Mundane Legal Order', in *Public Forgiveness in Post-Conflict Contexts*, eds. Bas van Stokkom, Neelke Doorn and Paul van Tongeren, 65–89. Cambridge-Antwerp-Portland: Intersentia, 2012.

Waldron, Jeremy. 'Torture and Positive Law: Jurisprudence for the White House', *Columbia Law Review* 105 (2005): 1681–1750.

Wouters, Jan and Frederik Naert, 'Of Arrest Warrants, Terrorist Offences and Extradition Deals: An Appraisal of the EU's Main Criminal Law Measures against Terrorism after "11 September"', *Common Market Law Review* 41 (2004): 909–935.

Part 1

Justice

Chapter 1

Judging the past: three ways of understanding time

Antoine Garapon

The way that governments treat their citizens has long been subject to review by courts and is the bedrock of the rule of law. Now, however, political action that was legal at a certain time (e.g., slavery or colonial administration), or beyond the scope of legality (warfare, for example) can be, or even *should* be, punished by either national or supranational courts. Once, this kind of 'damage', caused in the past, was widely believed to be the price that should be paid to build a State, keep an empire or win wars. Nowadays, this view has been abandoned. The Holocaust, colonization and the Balkan wars are examples of a new public expectation to submit history to judicial review, that is to say, to subject political action to examination in court proceedings under criminal law.[1]

Before this major shift, the State could only be held accountable by its own courts if it was questioned by its citizens. Now, some activists, backed up by cause lawyers, commence proceedings in the names of victims (or descendants of victims) against State's actions, seeking compensation decades after the events occurred. One example of this is the claims brought against the French national railway company (SNCF) by those who were deported by train during World War II and survived.

Previously, politics and criminal justice were idealized as two distinct, even irreconcilable areas: States made history, while the courts dealt with acts that did not form part of history. Courts revised acts driven by interests concerning relations between individuals. Today, the new role of revising history has also been

1 Nomi C. Lazar in her contribution to this volume insists on the pivotal role of constitution, and more precisely of preambles, in joining 'past events to a projected future'. Through an official interpretation of the past, constitutions shape the future (either in terms of continuity such as in Hungary or in terms of rupture as in China). I would insist on another aspect of the crucial role of legal and political institutions in dealing with time. The aim is similar – ensuring continuity – not by shaping the future in reference to the past, but by finding means of overcoming a terrible past; and not through constitutions but through trials. What is at stake here is no longer to give shape to the flow of time but rather to restore this flow because a horrible past blocks it. If for Nomi Lazar, the crucial role is given to constitutions and to preambles, here courts are at the forefront.

assigned to courts. As a result, the proper division of labor between justice and politics has been called into question. Many people now believe that courts should purge history of its crimes and judge past policies, reducing them to their criminal dimension. The courts are no longer responsible only for punishing a few wayward soldiers but are now tasked with punishing political or military officials who have enjoyed immunity for their conduct in the past. In this context, heads of staff or senior politicians have been charged with criminal offences, not for abuses but rather for their political choices. Or, better said, these officials may be prosecuted for the consequences of their decisions in people's lives. Such juridification bears witness to a new attitude many Western societies have developed towards the past; this is a change in the connection between past, present and future, and a novel order of historicity ('régime d'historicité'), to use the concept of François Hartog.[2]

This evolution of historicity is part of what Coral Bell terms 'a normative shift':

> The Pope's apologies to Muslims for the sins of 12th-century Crusaders, the crises over Kosovo and East Timor, the prosecution of Augusto Pinochet, the rows in the International Whaling Commission, the harangues of Slobodan Milosevic from his dock at The Hague, the belated compensation to the victims of Nazism – all these phenomena are improbably connected by a single invisible thread: normative shift. In the Western world of the last few decades, the phenomenon of normative shift – by which I mean simply the social process of changing domestic or international rules about what is deemed acceptable or unacceptable behaviour – has been a factor in decisions ranging right up to military action, and even the form such action has taken.[3]

To understand this new attitude towards history, I suggest it is useful to draw a distinction between three different ways of understanding time:

1 Time as specific to our modern era: justice reflects a 'past that does not pass'; i.e., a past that we do not manage to leave behind and we call upon justice to provide closure. Justice does this by bringing the past to the present, by investigating crimes of the past.
2 Time as a specific *moment* in which the past is enacted again on the symbolic stage of the criminal trial. High profile trials (such as Eichmann (1961), Barbie (1987) or Papon (1998)) are supposed to reach political catharsis.

2 François Hartog, *Régimes d'historicité: Présentisme et expériences du temps* (Paris: Le Seuil, 2002). This idea is very close to what Nomi Lazar in her contribution to this volume calls 'conceptions of the flow of time'. But this temporal frame seems to do more than shape our understanding of specific political events: it connects past, present and future. This framing of time may insist on continuity or focus on the present, and can be obsessed in overcoming a past perceived as criminal.

3 Coral Bell, "Normative Shift", *The National Interest*, 2002 (70), 44–54, accessed March 13, 2017, http://nationalinterest.org/article/normative-shift-529.

3 Time as an articulation between space and the world-system. This shift signals a reconfiguration of this connection. Contrary to great historical narratives (the Christian or the Marxist ones, for example) that reported the unraveling of history in a way that is beyond the temporal, this new order of historicity introduces a tension between the secular time of States and conflicts and the utopian time of justice and human rights.

'A past that does not pass': a new order of historicity

Under the previous order of historicity, the past and the present were related to a better future. Present hardship was endured for the sake of a future 'full of promise'.[4] Today, the present and the future are seen from the perspective of the past; with the burden of the overwhelming debt of the Holocaust. Thus, we have moved away from an order of historicity dominated by the future – that is to say, from Progress, Growth and Revolution – to a regime obsessed with the past; indeed, by a 'past that does not pass'. The past no longer entrusts us with a glorious heritage that we must nurture. Instead, it leaves us with liabilities that must be met – crimes for which penance must be done in the name of our forefathers, debts that must be repaid (and which may justify claims for compensation before civil courts).[5]

In such a context, in which the way of seeing the past has changed dramatically, dealing with historical injustice may take several forms:

- criminal proceedings, which are obviously popular because of the public attention they arouse (think of the Eichmann trial);
- truth and reconciliation commissions, specifically organized to deal with mass crimes, the most famous of which being the Truth and Reconciliation Commission in South-Africa;
- civil law suits, e.g., by the descendants of slaves seeking reparations.

Reparations can also be symbolic, as in the speech by Jacques Chirac in 1995 acknowledging the responsibility of the French state for the deportation of Vel d'hiv (a stadium in which ten thousand Jews were interned in 1942), or the kneeling of Willy Brandt before the Warsaw ghetto monument. All these forms of justice serve the same objective: to overcome a painful history to which we still feel bound, to conclude a past which we remain indebted to.

Even if the first signs of this shift came early in the 20th century, it appeared more clearly after the thirty-year economic and welfare boom following World

4 This is what Nomi C. Lazar in her chapter in this volume calls a 'progressive conception of the flow of time when, for instance, we assume that living conditions for each generation will be better than those of previous generations.'

5 On this subject, see Antoine Garapon, *Peut-on réparer l'histoire?: Colonisation, esclavage, Shoah* (Paris, Odile Jacob, 2003).

War II. This trend did not occur right after the traumatizing events of the first half of the 'terrible 20th Century'. Rather, it started a generation later, in the 1980s. Just after the war, when survivors returned from the Nazi camps, they were more concerned with recovering and building an ordinary life. Some tried to express what they endured but this went largely unheeded.[6]

This new order of history seems characteristic of a time going in the opposite direction when compared to the normal flow of time. Rather than progressively moving towards oblivion by healing wounds, time seems to function exactly in the opposite way: resentment gradually grows as the event becomes more distant in time.[7] Although the crimes may be declared imprescriptible, they nevertheless seem less and less tolerable as time passes,[8] like debt that increases inexorably with interest over time. However, even while acts of repentance, trials for crimes against humanity or other remedies flourished during the 1990s, this new order of historicity began to operate well before then. Some historians trace it back to World War II, where the Allies declared that convicting war criminals was one of the aims to engage in war.[9]

A discontinuous view of history

This shift in the order of historicity changes both the way in which we do history and the way in which we do justice. This new order is reflected in a new perception of history that first appears in the work of historians. As Henri Rousse explains: 'Writing history is no longer only an exercise of understanding and reflection, but a confrontation, a combat with the ever-present past, […] Hence the notion, both crucial and ambivalent, of a necessity to 'control the past' (*Vergangenheitsbewältigung*) that, from the 1950s–1960s, characterizes the attitude of the Germans towards their history.'[10] Here, we are not so much dealing with intellectual control but rather with moral control. We are concerned less with grasping historical significance than we are with ending the scandal that gave rise to it. In this view, history becomes a way of breaking the silence, which in the end is a tacit way to approve wrongdoings.

Why is it more difficult to speak peacefully of the Holocaust than of the looting of Constantinople? The answer is that we feel indebted towards the victims of the Nazi period and not towards the victims of an event that took place several

6 Recall that the first manuscript of Primo Levi was rejected by the publishing house Einaudi In January 1947.
7 Vladimir Jankélévitch, "Should We Pardon Them?", trans. Ann Hobart, *Critical Inquiry* 22, no. 3 (Spring 1996): 552–572.
8 The topic of imprescriptibility is taken up in more detail in the contribution of Luigi Corrias to this volume.
9 Henry Rousso, *La dernière catastrophe: L'histoire, le présent, le contemporain* (Paris: Gallimard, 2012), 126.
10 Rousso, *La dernière catastrophe*, 136.

centuries ago. Henri Rousso,[11] like Paul Ricœur and Ernest Renan,[12] sees in such a change the weight of the dead – a response to a duty to our ancestors with whom we are not at peace. It is worth noting the persistence of this anthropological feature that does not vanish in modern times.

This new order of historicity fuels a *discontinuous* view of history, as opposed to what Marxists called the 'course of history', in which history has an end. In contradistinction to this representation, the new view is focused on putting an end to an overwhelming past. While progress, revolution or the Kingdom of God used to spur humans to action and give them hope (sometimes too much, as Camus would say, because it ends in 'intoxicated consent'), the new order of historicity is much more pessimistic:

> It no longer belongs to the register of positivity, along with updated and claimed traditions, for example exemplary history that should guide the present into the future, but of negativity, such as a past that has taken the shape of a burden that has to be affronted or eliminated.... Our order of historicity is largely defined as the difficulty of overcoming the memory of recent major disasters, to reconnect with historical continuity.[13]

Whereas historians usually argue about the meaning of past events, while trying to track down causations, within this order they are often focused on giving a description of mass atrocities. The debate swings from the historic meaning to the moral significance of the past. Reading history through the eyes of an Inquisitorial Judge, who investigates crimes, is part of this new order of historicity, which ignores the chain of causation and gives priority to the moral perspective as opposed to the understanding of history. On the other hand, in an attempt to give a meaning to the horror itself, the historian puts events into context by looking for historical explanations; i.e., the reasons that gave rise to the events. The historian acknowledges the radical and monstrous novelty of the event. However, instead of mastering the event by going back to its underlying causes, she chooses to devise new criminal and non-historical categories to justify it. In short, this is the major difference: Holocaust historians leave historical time to be able to position themselves in the realm of morality, and therefore make normative judgements.

This shift also has an impact on the ordinary judicial system. Venturing through history, justice slightly changes its nature and goes far beyond its ordinary scope. So, justice no longer deals with past actions, but with actions whose consequences have not yet been revealed. Justice no longer has the task of simply narrating the past and providing definitive closure, it is now being implicitly mandated to 'act'on history. However, ordinary justice cannot deal with a violent past in the same way it deals with the present. In dealing with past atrocities, the judgment as

11 Rousso, *La dernière catastrophe*, 173.
12 Ernest Renan, *Qu'est-ce qu'une nation?* (Paris: Bordas, 1991).
13 Rousso, *La dernière catastrophe*, 23.

a legal act organizes the future and frees the past. Indeed, the direct effect of the performance of the trial consists of building a specific time that puts the past in the present and tries to organize the past:

> The work of these new kinds of courts of justice produces, *nolens volens*, the first historical narrative of the disaster, namely, the first coherent analysis of the event based on traces of evidence, submitted to adversarial proceedings and they try to make sense of it.[14]

A monstrous event[15]

The continuity of the past seems to have been interrupted by a 'monstrous event'. The normal course of events is interrupted by a catastrophe that cannot be integrated into prior history. The monstrous event shares with a disaster the characteristic of being incongruous and disruptive. Indeed, the event introduces another type of meaning altogether: it can no longer be understood by comparing it with other events; rather, it must be understood by comparing it to history as a whole, through its moral weight. This is why the science of history is less concerned about creating an in-depth narrative than with describing events the way justice does. This is because justice is interested in facts only and not in the reasons which led to them. This type of analysis can be applied to terrorism, which today is no longer seen from a historical and political perspective; namely, as the violent expression of a claim or a dispute, but rather as a natural event – a catastrophe.[16]

Not only does this type of history focus on events to the detriment of interpretation, these events are seen from the point of view of a specific personal experience: suffering. This new way of writing history no longer considers the past as a whole and in so doing it leaves the present out. We now understand the past through the lens of unjustifiable suffering, something no causal analysis can rationalize. This new way of reporting history *de-totalizes* history as it was previously understood. Indeed, by putting victims before everything else, we give up on perceiving history as a whole, in the hope of obtaining a permanent closure.

In contrast, the essence of criminal justice belongs to a dimension, of values and norms, which is a-historical by definition. An ordinary crime cannot be considered as a unique 'event', for its meaning is immediately reduced by the legal characterization to *déjà vu*. The monstrous event will be classified as a criminal matter, but it does not take long to understand that criminal categories are fragile and, above all, they risk being counter-productive by making 'events'out of ordinary crimes.

Such an order of historicity has a dual effect. On the one hand, it removes any specificity from the historical event by categorizing it in a legal offence category.

14 Rousso, *La dernière catastrophe*, 126.
15 Pierre Nora, "L'événement monstre", *Communications* 18, no. 1 (1972): 162–172.
16 For more on this point, see: Antoine Garapon and Michel Rosenfeld, *Démocraties sous stress* (Paris: PUF, 2016).

On the other hand, it creates the necessity for new legal categories in order to grasp its unique nature. The notion of a crime against humanity is a tailored concept designed to deal with violence perceived as unprecedented. The category of 'genocide' used after the Holocaust has now been extended to facts that took place several centuries before without fear of anachronism. The same may be said about the 2001 French legislation which retrospectively categorized slavery and western responsibility for it as 'crimes against humanity'.[17] The concepts of crime against humanity and genocide thus work as substitutes for historical categories designed to understand the past. Yet, this tends to hinder the historian's understanding of facts, her search for the 'cluster of objective causes', which would clarify and explain the event. More importantly, when one tries to understand the cause of a crime, one may very soon be suspected of attempting to excuse it.[18]

If history is made by wars and nations, in the period of 'post-history' in which we live crime has become a founding event. Of war, we remember less the struggle between nations than the devastation caused to civilians. Even the memory of the soldiers of World War I has shifted from heroes to victims during the 20th century, until the rehabilitation of those mutineers who were executed in 1917.[19] But if crime has become the imaginary and negative foundation of politics for a certain number of Western nations, it is also due to the specific forms of violence that emerged during the 20th century, including 'administrative massacres' or the extermination of whole categories of civilians by national armies. The foundational crime is not war, but the total collapse of a political community.[20]

Crime in everyday life does not make history: in the cases that are predefined by criminal law, their meaning is given immediately – and they are stigmatized – and for that reason are not subject to political discourse. Therefore, victims of a crime face a challenge when they want it to be categorized as a 'crime against humanity' or, better still, as 'genocide', because *ipso facto* they make their case disputable.

'Liquidate' history?

Compensation or punishment '*liquidates*' history as seen in various civil proceedings for damages that claim to purge the past by paying off or 'liquidating' a debt. In French, the term 'to liquidate' means to clear oneself or pay off a debt or to get rid of something or even someone (e.g., 'liquidating' a political opponent). Such a liquidation of history by law goes hand in hand with the growth of economics as the new 'discourse of truth' of our times, which also makes use of the liquid

17 Rousso, *La dernière catastrophe*, 144–145.

18 That brings us to the debate between Hannah Arendt and Karl Jaspers on how best to deal with Nazi crimes, see Hannah Arendt and Karl Jaspers, *Correspondence (1926–1969)*, trans. Éliane Kaufholz-Messmer (Paris: Payot, 1995).

19 On this subject, see Nicolas Offenstadt, *Les Fusillés de la Grande Guerre et la mémoire collective (1914–1999)* (Paris: Odile Jacob, 1999).

20 On this topic, see: Antoine Garapon, *Des crimes qu'on ne peut ni punir, ni pardonner: Pour une justice internationale* (Paris: Odile Jacob, 2002).

metaphor (a 'liquid world', says Zygmunt Bauman). Globalization through economics and international criminal law acts as a precursor to a world that is fully coordinated by the law and the market. This view replaces the former Westphalian model founded on sovereignty of states. Just like global markets, international criminal justice is commonly understood as either a tool that downsizes the scope of sovereignty, or as a way to minimize the influence of politics by penalizing its abuses.

The period between the fall of the Berlin Wall and the terrorist attacks in New York and Washington, D.C., was a very special one, both disappointing and hopeful. One of these hopes was to settle the debts of history to make a fresh start for the world. This attempt to settle the past, as it was planned in the Durban conference in South Africa from 2–9 September of 2001, failed. A couple of days later, the attacks of 11 September 2001 reminded the world that war was still present. However, these attacks did not put an end to the idea of judging crimes of the past.

Putting the past in the present: the moment of justice

To reduce the moral weight of the past, the new order of historicity sets time aside to concentrate on the moment of the trial only. The particular moment of the trial isolates ordinary time that is lived as duration: the trial *suspends time*. It combines two distinct and complementary temporalities: a past that is called upon (by way of discourse and the symbolic framework of the trial) and an all-powerful present (capable of acting in the past). Past crimes were often more or less known already; they were present, but as a dull, heavy and untouchable knowledge. However, the trial works to fix the crime, to reactivate it in a unity of time, place and action. The trial collapses the distance between past and present: through the staging of an event in the past whose consequences are still felt in the present, the trial makes it artificially contemporary. This revitalization of the event along with the emotions related to it are at odds with the distancing and objective attitudes one would expect from an historian.[21]

'The moral inversion of time'

Historical crimes are declared to be beyond any statute of limitation, in other words, they are insensitive to the passing of time. Statutes of limitation appear to be a way to surrender to the omnipotence of time. However, statutes of limitation run the risk of freezing the resentment of victims as well as the guilt of those who caused the event and even of those who let it happen: all of these outcomes 'block access to the human dimension of choice: the future.'[22] Indeed, to quote Jean Améry:

21 'This amnesia', argues Henri Rousso, 'literally constitutes the putting of the past in the present, a process of remembrance that is opposite to that of the historian', see Rousso, *La dernière catastrophe*, 266.

22 Jean Améry, *Par delà le bien et le mal. Essai pour surmonter l'insurmontable*, trans. Françoise Wuilmart (Arles: Actes sud, 1995).

> It is the right and privilege of man, that he does not have to declare that he is in agreement with any natural event and therefore with any organic growth of time. What is past is past: this sentence is as true as it is the enemy of morals and the mind. The moral strength of the Resistance [in WWII] contains protest and revolt against reality that is only reasonable as long as it is moral. The moral man requires that time be abolished.[23]

The trial encompasses two versions of time: it goes into the past while it takes place in the present. The purpose of the trial is not to abolish time but morally to correct what took place by adding moral consequences to material ones. For example, Jean Améry was tortured during World War II and waited for justice to encounter his torturer again. If it had happened, this second meeting (the first meeting being at the time of the torture) would not have been intended to wipe out the past – how could it? – but to undo the 'normalization' of the event which had occurred with time. This is what Améry calls the '*process of moral inversion of time*'. Our modern era tries to rid itself of the accusation that it has implicitly turned a blind eye on historical crimes by not officially confronting them.

The legal context and the specific lay-out of the 'legal game', both indispensable for the achievement of justice, work to relativize authority: the former general seems naked without his uniform, wearing only a suit in The Hague. Moving from a historical fact that took place in the real world to a ritualistic context makes dictatorship lose its numinous force.[24] The past event is replayed, having at least one of the protagonists of the original event physically present as one of its actors in the renewed enactment. He has to confront the accusation publicly. Nothing is decided in advance: that is why the trial is, for Hannah Arendt, akin to a game, not a ceremony.[25] In this way, the temporality of history is reopened and made available to human action – but shifted into the sphere of morals (not into the sphere of the physical world, which is gone forever). The *suspension* of time during the trial, while being on stage, makes way for the *restoration* of the past. These two elements make up the *specific temporality* of the trial, on which our contemporaries rely to master a monstrous past.

The experience of the irreparable

The first step in this attempt to control the past is to describe it in the two meanings of the term: to shape it and to make it present again. The monstrosity of the crime – and not only its magnitude – makes it unprecedented. The monstrosity of a crime against humanity, said Hannah Arendt, is that 'contrary to any criminal wrongdoing, [it] exceeds and goes beyond the scope of all legal

23 Améry, *Par delà le bien et le mal.*
24 Améry, *Par delà le bien et le mal.*
25 See Hannah Arendt, *Eichmann in Jerusalem: A Report on the Banality of Evil* (New York: Viking Press, 1963).

systems.'[26] However, she adds, 'by the very nature of these cases, the only tools available to us are those of the law to judge and condemn and neither legal concepts nor political structures can represent them adequately.'[27]

The radical novelty of historical crimes of the 20th century makes it difficult to determine the type of criminal offence that was committed according to conventional forms of criminal proceedings. This willingness to revise 'historical' events challenged traditional forms of the legal trial, which promptly showed its limitations. First, practical limitations emerged. For example, just to get an idea of the magnitude of the problem, in 1994 Rwandan authorities detained over 100,000 people suspected of genocide. To judge them according to the rule of law would have absorbed all the legal capacities of judgment of the totality of French courts for over 50 years. The International Criminal Court spent several years, and several hundred million dollars, in the trial of two people, and acquitted one, for serious violations of human rights in the Ituri conflict in the Democratic Republic of the Congo, in which some 50,000 people were killed. Second, the normal application of criminal law also faces more substantial obstacles. One obstacle being that the behavior of the accused was often legal at the time of the commission of the crime – for instance, when they were carrying out legitimate orders. These historical crimes do not arise from a transgression of the law, but from a perversion of the law that enabled the commission of a mass crime.

It is not simply because of a lack of resources or difficulties in finding evidence that justice is stymied, but for a deeper reason. Only if all the arrested perpetrators of these wrongdoings were judged would one have the feeling that justice met public expectations. But is that so certain? In the revision of monstrous events, justice reaches a political level. The choice to treat political violence like ordinary legal offenses is overtaken by reality: there remains an irreducible disproportion between the magnitude of the politics on the one hand and the ordinary nature of law courts on the other.

Reconciliation with our political condition

To resolve these inadequacies in the law while recognizing, as Hannah Arendt has said, that it is the only recourse we have, justice in respect of history tries to search for the truth directly, without using restrictive rules of court proceedings. However, this attempt reinforces the contradiction more than that it resolves it. In fact, the truth that these new political structures, like the Truth and Reconciliation Commissions, seek is not the same as the truth that historians seek. Consequently, these truths may at any time be refuted by historians. The truth the Commissions

26 Hannah Arendt, "Letter to Karl Jaspers", 18/8/1946, in Hannah Arendt and Karl Jaspers, *Correspondence (1926–1969)*, trans. Éliane Kaufholz-Messmer (Paris: Payot, 1995).

27 Arendt, "Letter to Karl Jaspers", 18/8/1946.

may reach is that of the reality of abuse seen through the eyes of the victims. It is a subjective truth (for which the South African TRC was criticized).[28]

Can there be other forms of truth? Attempts at finding truth are caught up in the following contradiction: the need for a shared history, on the one hand; and the impossibility of having a shared history since we live in a liberal society that allows everyone to have his or her own version of history.[29] Since the new regime is democratic, it cannot *impose* a form of 'sacred history' that separates good from evil: that would contradict its liberal nature. Thus, the new liberal regime gives the floor to the different parties, including to the perpetrators who appear as ordinary men (a recurring theme in the literature on transitional justice).[30]

Nor can 'new' justice make the same mistakes than the ones it pretends to correct; that would reproduce the evil that it seeks to remedy. Therefore, it distances itself from ordinary criminal justice. The latter often leads to a decision which involves the temporary or definitive exclusion of a member of the society. Truth and Reconciliation Commissions seek reconciliation. Reconciliation aims directly at long-term action and does not pursue the abstraction or isolation of members of society. 'Losers disappear,' wrote Simone Weil, 'they are nothing.'[31] Reconciliation must also give attention to the now defeated person, the former offender. This task is a difficult but necessary one to make a difference.

There are, however, many other ways to do justice to the past besides staging trials or convening commissions; some options are not judicial-like at all. It is the case of collective memory work that sheds new light on the past. One must learn to live with one's past and not repeat the phenomenon of the scapegoat by shouting at a handful of criminals, who yesterday were called 'others', as if they were the source of all evil. If history is in danger of falling into the trap of reproduction, the work of judging history must necessarily expand. Remembering crimes leads to introspection of the political community beyond this one piece of history, it challenges mankind to confront its barbarism. This is what Karl Jaspers meant when he spoke of 'metaphysical guilt'.[32]

Tragedy as a tool for taming evil

On the judicial stage, the irresolvable tensions between the community and the individual are well described: the story of the victims, the political climate,

28 See the debate after the publication of Antjie Krog, *Country of my Skull: Guilt, Sorrow and the Limits of Forgiveness in the New South Africa* (New York: Penguin Random House, 2000).
29 See Mark Osiel, *Mass Atrocity, Collective Memory, and the Law* (New York: Transactions, 1997), and Kora Andrieu, *La justice transitionnelle* (Paris: Gallimard, 2012).
30 See Christopher R. Browning, *Ordinary Men: Reserve Police Battalion 101 and the Final Solution in Poland* (New York: Harper Perennial, 1992).
31 Simone Weil, *Œuvres complètes* (Paris: Gallimard, 1998), 289.
32 Karl Jaspers, *The Question of German Guilt*, trans. E. B. Ashton (New York: Fordham University Press, 2000).

individual destinies, foolish hopes and real suffering. Judging history offers a unique experience that involves both an ontological involvement in time and a declaration of political evil. More than ordinary justice, it pushes us to the limits of our human condition, forcing us to face the inexorable passage of time as well as our political milieu. However, one should not conclude that justice is powerless. Justice retains a stubborn desire to overcome this double confinement.

Historical justice must perform a double task that may appear contradictory: take note of evil while fighting it at the same time. This is what is required of historical justice, and this goal can only be achieved by taking advantage of the reenactment of the scene. For it is not enough simply to say things, one must show them: a trial does not only rely on words and texts but also on attitudes, gestures and silences. There is a mystery of life that one can only understand through staging and acting it out. The stage allows the exchange of experiences: whoever looks at the action on stage can identify himself with the actors and, especially, with the creditor of the moral debt (i.e., the victim). It enables the staging of political evil and tries to reverse it, sometimes in a dramatic manner. The staging of evil in history can both attest to and challenge this evil; both operations being concomitant and visually experienced.

The tragedy of *The Oresteia* by Aeschylus illustrates these points. The last play in the trilogy, *The Eumenides*, ends with the conversion of the Furies (*Erinyes*) into Eumenides, which means that the infernal goddesses of vengeance turn into benevolent goddesses, guardians of the institutions of the city. In this way, the tragedy puts an end to the curse of Atreus, not by rejecting the vengeance, but by its introjection. Striving to be just, in the context of historical justice, is to tear oneself away from the permanent temptation to put oneself in the place of the victims in order to avenge them and thereby perpetuate the cycle of violence.

This approach enables us to understand the judgment of history as an ongoing conspiracy that does not *replicate* the violence but *converts* it. The incorporation of evil into history leads us to consider the judgment of history as a *transformation* of a terrible threat of revenge into a civic pact. As Hegel wrote: 'The Furies were sleeping and the crime woke them.'[33] The Furies said that violence is still there, that it is impossible to eliminate it and that therefore one should think of justice as incorporating the past violence and comparing it to violence standing alone – what we do – and not in a *segregated* way. That is also the meaning of the last sentence of Albert Camus' *The Plague*:

> The plague bacillus never dies or disappears for good; that it can lie dormant for years and years in furniture and linen chests; that it bides its time in bedrooms, cellars, trunks and bookshelves; and that perhaps the day will come when, for the bane and the enlightenment of men, it would call up its rats again and send them forth to die in a happy city.[34]

33 Georg W. F. Hegel, *Elements of the Philosophy of Right*, ed. Allen W. Wood (Cambridge: Cambridge University Press, 2003) section 101, *Zusatz*.

34 Albert Camus, *The Plague*, trans. Stuart Gilbert (London: Penguin, 1960).

The case of modern Germany is exemplary in this regard. The monstrosity of the crimes of Nazism resulted in a Constitution that places human dignity above everything else. Reunification was accompanied by an official declaration that recognized the responsibility of all Germans for Nazism and that affirmed the weight of the past in the creation of a common national future. Recognizing the horrors of history gave this great country the energy for its rebirth as a tolerant, responsible member of the community of nations.

'Living with it': a new relationship with the world

The new order of historicity, in its attempt to excise a crushing past, does not emerge scot-free from its confrontation with it. The moment of the trial modifies the post-trial time. The latter cannot be a return to *status quo ante* (that can exist in ordinary justice). It cannot purge vices in the same way as ordinary justice seeks to, when a troublemaker is locked up or a criminal is temporarily excluded from society. We are now condemned to 'live with' our past, without accommodating it, but without refusing it either.

Attending to the tragedy of our finitude invites us to 'live with it': this is the main lesson we draw from the re-enactment. We must live with criminals and with their victims. Because yesterday's enemies and people with whom we used to have asymmetrical relationships (e.g., people from former colonies and excluded people) now live among us. For example, in France globalization has brought together as co-nationals: (descendants of) former slaves, colonized people, or Jews deported by the French police, Harkis (who were abandoned during the Algerian war of decolonization), and former members of the Algerian National Liberation Front (against whom the French fought during the same war). That is why the principle of non-discrimination is so valuable. 'Live with it' is the founding experience of globalization; it implies a new relationship with space that is not closed on itself but has been opened by law; by a law that ensures the fundamental rights of everyone.

The new order of historicity finds a way out of these deadly conundrums, by *linking* the past, present and future in a new way; i.e., by converting a weighty history into a vigilant memory. The momentum of the trial opens a new political moment, where past, present and future are intertwined in a new constitution. At this point, the constitution that might be formulated is based on a past that is not expelled from collective memory, but that is incorporated in it (e.g., in the German Constitution with the inclusion of human dignity as a right or, to some extent, in the European Convention on Human Rights). This is a way of constructing a future that is not only dreamed of, but which is also planned. These fundamental texts, either national constitutions or regional conventions enforceable through national courts, aim for a continuity in the future. To use the words of Nomi Claire Lazar: the constructed shape of past events, here mass atrocities, 'strongly implies the shape of things to come.'[35] After having been

35 Nomi C. Lazar, in this volume.

acknowledged, those crimes are thereby converted into positive norms aimed at future control; they do not function as directions for the future, but rather as unsurpassable boundaries.

From a present time that carries the past neither as a burden nor a threat, but rather as an opening to the future that limits its own capacity, taking the new order of historicity, we must distinguish the moment of justice from the emergence of a new utopia. In other words, we must distinguish the present, according to a philosophy of history, that is best characterized by spatial metaphors. For Albert Camus, the end of a belief in a sense of history does not result in the abolition of the idea of hope.[36] However, hope is no longer part of a utopian future from another world that is un-tuned to present actions: on the contrary, remembering crimes gives hope in the present because the revision of history can create tools to prevent the repetition of such monstrosities.

A new way of allocating institutions to space and time

The Westphalian system, which allowed for the coexistence of states that did not share common values, replaced the mediaeval one based on the concept of just war.[37] We could argue that the new articulation between states taking place after the Westphalian system shares some common traits with the previous one. Judging history inaugurates a new world-system (largely utopian) that connects domestic and international law in a new way that offers an alternative to the Westphalian model. To understand this new world order, we must be careful not to view international criminal justice as part of a narrative on human progress, like some culminating event in history that would overcome the barbarism of war once and for all. Instead, we should consider the institution of the International Criminal Court, for example, as an interface between specific forms of violence and a new design of the world (that began in Nuremberg).

It is worth recalling the major conflicts that shook the 20th century that have found their epilogue in the creation of a jurisdiction intended to overcome the aporia of history by making a new world order possible. World War I led to the creation of the International Court of Justice (ICJ) and to the trial of Wilhelm II (that was aborted); World War II gave birth to the Nuremberg and Tokyo trials and the end of the Cold War enabled the creation of the International Criminal Court (ICC). The first tribunal was supposed to defuse potential conflict between states through international law; the second group launched the idea of international criminal justice; and the third court is now trying to institutionalize and implement a court of justice based on the principle of complementarity.

36 Albert Camus, *Le Mythe de Sisyphe* (Paris: Gallimard, 1942).

37 For an overview of this argument, see Carl Schmitt, *The Nomos of the Earth in the International Law of the Jus Publicum Europaeum*, trans. G. L. Ulmen (New York: Telos Press, 2003).

In space: the principle of complementarity

The principle of complementary jurisdiction is pioneering a whole new concept of international (even global) justice. Indeed, it redesigns the very notion of unity by bringing the world together. It highlights the shift in the concept of justice from an international Westphalian worldview to transnational justice based on the principle of universal jurisdiction. Recall the Nuremberg trials where the judges were from one side of the conflict and justice was in the hands of the victor, compared to supranational courts where the community of nations stands in judgment over a few of its members (the international criminal tribunals) on the other.

The principle of complementarity has changed the whole landscape of the administration of justice; it is no longer simply left to the parties in conflict. Instead, under this conception of international justice, justice is regarded as a viewpoint that is shared between the national and supranational levels, assuming both partake in a common idea of justice, which is a precondition for the legitimacy of the principle of complementarity. In other words, complementarity rests upon the notion that depending on what States or people (if we include the reconciliation framework) can achieve in terms of justice, there may not be a need to refer a case to a supranational court. Providing justice in very concrete terms has now become a (possible) task for the whole of humanity, for State institutions, as well as for people concerned all over the world. This task puts flesh on the bones of cosmopolitanism.

Indeed, 'complementarity' assumes a common conception of justice, and a common understanding that crimes against humanity are a negative but common experience of humanity. We no longer see the tragic fate of victims as inevitable, but as the most universally applicable experience of mankind: suffering that we all share. Hence, complementarity is not only a mechanism for the Prosecutor of the ICC to bypass cases: it carries with it the hope for a more humane world. The principle of complementarity does not negate state sovereignty or remove the idea of borders between nations, but it does make them more permeable. Complementarity introduces a new relationship between exteriority and interiority that characterizes a new way of looking at space and time: they are no longer mutually exclusive but may be combined in novel ways. This new exteriority/interiority relation is first apparent in space. The best example in this regard is Europe. European courts, and the European Court of Human Rights in particular, are neither outside of European countries (because there is at least one representative of each country presiding) nor totally inside. Furthermore, national judges are the first to enforce European law. In line with the complementarity principle, national judges remain the first ones under the duty to implement laws with common principles that are most frequently contained in international agreements.

While the previous (legal) system of the world was structured around the relationship between self and others, in this new system the other is no longer kept distant but is internalized or 'introjected' (to use a psychoanalytical metaphor). The common reference becomes *both* internal and external. But it would be unrealistic to believe in a complete merging of the two, just as much as it would be to think that one could return to the ancient world. Thus, from a legal point of view, the international system must be understood in a new way. No longer can it be grasped as relations between States only, neither as one global zone. Rather, it should be seen as a community that shares some basic moral standards. The world can be reduced neither to the combination of all States, nor to a universal monarchy, but it might be understood 'as a regulative idea of the nation and homeland: which prevents nations from closing in on themselves entirely, which points towards something else.'[38] This 'other' of territories merges with the idea of human rights. In this way, as Bergson put it, 'it is not through enlargement that one goes from a closed to an open society, from the City to Humanity. The idea of the world is even contrary to that of the City, it does not mean all the cities but what does not fit into the shape of the City.'[39]

In time: veritas filia temporis

Such a relation between interiority and exteriority introduces a time lag between moments of political action and justice. The possibility of intervention opens a particular time, that is neither the end of history nor the time and space locked in by a nation. It is from its longest temporality, and at a rhythm that does not correspond to the owners of political power, that justice derives its power. In the short term and practically speaking, political power trumps justice because it maintains public order. However, this power only lasts for as long as it runs, while justice has time for itself: it can intervene after a shift in power, a long time after the facts. *Veritas filia temporis*: patience is the best officer of the court. The division of power is not only spatial; it is also temporal.

Epilogue: justice as a spiritual power

In this new temporality – that cannot be more eschatological than apocalyptic – history is replaced with the construction of a new world space. Justice remains partly unavailable to politicians, without claiming to be the substitute of politics: it is a kind of *raison d'état* in the medieval sense of the term (which is exactly the opposite of the modern meaning of the term).[40] Progress has not disappeared. Historicity remains, but it is no longer the world politically constructed by people or revolutionary movements. It is instead the result of the increasing dominance of jurisprudence, of a sort of global *common law*. Justice now embodies a power of a spiritual nature that confronts temporal powers.

38 Pierre Ganancia, "L'idée de nation d'un point de vue cosmopolitique", lecture delivered at the IHEJ as part of the Philosophy of Law Seminar, November 18, 2006 on file with the author.
39 Cited in Ganancia, "L'idée de nation d'un point de vue cosmopolitique".
40 Michel Senellart, *Machiavélisme et raison d'État* (Paris: PUF, 1989).

The analogies between the configuration of our world, at least as it is dreamed, and medieval Christianity, are striking. The principle of complementarity, which builds a bridge directly between international institutions and national courts, reminds one of the connections that existed between Rome and the local churches. It gives Europe a framework that is reminiscent of Christendom before the formation of States, where the Church played a spiritual role. Today, the reference is no longer religious but legal: human rights supersede sovereignty, or, in other words, Christian virtues that, hopefully, will not go mad.[41]

Bibliography

Améry, Jean. *Par delà le bien et le mal. Essai pour surmonter l'insurmontable.* Translated by Françoise Wuilmart. Arles: Actes sud, 1995.

Andrieu, Kora. *La justice transitionnelle.* Paris: Gallimard, 2012.

Arendt, Hannah. *Eichmann in Jerusalem: A Report on the banality of evil.* New York: Viking Press, 1963.

Arendt, Hannah and Karl Jaspers. *Correspondence (1926–1969).* Translated by Éliane Kaufholz-Messmer. Paris: Payot, 1995.

Bell, Coral. "Normative Shift" *The National Interest*, 2002. http://nationalinterest.org/article/normative-shift-529.

Browning, Christopher R. *Ordinary Men: Reserve Police Battalion 101 and the Final Solution in Poland.* New York: Harper Perennial, 1992.

Camus, Albert. *Le Mythe de Sisyphe.* Paris: Gallimard, 1942.

Camus, Albert. *The Plague.* Translated by Stuart Gilbert. London: Penguin, 1960.

Chesterton, Gilbert K. *Orthodoxy.* 1908.

Garapon, Antoine. *Des crimes qu'on ne peut ni punir, ni pardonner: Pour une justice international.* Paris: Odile Jacob, 2002.

Garapon, Antoine. *Peut-on réparer l'histoire?: Colonisation, esclavage, Shoah.* Paris: Odile Jacob, 2003.

Garapon, Antoine and Michel Rosenfeld. *Démocraties sous stress.* Paris: PUF, 2016.

Hartog, François. *Régimes d'historicité: Présentisme et expériences du temps.* Paris: Le Seuil, 2002.

Hegel, Georg W. F. *Elements of the Philosophy of Right.* Edited by Allen W. Wood. Cambridge: Cambridge University Press, 2003.

Jankélévitch, Vladimir. "Should We Pardon Them?" Translated by Ann Hobart. *Critical Inquiry* 22, no. 3 (Spring 1996).

Jaspers, Karl. *The Question of German Guilt.* Translated by E. B. Ashton. New York: Fordham University Press, 2000.

Krog, Antjie. *Country of my Skull: Guilt, Sorrow and the Limits of Forgiveness in the new South Africa.* New York: Penguin Random House, 2000.

Nora, Pierre. "L'événement monstre" *Communications* 18, no. 1 (1972): 162–172.

Offenstadt, Nicolas. *Les Fusillés de la Grande Guerre et la mémoire collective (1914–1999).* Paris : Odile Jacob, 1999.

Osiel, Mark. *Mass Atrocity, Collective Memory, and the Law.* New York: Transactions, 1997.

Renan, Ernest. *Qu'est-ce qu'une nation?*Paris: Bordas, 1991.

41 Gilbert K. Chesterton, *Orthodoxy* (1908).

Rousso, Henry. *La dernière catastrophe: L'histoire, le présent, le contemporain*. Paris: Gallimard, 2012.
Schmitt, Carl. *The Nomos of the Earth in the International Law of the Jus Publicum Europaeum*. Translated by G. L. Ulmen . New York: Telos Press, 2003.
Senellart, Michel. *Machiavélisme et raison d'État*. Paris: PUF, 1989.
Weil, Simone. *Œuvres complètes*. Paris: Gallimard, 1998.

Chapter 2

Law at the right time: a plea for slow law in hasty times

Bart van Klink

Law's untimeliness

According to Willem Witteveen, '[s]low law is the true art of legislating'.[1] Law seems to be either too late or too soon, but never 'in time'. It is often too late, because at the very moment that a statute is promulgated, after a lengthy legislative process, the social norms codified in the law may have changed. In adjudication, there is a growing pressure on judges to act quicker, so that more cases are decided in less time.[2] Increasingly, the legal forms that structure the process of law-making and law application are seen as a hindrance to what people seem to desire: justice on direct demand. As Ernst Jünger observes: 'and even the fastest beat of legislation lags behind the march of life, which in each moment demands its right'.[3] At the same time, law sometimes appears to come too soon. People are not always ready for the norms that the law offers. Legislation with a high aspirational character, such as non-discrimination law or environmental law aiming at sustainable development, often meets with resistance in society. Moreover, the legislature is sometimes accused of issuing legislation too quickly, without having taken enough time for deliberation and reflection. As a result, the legislation may be of a bad quality, as for instance the phenomenon of 'ad hoc legislation' shows.[4]

1 Willem Witteveen, De wet als kunstwerk: Een andere filosofie van het recht (Amsterdam: Boom, 2014), 406 (my translation). I would like to dedicate this article to the memory of Willem Witteveen, my former supervisor who tragically died at the MH17 crash. After having written the first draft of my paper, I found out that he made a similar (though very short) plea for 'slow law' in his last book, which was published posthumously.

2 See Lyana Francot and Sophie Mommers, 'Picking up the Pace – Legal Slowness and the Authority of the Judiciary in the Acceleration Society (a Dutch Case Study)', *International Journal of the Legal Profession*, 23 (2016): 1–19.

3 Ernst Jünger, *Das abenteuerliche Herz* (Stuttgart: Klett-Cotta, 1987), 54 (my translation).

4 Ad hoc legislation is promulgated in reaction to a particular incident and is meant to apply to this case only, cf. Anna Jasiak, *Constitutional Constraints on Ad Hoc Legislation: A Comparative Study of the United States, Germany and the Netherlands* (Nijmegen: Wolf Legal Publishers, 2010).

In this chapter, I will address the question whether there is a right time for the law. To what extent should the law look back to the past and anticipate future developments? My research focuses in particular on modificatory legislation that aims at changing current or traditional ways of thinking and behaviour. However, it applies as well to other authorities who are engaged in acts of modificatory law creation, such as courts in ground-breaking rulings. In the sociology of law, there is long tradition of scholars warning against legislation that runs out of time with the present state of affairs. This self-acclaimed realist position is nicely captured in the famous (or notorious) aphorism attributed to William Graham Sumner: 'Lawways cannot change folkways.'[5] That seems to imply that law is never a suitable instrument for emancipatory or revolutionary goals. However, there are examples that demonstrate that law can contribute to and reinforce social change, such as the European Charter of Human Rights and the landmark decision *Brown vs. Board of Education* by the US Supreme Court (1954). I intend to identify some principles that could guide the legislature (or other bodies of law creation) in deciding when it is the right time for making seemingly untimely law and how to do this, that is, by means of which legal forms. By prescribing a certain way of doing things by law, there is an inherent slowness in the forms that constitute law. Should law move quicker and be more responsive to dynamic developments in technology and morality? Or should it, on the contrary, slow down and act as a safeguard against all too sudden changes and amendments? I prefer the latter. In my view, slowness is exactly what is called for in these hasty times.

Firstly, I will explore some reasons why law may be reluctant to change and not suited for causing social change. I will start this exploration with Sumner's classic study of the folkways, which still constitutes one of the most articulated and intriguing criticisms of law as an instrument of change, based on extended empirical research in many parts of the world throughout history. Secondly, I will argue, building on Oakeshott's notion of radical temporality and current hermeneutic theories of legal interpretation, that law – just like everything else in the world – cannot be immunized against change and is itself part of the ongoing process of social change – either as a hindrance, or a stabilizer or a catalyst. Thirdly, I will explore in what way legislation could or should contribute to changes in society. How may the law deal in a prudent way with the constant social pressure to change and to cause change in its environment? Finally, starting from the concept of legal forms (as developed in my inaugural lecture, see below), I will identify some normative principles that may guide the process of legal change – in the impatient anticipation of the New.

Resistance to change

In the modern experience of time, time is always moving quickly. Due to rapid changes in our environment, caused by technological inventions and innovations

5 Although the exact phrasing cannot be found in this work, the reference is to William Graham Sumner, *Folkways: A Study of the Sociological Importance of Usages, Manners, Customs, Mores, and Morals* (New York: Dover Publications, Inc., 1959 (1906)).

(among other things), we seem to have lost control over time. We have to rush in order to catch up with the latest developments and trends. According to Odo Marquard, the essence of human existence is no longer characterized by reflexion – 'I think, therefore I am', as Descartes put it – but by hastiness: 'I am in a hurry, therefore I am.'[6] Because we are constantly in a hurry, we do not have time enough to reflect and to relax. In reaction to the experienced acceleration of time, attempts have been made to slow down time. Marquard argues that people, because of their finality and fallibility, have no other choice than to develop a 'sense for slowness'.[7] 'Slow' has become a popular catch phrase for all kind of activities: slow food, slow money, slow sex, slow science, slow politics, and so on. In politics, at least in western European states, one can see that, after a period of progressive, future-oriented politics, mostly of a (neo-)liberal or social democratic kind, in the last decade conservative and populist parties (from left to right), aiming at a restoration of the nation-state and the traditional values it embodies, are on the rise again.[8]

Slowness may be revaluated in many fields of society, as an antidote to an overall sense of stress and time pressure; in law, however, in particular from perspectives external to the legal system, it is not very much appreciated. Comparing the temporal conditions of law and science, Latour notices: 'Common sense finds the slowness of both law and science incomprehensible (…). What a waste of time! How slow!'[9] Law and science are both engaged, as Latour says, in the 'production of doubt'[10] which, from the internal perspective of scholars and judges respectively, necessarily takes time in order to preserve quality. People have no patience for that and, in Latour's view, understandably so: 'And yet common sense is right: *things have to be brought to an end.*'[11] Here, the ways of law and science part: in adjudication, the judge has to take a final decision, after having doubted and deliberated for a long time as the legal procedure prescribes; in science, on the contrary, every result is temporary and can be questioned by future research in an endless quest for knowledge.[12] According to Latour, slowness is a fundamental quality of the law. Unlike science, law aims at stabilising its system of rules: 'A

6 In German: 'Ich eile, also bin ich', quoted in Harald Weinrich, *Knappe Zeit: Kunst und Ökonomie des befristeten Lebens* (München: Beck, 2008), 165 (my translation).

7 Quoted in Weinrich, *Knappe Zeit*, 165. In the original text Marquard writes 'slowness' in the plural ('Langsamkeiten').

8 At the last European elections, conservative or right-wing parties have won or have increased their support in many countries (for instance in Denmark, Hungary and Poland).

9 Bruno Latour, *The Making of Law: An Ethnography of the Conseil d'Etat*, tr. Marina Brilman and Alain Pottage (Cambridge: Polity Press, 2013), 220–221.

10 Latour, *The Making of Law*, 221.

11 Latour, *The Making of law*, 221 (original italics).

12 As Weber notices, it is the fate and purpose of any scholar that his research is refuted by future research cf. Max Weber, *The Vocation Lectures: 'Science as a Vocation' and 'Politics as a Vocation'*, ed. David Owen and Tracy B. Strong; tr. Rodney Livingstone (Indianapolis, Indiana: Hackett Publishing Company, 2004), 11.

premium is put on legal stability but there is no such thing as scientific stability.' Therefore, law resists radical change:

> Although one might speak admiringly of 'revolutionary science', 'revolutionary laws' have always been as terrifying as courts with emergency powers. All those aspects of law that common sense finds so irritating – its tardiness, its taste for tradition, its occasionally reactionary attitudes – are essential to law's functioning.[13]

Law seems to be essentially conservative: it sticks to established practices and is reluctant to give up what it has acquired in decades of experience. As Přibáň argues, 'law is not primarily a matter of social experimentation'.[14]

Itself wary of change, law is not likely to bring about radical changes in its environment. Law's failure to modify current patterns of behaviour in society is a recurrent theme in the sociology of law, as is exemplified in Sumner's classic study of the folkways.[15] In his view, '[w]orld philosophy, life policy, right, rights, and morality are all products of the folkways.'[16] From its early beginning until the present day, society is trying to find strategies to cope with the outside world in order to improve its life conditions. These strategies, when they have been proven to be successful and have settled themselves in actual behaviour, make up the folkways.[17] According to Summer, '[t]he life of society consists in making folkways and applying them.'[18] However, 'making folkways' is a misleading expression, because folkways develop themselves, not as a product of an act of human creation, but incrementally in reaction to changing life conditions. Folkways develop themselves in the same way as a language is developed: not by conscious intervention from speakers, but in the practice of speaking itself.[19] In the mores,[20] 'is' and 'ought' collide or, more correctly, the 'ought' is reduced to the 'is':

13 Latour, *The Making of Law*, 242–243.
14 Jiří Přibáň, *Legal Symbolism. On Law, Time and European Identity* (Aldershot: Ashgate, 2007), 54.
15 In his Social Working Approach, Griffiths is also very pessimistic about law's possibility to bring about fundamental changes in society cf., e.g., John Griffiths, 'The Social Working of Legal Rules,' *Journal of Legal Pluralism and Unofficial Law* 48 (2003): 1–84.
16 Sumner, *Folkways*, 29.
17 In his lengthy study of the folkways, Sumner never clearly defines this concept. Sometimes 'folkways' is used as a synonym for the mores (see footnote 20), at other times it seems to refer to established patterns of behaviour only (that is, the mores minus the intellectual 'superstructure'). In what follows, I will use these concepts interchangeably, as Sumner mostly does.
18 Sumner, *Folkways*, 34.
19 This analogy is discussed in Sumner, *Folkways*, 136, and is very similar to De Saussure's description of the development of language cf. Ferdinand de Saussure, *Course in General Linguistics*, ed. Charles Bally and Albert Sechehaye, tr. Roy Harris (La Salle, Illinois: Open Court, 1983).
20 The mores are 'the ways of doing things which are current in society to satisfy human needs and desires, together with the faiths, notions, codes, and standards of well living

because this is done currently, one has to do it. 'In the folkways, whatever is, is right.'[21] Folkways have 'the normative force of the factual', as the Austrian legal scholar Georg Jellinek would say.[22]

Although folkways have an indisputable authority for the here and now, they do vary in time and place. Folkways change over time, but in most cases not as a result of rational invention and intervention. '[C]hanges in history are primarily due to changes in life conditions. Then the folkways change.'[23] Sumner is very sceptical about the possibility of legislation to make or change the mores. Social engineering is doomed to fail: 'The habit of using jural concepts, which is now so characteristic of our mores, leads us into vague and impossible dreams of social affairs, in which metaphysical concepts are supposed to realize themselves, or assumed to be real.'[24] As an example Sumner refers to legislation against race discrimination in the United States in his time, at the beginning of the 20th century. In his view, the blacks and whites were at that point of history more separate than ever. We are, according to Sumner, nothing more than spectators looking at a 'great natural convulsion':[25] we cannot influence and foresee the ways in which the mores will develop themselves. The outcome of this process does not depend on ethical views 'any more than the volcanic eruption on Martinique contained an ethical element.'[26] The two races may eventually learn to live together, Sumner believes, but that will take time. Mores change gradually, 'by slow and long-continued effort'.[27] For that reason, legislation is doomed to fail, just like preaching: 'The favourite methods of our time are legislation and preaching. These methods fail because they do not affect ritual, and because they always aim at results in a short time.'[28]

In order to be effective, legislation has to adapt itself to the mores instead of trying to modify them. The only thing politics can do is preserving the current state of affairs: 'All the political institutions of a modern state are conservative in the sense that they retain and sustain what is and what has been, and resist interference or change.'[29] Like Latour, Sumner considers slowness to be a necessary

which inhere in those ways, having a genetic connection with them' (Summer, *Folkways*, 59).

21 Sumner, *Folkways*, 28.

22 On the different meanings of Jellinek's notion of the normative force of the factual, see Bart van Klink and Oliver W. Lembcke, 'Exploring the Boundaries of Law: On the Is-Ought Distinction in Jellinek and Kelsen' in *Facts and Norms in Law Facts and Norms in Law: Interdisciplinary Reflections on Legal Method*, ed. Sanne Taekema, Bart van Klink and Wouter de Been (Cheltenham: Edward Elgar Publishing, 2016), 201–223, 204–209.

23 Sumner, *Folkways*, 35.

24 Sumner, *Folkways*, 66.

25 Sumner, *Folkways*, 78.

26 Sumner, *Folkways*, 78.

27 Sumner, *Folkways*, 87.

28 Sumner, *Folkways*, 96.

29 Sumner, *Folkways*, 167.

quality of law. By codifying and enforcing the mores that are widely accepted in society, law provides for stability. Only when the folkways have changed substantially and permanently, law will have to follow, reluctantly and slowly. However, Sumner is not against change per se. He does believe that the innovation of the mores is necessary: 'The folkways need constant rejuvenation and refreshment if they are to be well fitted to present cases, and it is far better that they be revolutionized than they be subject to traditional changelessness.'[30] But, in his view, the source of change lies in society and its living conditions, not in legislation or policy.

Radical temporality

Although law seems to resist change, there is no escape from it. Despite all attempts to turn back time or to slow it down, no one can keep time from moving on. As Heraclites said presumably, 'All things move and nothing is at rest.' Because everything changes, 'you cannot step twice into the same stream'.[31] According to Oakeshott, the universal condition of human existence is characterized by 'radical temporality'.[32] That means, in practical experience,[33] 'reality is asserted under the category of change'.[34] Through our actions, we are always engaged in altering the world as is it, even when we intend to preserve it: 'all human actions belong to the realm of change, including actions to bring changes to conclusive closure'.[35] What is constant in practical experience is, paradoxically, the 'possibility of change'.[36] Change is not a mere possibility of our world of practical action, but change and instability define and determine our world. This follows, in Oakeshott's view, from the human 'ordeal of freedom'.[37] As human beings, we are bound to be free. Our course of action is not determined, but in most situations we have a variety of options from we which can, and have to, choose. Because

30 Sumner, *Folkways*, 634–635.

31 Quoted in Plato's *Cratylus*, 401d and 402a, cited and discussed in Francesco Ademollo, *The* Cratylus *of Plato: A Commentary* (Cambridge: Cambridge University Press, 2011), 203 ff.

32 This notion is not used by Oakeshott himself, but by Fuller in order to describe Oakeshott's view of the human condition in practical experience, cf. Timothy Fuller, 'Radical Temporality and the Modern Imagination: Two Themes in the Thought of Michael Oakeshott' in *A Companion to Michael Oakeshott*, ed. Paul Franco and Leslie Marsh (University Park, Pennsylvania: The Pennsylvania State University Press, 2012), 120–133, 121.

33 As opposed to historical and scientific experience, which Oakeshott has discussed earlier in his study of the various modes of experience: 'Science assumes a world of stable, unchanging, quantitative fact; history assumes of world of unchanging past fact; practice assumes a world of mutable, transient fact', cf. Michael Oakeshott, *Experience and Its Modes* (Cambridge: Cambridge University Press, 2002), 263.

34 Oakeshott, *Experience and Its Modes*, 273.

35 Fuller, 'Radical Temporality and the Modern Imagination,' 121.

36 Oakeshott, *Experience and Its Modes*, 267.

37 Fuller, 'Radical Temporality and the Modern Imagination,' 123.

change is produced by a conscious reworking of the past, the past can never in itself determine the course of history; it offers a range of possible directions where to go and how to proceed.[38] In practical activity, we aim at improving the practice at hand, building on the values that are already part of that practice. As 'incomplete beings', we are 'searching for completion'.[39] We are never satisfied and always trying to reconcile the world as it is with how we want it to be: 'Practice is never the mere assertion of the present; it is essentially action, the alteration of 'what is' so as to make it agree with "what ought to be".'[40] There is no final destination, no end of history – only a becoming of something that was in some sense already there, *ad infinitum*.

In current hermeneutic theories of legal interpretation, the radical temporality of law is widely acknowledged.[41] As MacCormick argues, 'legal rules, principles, and doctrines are themselves time-bound, have themselves a history of critical development over time.'[42] How this critical development may take place, is elaborated in Dworkin's theory of constructive interpretation. He compares, famously, legal interpretation to the writing of a chain novel. Through interpretation, law is developed and thereby changed: every legal decision (at least in hard cases[43]) adds a new chapter to the previous ones. According to Dworkin, the judge should offer an interpretation which not only has to be in accordance with the law as it is (referred to as the 'dimension of fit'), but also shows the legal system in its present state in its best light, that is how it ought to be following her own political morality (the 'dimension of substance', also referred to as the 'dimension of justification').[44]

Earlier, Hans-Georg Gadamer developed a similar notion of legal interpretation within the context of his general hermeneutic philosophy of understanding. In his view, understanding involves a fusion of horizons – the 'familiar' horizon of the present in which the interpreter is situated and the 'strange' horizon of the continuing tradition from which the text speaks. Both horizons are never completely present to themselves but are constituted, over and over again, in the act of

38 Referring to Heidegger, Nousiainen (1995: 32) argues that time offers a 'structure of possibilities', cf. Kevät Nousiainen, 'Time of Law – Time of Experience' in *Time, Law, and Society. Proceedings of a Nordic Symposium Held May 1994 at Sandbjerg Gods, Denmark (ARSP-Beiheft 64)*, ed. Jes Bjarup and Mogens Blegvad, (Stuttgart: Franz Steiner Verlag, 1995), 23–39.

39 Fuller, 'Radical Temporality and the Modern Imagination,' 121.

40 Oakeshott, *Experience and Its Modes*, 247.

41 In contrast to, for instance, originalism which desperately tries to keep the law from changing by holding on to the original intent of the legislator or the law's original meaning, see further below.

42 Neil MacCormick, 'Time, Narratives, and Law' in Bjarup and Blegvad (ed.), *Time, Law, and Society*, 111–125, 123. I thank Maks Del Mar for bringing this text to my attention.

43 According to Gadamer, this applies to standard cases as well (see below).

44 Ronald Dworkin, *Law's Empire* (Cambridge Mass.: Harvard University Press, 1986), 230–231.

understanding which brings them together. This means that not only the temporary horizon widens by accommodating 'new' understandings, but the past horizon is also changed when approached from a contemporary point of view: 'In as much as the tradition is newly expressed in language, something comes into being that had not existed before and that exists from now on.'[45] This is what Gadamer calls 'effective-history' (in German, *Wirkungsgeschichte*): the past lives on and works on in the present, while the present continues to affect the past. Time – the temporal distance between the production and the reception of a text – is not a 'yawning chasm' but a positive and productive factor in the understanding of a text. Every interpretation not only reproduces a pre-given meaning, but also adds something new to the existing canon of interpretation. The distance in time allows the 'true' meaning that is enclosed in a case to come out fully into the open. However, Gadamer rejects the notion of an 'ultimate sense': '[T]he discovery of the true meaning of a text or a work of art is never finished; it is in fact an infinite process.'[46]

For Gadamer, legal interpretation is the paradigm example of understanding, expressed in the notion of application. He criticizes the originalist idea that application is only a matter of reproducing an original meaning or an original intent. 'The real meaning of a text, as it speaks to the interpreter, does not depend on the contingencies of the author and whom he originally wrote for. (...) Not occasionally only, but always the meaning of a text goes beyond its author. That is why understanding is not merely a reproductive, but always a productive attitude as well.'[47] It is not the purpose of law to be understood historically, but to be made concrete in the act of interpretation (which, of course, presupposes the historicity of all understanding). This means that a legal (or any other) text in every concrete situation is understood in a new way, different from before.[48]

From an external system-theoretical perspective, Priban applies Gadamer's notion of effective-history to the political act of constitution-making, but adds to it an ideological-critical twist. In his view, constitution-making (and legislation in general) involves not only the reproduction but also the production of meaning:

> However, the historical nature of society and cultural sedimentation also mean that every intentional act of constitution-making or legislation, though itself a

45 Hans-Georg Gadamer, *Truth and Method* (2nd English edition; London: Sheed and Ward, 1981), 419.
46 Gadamer, *Truth and Method*, 265.
47 Gadamer, *Truth and Method*, 263–264.
48 For a more extended description of Gadamer's theory of understanding, see Bart van Klink, 'An Effective-historical View on the Symbolic Working of Law' in *Social and Symbolic Effects of Legislation under the Rule of Law*, ed. Nicolle Zeegers, Willem Witteveen and Bart van Klink (Lewiston: The Edwin Mellen Press, 2005), 113–145, 130–134.

> product of culture and the social past, stretches out beyond historical limitations and remains constantly subject to new interpretations, manipulations and elaborations.[49]

In our modern society, tradition offers a 'rich source of possibilities of meaning'[50] which is explored and exploited for present political purposes. With another reference to Gadamer, Přibáň claims that constitution-making has to be seen as 'actively manipulating prejudices'.[51] In Gadamer's view, understanding is not possible without playing off one's own fore-meanings and prejudices. Prejudices are to be conceived not so much as a hindrance but as a necessary condition to understanding: without them, a text cannot open itself to its interpreter. Playing off these prejudices means that, in the interpretative process, some of them will be proved to be wrong, while others will be confirmed. According to Přibáň, in the act of constitution-making prejudices are actively and consciously manipulated in order to create support for the existing legal and political order. That means, however, that tradition, as an authoritative source of new legislation, is no longer capable of fulfilling its stabilising function: 'The conservative power of tradition is eliminated because the present is always an innovative present breaking away and reconstructing the seemingly homogenous flow of history and tradition.'[52] According to him, modern law is characterized by flexibility and changeability. Increasingly, legislation has become an instrument or 'a major vehicle of social change in modern society'.[53] In times of revolution, (constitutional) law is able to give stability and legitimation to the new order by reproducing old and established legal symbols, but adapting (or 'manipulating') them in such a way that it suits the purposes of the new regime.

Innovation and continuity

When we compare the findings of the previous two sections, we seem to be confronted with an antithesis. From a sociological point of view, as Summer's study of the folkways was at pains to demonstrate, law is unfit as an instrument of social change but is bound to follow the mores prevailing in a given society. Its proper function is codification, not modification. On the other hand, from a (critical) hermeneutic perspective, law never merely confirms existing social norms and values – as far as they are contained in the law or read into it – but, in its application to a specific case, always changes them to a greater or lesser degree. Whether the law is successful in affecting change in social reality, is a matter of

49 Přibáň, *Legal Symbolism*, 51.
50 Přibáň, *Legal Symbolism*, 51.
51 Přibáň, *Legal Symbolism*, 52.
52 Přibáň, *Legal Symbolism*, 52.
53 Přibáň, *Legal Symbolism*, 54.

willingness of the law addressees to comply with the law and, therefore, of law's authority (or its persuasiveness or force, if authority alone is not sufficient[54]).

Building on Oakeshott's notion of radical temporality, I would argue that law is inevitably involved in a process of permanent change. The law can bring about change, both internally within the existing system of norms and externally in the relation to its environment, roughly speaking in three different ways. To begin with, the law can anticipate desired future social norms by implementing ideals which are supported by a minority in society, the moral avant-garde so to speak (with enough political power though to legally enforce its morality), while the majority is still hesitant or even hostile towards them. In that case, we may speak of modificatory legislation. Examples are anti-discrimination or environmental laws which, at least when they were first issued, met with much resistance in society and were considered to be largely symbolic.[55] If the law is successful in modifying current patterns of thinking and behaviour – which in most cases it will not be, as Sumner and many other legal sociologists attest – it causes rapid changes in society. Subsequently, the law may reinforce emerging social norms which, though not accepted by everyone, are on their way to becoming more and more established. By doing so, the law figures, not so much as a forerunner, but primarily as a catalyst of social change which was already set in motion by developments elsewhere in society. In that case, law may accelerate these processes of social reform and give them stability by means of what Jellinek would call 'the factual force of the normative'.[56] Finally, the law may apparently simply adopt and confirm widely accepted social norms, such as the prohibition on theft or murder. As a result, the social norms at hand are stabilized and, for the time being, immunized against further development. However, by merely reproducing established social norms the law makes them subject to change, that is to a creative production of meaning. The social norms at hand become part of the hermeneutic process of law application by which they are transformed so that they not only fit the existing system of legal norms but also do justice to changing circumstances and evolving moral and political opinions. In other words, codification gives inevitably way to modification. More radically, codification can be seen as a kind of modification: by trying to fixate what is in constant development, it changes the social and legal meaning of the law. A sheer repetition of the same norm in different times turns it into a

54 According to Hannah Arendt, *Between Past and Future: Eight Exercises in Political Thought* (New York: Penguin Books) 2006, 93, authority excludes *potestas* or power – 'where force is used, authority has failed' – as well as persuasion: 'Authority (...) is incompatible with persuasion, which presupposes equality and works through a process of argumentation. Where arguments are used, authority is left in abeyance.'

55 In my PhD thesis, Bart van Klink, *De wet als symbool. Over wettelijke communicatie en de Wet gelijke behandeling van mannen en vrouwen bij de arbeid* (Deventer: W.E.J. Tjeenk Willink, 1998), I investigated the phenomenon of symbolic legislation, in particular in the field of anti-discrimination legislation.

56 See note 22.

different norm, because the social context which co-determines its meaning will change constantly.[57]

So in all these cases the law is in one way or the other involved in the process of social change, either by seeking to anticipate, accelerate or resist it. The distinction between these three modes of change is gradual, not fundamental, and it can be matter of debate whether a specific instance of legislation has to count as modifying, reinforcing or codifying, depending on whether one considers the social norms contained in the law to be anticipated, emerging or already fully established in social practice. Moreover, in the course of time, an instance of legislation can switch from one mode to the other, for instance from modifying to reinforcing, when the legal norms provided by a statute are becoming more and more accepted, which seems to be the case with environmental law.

Although the law is involved in a process of permanent change, it still makes sense to raise the question in what way the law has to change by trying to affect change or to react to changes in its environment. What the sociological and the hermeneutic philosophical perspective have in common is a resistance to radical change. Radical change is a change that does not somehow build on already established social practices and the norms and values contained and emerging in these practices but instead tries to break away from traditional and customary ways of doing things, to create – when necessary by violent means – a new beginning or a clean slate, in the name of religion, rationality, universal rights or some other transcendental value. As Marquard argues, we never start from scratch when we are construing our world, both in the private and in the public sphere. We may be critical towards the way we have been doing things so far, but the criticism never applies to our world in its totality but only to certain parts of it that may have to be changed.[58] Moreover, the change does not come from nowhere but departs from earlier experience: we use the resources from our past to build our future.[59] As human beings we always lack something and what we lack in particular, according to Marquard, is time.[60] We do not have time to escape entirely from our past and to redesign our world *ab novo*. Our mortality compels us to conventionality. We may be living in a post-conventional era, as is often claimed. However, we still cannot do without conventions and customs. On the contrary,

57 As Lindahl puts it: '*Legal interpretation is, as a hermeneutic process, a differentiating repetition of normative meanings*', cf. Hans Lindahl, 'Rechtsvorming als politieke representatie: De kwestie van constitutionele toetsing' in *De rechter als rechtsvormer*, ed. Erik-Jan Broers and Bart van Klink (Den Haag: Boom Juridische uitgevers, 2001), 173–196, 192 (original italics; my translation).

58 As Marquard argues, we are 'partialkritisch' (partially critical), not 'totalkritisch' (completely critical), cf. Odo Marquard, *Skepsis in der Moderne* (Stuttgart: Philipp Reclam jun. 2007), 17.

59 This idea is nicely captured in the title of one of his collections of philosophical essays: *Zukunft brauch Herkunft*, see Odo Marquard, *Zukunft braucht Herkunft* (Dittingen: Reklam Verlag, 2003).

60 'Der Mensch als Mängelwesen ist vor allem das Zeitmangelwesen,' cf. Marquard, *Skepsis in der Moderne*, 89.

we need them more than ever. In a world in which the future is increasingly uncertain and unfamiliar to us we have to resort, by way of compensation, more and more to the past.[61] To be able to bear the burden of innovation, we need at the same time a 'culture of continuity'.[62] Because of the temporal finality of human existence, innovation and continuity belong together.

Marquard characterizes his philosophy as sceptical. In his view, *scepsis* is a philosophy of finality: due to the shortage of time, we have to start from our contingent conventions and customs when arranging and rearranging our world. *Scepsis* is 'the willingness to accept one's own contingency'.[63] If we want to change our normative order, we have to do it on a small scale, incrementally and slowly. As Marquard states, '[s]mall (that means: slow) is beautiful.'[64] Slowness, one could say, is a coping strategy that enables us to deal with our fast-changing world. It gives us time to reflect and react in a prudent way to new situations, building on practical knowledge and experience acquired in the past.[65] By developing a 'sense of slowness', we learn to discover the changes that are both desirable and feasible.[66] Politically speaking, *scepsis* is a moderate, middle position which avoids the extreme right as well as the extreme left. It does not intend to change the world by revolution, but only step by step, by means of small corrections. It negates the 'conformism of negation', that is the common intellectual inclination to reject entirely the current state of affairs (which Nietzsche diagnosed as nihilism[67]). According to Marquard, one has to have a little faith in the world as it is.[68]

A similar rejection of radicalism and affirmation of incremental change can be found in Michael Oakeshott's political philosophy. Oakeshott makes a general distinction between the 'politics of scepticism' and the 'politics of faith', which are related to different conceptions of government.[69] The politics of faith aims at

61 'Je mehr die Zukunft modern, für uns das Neue, das Fremde wird, desto mehr Vergangenheit müssen wir (...) in die Zukunft mitnehmen', cf. Marquard, *Skepsis in der Moderne*, 92.
62 Marquard, *Skepsis in der Moderne*, 89 (my translation).
63 Odo Marquard, *Individuum und Gewaltenteilung* (Stuttgart: Philipp Reclam jun., 2004), 79 (my translation). As Alexy argues, contingency in law is a reflected kind of contingency: '[T]he contingency of law is not pure facticity. It is a reflected contingency which is on the one hand relative to time and on the other hand transcending time while striving for the realization of the regulative idea of practical truth or correctness.' See: Robert Alexy, 'Law, Discourse, and Time' in Bjarup and Blegvad, (ed.), *Time, Law, and Society*, 101–110, 110.
64 Marquard, *Individuum und Gewaltenteilung*, 77 (original text in English).
65 See on this point also Hermsen, as discussed above.
66 See Weinrich, *Knappe Zeit*, 165.
67 According to Carr, Nietzsche conceives of nihilism 'as a condition of tension, as a disproportion between what we want to value (or need) and how the world appears to operate'. See Karen Carr, *The Banalisation of Nihilism* (New York: State University of New York Press, 1992), 25.
68 Marquard, *Individuum und Gewaltenteilung*, 112.
69 Michael Oakeshott, *The Politics of Faith and the Politics of Scepticism: Selected Writings of Michael Oakeshott*, ed. Timothy Fuller (New Haven: Yale University Press, 1996);

changing the world top-down according to a pre-established plan in order to achieve specific goals. In modernity, according to Oakeshott, two moral aspirations are prevailing: perpetual peace and ever-expanding prosperity.[70] After the attacks of '9/11', the dominant collective goal in many Western countries has become safety. In our era of modern rationality, law is seen predominantly as an instrument that can be used for whatever purpose.[71] The politics of scepticism, on the contrary, does not consider government to be a common enterprise directed at achieving certain shared goals (referred to as 'teleocracy').[72] It is suspicious of ideology and big plans. It prefers to leave the choice of goals as much as possible to the members of the community themselves. In Oakeshott's view, the Rule of Law constitutes a civil association based on the authority of non-instrumental rules which impose on its associates the obligation to respect the conditions prescribed in the law (or 'nomocracy').[73] Within the Rule of Law, peace, prosperity or safety are no collective goals but formal conditions that enable citizens to fulfil their own needs and pursue their own goals.

This position may be deemed conservative, in the sense that it tries to preserve what has been proven to be valuable in our social practices. However, it departs from the nostalgic kind of conservatism that tries in vain to keep the world as it is. Again, change is inevitable.[74] According to Oakeshott, there always is a discrepancy between the 'here and now' and how we would like the world to be. In practical experience, we are never fully satisfied with how things are and we are continuously looking for ways to improve our current situation, to bring the 'is' as much as possible in accordance with the 'ought'. Customs are helpful in mediating this tension. Although 'is' and 'ought' are destined to remain separated (we will never be fully satisfied), we can find in our past arrangements and our future projections clues for how to move on: 'How we ought to be is embedded in what we have been and imagine ourselves becoming to be.'[75] If we want to change our present situation we start, by necessity, from knowledge acquired in the past: '[W] here change seems to be going is a matter of intimations extrapolated from what

further discussed in: Michael Oakeshott, *On Human Conduct* (Oxford: Clarendon Press, 1975) and Michael Oakeshott, 'The Rule of Law' in Michael Oakeshott, *On History and Other Essays* (Indianapolis: Liberty Fund, 1999), 129–178.

70 Cf. Lon L. Fuller, *The Morality of Law (Revised Edition)* (New Haven: Yale University Press, 1969), 129.

71 Against the current instrumentalist conception of law, Witteveen defends in his last book *De wet als kunstwerk* the notion of law as an artefact or piece of art (the Dutch word 'kunstwerk' covers both meanings).

72 Oakeshott, *On Human Conduct*, 205.

73 Oakeshott, *On Human Conduct*, 203.

74 In the essay 'On Being Conservative', Oakeshott explains his notion of conservatism; see Michael Oakeshott, *Rationalism in Politics and Other Essays* (London: Methuen, 1962), 168–196. On the different meanings of his conservatism, see also *The Meanings of Michael Oakeshott's Conservatism*, ed. Corey Abel (Exeter: Imprint Academic, 2010).

75 Fuller, 'Radical Temporality and the Modern Imagination', 124.

we already know in experience.'[76] That does not mean that the past determines the course of history. What the past offers are indications or intimations, no 'necessary implications'.[77] Therefore, Oakeshott rejects the idea of universal rules or principles, such as human rights, which are supposed to transcend the concrete historical legal order. The only change the law can bear, is change that is effected from within the law itself.

Legal forms and legal change

As Kelsen argues, law regulates its own creation.[78] It contains legal norms which prescribe how new legal norms have to be enacted. A legal norm is not created from nowhere, but is enacted in a certain moment of time by a competent authority, following a prescribed procedure. In the process of its enactment, the legal norm acquires a specific format: the norm may contain a prescription, permission or a prohibition, which can be phrased as a (more or less) strict rule or a general clause, which is valid for a restricted or an unspecified period of time and applicable to a particular group in society or to all citizens, and so on. After that, when the norm is applied or maintained in concrete cases, also specific procedures are followed. The administration takes a decision, within a limited time frame as required by the law, and gives the opportunity to the parties involved to object to the decision taken. If the case is brought before the court, the judge will first hear both parties before she gives her verdict for which legally sound arguments have to be given. Earlier I have called this aggregation of forms that regulate in which manner legal norms are first created and subsequently applied, executed and maintained, *legal forms*.[79] A great variety of legal forms can be found on all levels of the legal system, starting from the creation of a general legal norm to its application on concrete cases. They involve many different aspects of the enactment and execution of the law, such as:

i *Time*: the period in which the administration or the court have to take a decision and the parties involved can object against it; the period in which a bill can be amended by member of Parliament; the amount of speaking time granted to the parties in a trial; the length of a sentence; et cetera.

76 Fuller, 'Radical Temporality and the Modern Imagination', 122. As Gerencser argues, two types of knowledge are necessary for attending to the arrangements of society: *technical* knowledge (concerning formal procedures and strictures) and *historical or practical* knowledge. See Steven Gerencser, 'Oakeshott on Law', in Paul Franco and Leslie Marsh (ed.), *A Companion to Michael Oakeshott*, 312–335, 315.

77 Fuller, 'Radical Temporality and the Modern Imagination', 124.

78 Hans Kelsen, *General Theory of Law and State*, tr. Anders Wedberg (New Brunswick, New Jersey: Transaction Publishers, 2006), 124 (see further below).

79 Bart van Klink, *Rechtsvormen: Autonomie van recht en rechtswetenschap* (inaugural lecture, Vrije Universiteit Amsterdam) (Den Haag: Boom Juridische uitgevers 2010), 27 ff.

ii *Space*: the domain in which a legal norm is valid, geographically and legally speaking; the ordering and arrangement of legally relevant locations, among which court rooms, town halls and prisons; symbolic divisions of space, for instance between the public and the private domain.
iii *Distribution of roles*: the authorities who are competent to carry out legally relevant actions (such as submitting a bill, taking a decision, or making a contract); the relationship (hierarchical or not) between these authorities; the tasks and powers assigned to them.
iv *Language use and discursive structures*: language use concerns the way in which a statutory norm or a legal decision by the administration or court is phrased, justified and explained, including the vocabulary used, the tone and style. Discursive structures are the possibilities of consultation, deliberation and public participation offered by the law, which precede the enactment or execution of a legal norm or follow after that.
v *Modalities of enforcement and control*: a broad category which comprises all means by which the law takes care that its norms are observed, either by force (through the use of sanctions) or by persuasion (via education, information and recommendations). In order to secure that the law is enforced in a lawful manner, structures of supervision and judicial review have to be installed.

In the various legal orders and legal domains, different choices are made regarding these aspects: the time for taking a decision or the speaking time may differ, the distribution of power is organized in a different way, the legal norms are phrased in more strict or more general terms, the sanctions are serious or largely symbolic, and so on. In a legal order dedicated to the Rule of Law the requirements are more strict regarding the aspects mentioned than in other political regimes. To give a few well-known examples: legal rules have to be phrased in general terms, so that they are applicable to specific groups in society or to all citizens, not to individual persons; strict rules are, in general, preferred over general clauses, because they are – generally speaking – more informative and therefore better equipped to provide for clarity and, therefore, legal security; in applying the law on concrete cases, the judge has to take her cue from previous legal decisions and she has to substantiate her decision.[80]

Legal forms are not fixed, but change over time: in the course of history obsolete legal forms are abandoned or simply disappear, new forms emerge and develop themselves, old forms are revised and reformed. Nevertheless, the existing aggregation of legal forms has a certain stabilizing effect on the entire legal system: the legal forms themselves ensure that established forms are not suddenly abolished or that, out of the blue, new ones are introduced. According to Luhmann, the legal system is both cognitively open and operationally closed.[81] That means that the

80 See further Fuller, *The Morality of Law*, 46–49.
81 Niklas Luhmann, *Law as a Social System*, tr. Klaus A. Ziegert (Oxford: Oxford University Press, 2004), chapter 2.

legal system is capable of receiving information from other systems, but it translates this outside information in its own code. Law is an autonomous system, because of its operational closure. It determines, on the basis of its own standards, what may count as valid law and what not. In other words, the legal system draws its own boundaries: '[O]nly the legal system itself can effect its closure, reproduce its operations, and define its boundaries.'[82] The law does react to changes in its environment, for instance under the influence of the public opinion. However, the law chooses itself the form in which it reacts to these changes: 'Change is not possible except through the legal system itself *choosing the forms* with which it accounts for the changes in public opinion, for instance by the prohibition of racial discrimination in public institutions (...).'[83]

The Rule of Law aims at protecting the legal system from radical change. By providing rules which are oriented to the future, it stabilizes expectations: 'The "Rule of Law" means that both the government and the citizens are bound for the future. (...) Rules bind generally, and for the future. They give individuals information of importance to their choices. This speaks against sudden and frequent changes.'[84] According to Marquard, administration and jurisdiction are 'compensation mechanisms' against the rush of modern life.[85] The same applies to legislation. Because of its extended and lengthy procedure, it takes a lot of time and effort before a bill is accepted (if it is accepted at all). The law is not resistant to change, but every proposal for change has to follow the legal forms which both enable and condition legal change.

There are several principles connected to the legal forms that proposals for legal change have to respect. I will discuss three of them here briefly, from three different perspectives, the legal, political and social perspective. To begin with, from a legal perspective, one of the main principles underlying the law as a legal system is *normative coherence*. As MacCormick argues, 'coherence stipulates that norms should not merely not contradict each other, but should also hang together purposively.'[86] That means that new norms have to fit within the existing system of norms. Kelsen calls this the 'principle of non-contradiction',[87] which must be presupposed in the idea of law; otherwise the notion of legality would be 'destroyed'.[88]

Subsequently, from a political perspective one may ask what changes are desirable. It is not my purpose, within the forum of science, to determine in which direction society, in my view, should be heading. However, starting from the Rule

82 Luhmann, *Law as a Social System*, 100.
83 Luhmann, *Law as a Social System*, 119 (my italics).
84 Mogens Blegvad, 'Time, Society, and Law,' in Bjarup and Blegvad (ed.), *Time, Law, and Society*, 11–22, 20.
85 Marquard, *Individuum und Gewaltenteilung*, 58.
86 MacCormick, 'Time, Narratives, and Law', 120.
87 Kelsen, *General Theory of Law and State*, 374–375.
88 Kelsen, *General Theory of Law and State*, 402.

of Law's central aim of providing stability, I would argue that legal norms should not be too much out of step with normative developments in society. I call this the principle of *political congruence.* Above, I identified three modes of change: firstly, the law can anticipate desired future social norms by implementing ideals which are supported by a minority in society; secondly, the law may reinforce emerging social norms which, though not accepted by everyone, are on their way of becoming more and more established; thirdly, the law may apparently simply adopt and confirm widely accepted social norms. (It is, of course, a matter of political judgment whether one considers the social norms at hand to be anticipated, emerging or already fully established in social practice.) Given the value of stability, the last two modes of change appear to be less problematic than the first one. The law may codify existing social norms, which Sumner seemed to consider the only thing the law can properly do. Priban rightfully warns against 'the proto-romantic perspective of the "deification of the factual"'.[89] According to him, in modern, rationally organized legal systems the 'mythical sources' of the folkways are replaced by the concept of legal validity.[90] That means, that social norms will inevitably be transformed when they are incorporated in the legal system. In other words, as I argued above, every codification gives way to modification. What Sumner failed to see was that the law can also operate as a catalyst of social change by reinforcing emerging social norms. Lawways may not be able to change folkways, but they can support some trends within the folkways and suppress others. A classic example is the case of *Brown vs. Board of Education* in the US. By banning racial segregation in education, the Supreme Court promoted the equal treatment of black and white people in other sectors of society. Moreover, the legal recognition of human rights (for instance, in the European Charter of Human Rights) may give support to social movements striving for justice. So one does not have to discard human rights out of hand as Oakeshott seems to do (see above), as long as their application is sensitive to local differences and historical particularities. Thereby, human rights will inevitably lose some of the absolute and universal character attributed to them.[91] It is the art of political judgment to create room for what, in the words of Jean-François Lyotard, is 'almost there'. In his view, this presupposes a passive or receptive attitude of waiting.[92] However, if future social norms are anticipated too rashly and impatiently (as in the first mode of change) problems of legitimacy arise: on what grounds can the moral avant-garde claim that its morality should be legally acknowledged and be imposed on the majority of society? Moreover, it causes problems of acceptance, which is connected to the

89 Přibáň, *Legal Symbolism*, 35.

90 Přibáň, *Legal Symbolism*, 12.

91 For reasons of time and space, I have to postpone the discussion of this point to a future article.

92 See Hermsen, *Stil de tijd*, 251–261. In this sense one could, with Corrias, speak of the 'passivity of law', cf. Luigi Corrias, *The Passivity of Law: Competence and Constitution in the European Court of Justice* (Dordrecht: Springer, 2011).

last principle below, that of empirical feasibility. Equally problematic, from the viewpoint of the Rule of Law, is the tendency described by Přibáň (see above) to cover up major changes in the legal and political order after a revolution by manipulating established legal symbols in the new constitution.

Finally, from a social perspective, it is obvious that the changes proposed should be realistic and viable, not only in technical or instrumental terms – are there enough, financial and other, resources available to effect the change – but also in social terms: Is the change accepted in society? Is there enough support? Does the change strived for not disrupt the social order? This may be called the principle of *feasibility*. (Whether a legislative proposal is feasible in this sense is, again, a matter of political assessment.)

Epilogue: the 'Novum'

There may never be a 'right time' for the law. The law is destined to be either too late, unable to keep up the pace with our fast-changing world, or too soon, offering aspirational norms for which people not seem to be ready. However, by connecting to what is already present and what is emerging in our social practices, it may make room for what is not yet there. What the three, principles discussed above – normative coherence, political conformity and empirical feasibility – amount to is the general idea that legal change should be slow, gradual and immanent. Only by changing our normative order slowly and gradually from within, building on the existing legal forms, normative traditions and social practices, is there sufficient time both for deliberation and reflection and for gaining support for the changes proposed. As Ernst Bloch indicates in *The Hope Principle*, time creates the space needed for change, improvement and a re-interpretation of what is already there.[93] With time comes hope – the hope that we can construct a better future by reconstructing our past. In our present arrangements, the new (or 'Novum') announces itself as a latent and real possibility – not necessarily, but hopefully for the good:

> Just as a Not-Yet-Conscious, which has never been conscious before, dawns in the human soul, so a Not-Yet-Become dawns in the world: at the head of the world-process and world-whole, is this Front and the vast, still so little understood category of the Novum. Its contents are not merely those that have not appeared, but those that are not decided, they dawn in mere real possibility, and contain the danger of possible disaster, but also the hope of possible, still not thwarted happiness, capable of being decided by human beings.[94]

93 See Hermsen, *Stil de tijd*, 153.
94 Ernst Bloch, *The Principle of Hope: Volume Two*, tr. Neville Plaice, Stephan Plaice and Paul Knight (Cambridge, Mass.: The MIT Press, 1995), 623–624.

Bibliography

Abel, Corey, ed. *The Meanings of Michael Oakeshott's Conservatism*. Exeter: Imprint Academic, 2010.

Ademollo, Francesco. *The Cratylus of Plato: A Commentary*. Cambridge: Cambridge University Press, 2011.

Alexy, Robert. 'Law, Discourse, and Time'. In *Time, Law, and Society: Proceedings of a Nordic Symposium Held May 1994 at Sandbjerg Gods, Denmark (ARSP-Beiheft 64)*, edited by Jes Bjarup and Mogens Blegvad, 101–110. Stuttgart: Franz Steiner Verlag, 1995.

Arendt, Hannah. *Between Past and Future: Eight Exercises in Political Thought*. New York: Penguin Books, 2006.

Blegvad, Mogens. 'Time, Society, and Law'. In *Time, Law, and Society: Proceedings of a Nordic Symposium Held May 1994 at Sandbjerg Gods, Denmark (ARSP-Beiheft 64)*, edited by Jes Bjarup and Mogens Blegvad, 11–22. Stuttgart: Franz Steiner Verlag, 1995.

Bloch, Ernst. *The Principle of Hope: Volume Two*, translated by Neville Plaice, Stephan Plaice and Paul Knight. Cambridge, Mass.: The MIT Press, 1995.

Carr, Karen. *The Banalisation of Nihilism*. New York: State University of New York Press, 1992.

Corrias, Luigi. *The Passitivity of Law: Competence and Constitution in the European Court of Justice*. Dordrecht: Springer, 2011.

Dworkin, Ronald. *Law's Empire*. Cambridge Mass.: Harvard University Press, 1986.

Francot, Lyana, and Sophie Mommers. 'Picking up the Pace – Legal Slowness and the Authority of the Judiciary in the Acceleration Society (a Dutch Case Study)'. *International Journal of the Legal Profession* 23 (2016): 1–19.

Fuller, Lon L. *The Morality of Law (Revised Edition)*. New Haven: Yale University Press, 1969.

Fuller, Timothy, Radical Temporality and the Modern Imagination: Two Themes in the Thought of Michael Oakeshott'. In *A Companion to Michael Oakeshott*, edited by Paul Franco and Leslie Marsh, 120–133. University Park, Pennsylvania: The Pennsylvania State University Press, 2012.

Gadamer, Hans-Georg. *Truth and Method* (2nd English edition). London: Sheed and Ward, 1981.

Gerencser, Steven. 'Oakeshott on Law'. In *A Companion to Michael Oakeshott*, edited by Paul Franco and Leslie Marsh, 312–335. University Park, Pennsylvania: The Pennsylvania State University Press, 2012.

Griffiths, John, The Social Working of Legal Rules'. *Journal of Legal Pluralism and Unofficial Law* 48 (2003): 1–84.

Hermsen, Joke J. *Stil de tijd. Pleidooi voor een langzame toekomst*. Amsterdam: De Arbeiderspers, 2011.

Jasiak, Anna. *Constitutional Constraints on Ad Hoc Legislation: A Comparative Study of the United States, Germany and the Netherlands*. Nijmegen: Wolf Legal Publishers, 2010.

Jünger, Ernst. *Das abenteuerliche Herz*. Stuttgart: Klett-Cotta, 1987.

Kelsen, Hans. *General Theory of Law and State* (translated by Anders Wedberg). New Brunswick, New Jersey: Transaction Publishers, 2006.

Latour, Bruno. *The Making of Law: An Ethnography of the Conseil d'Etat*, translated by Marina Brilman and Alain Pottag, revised by the author. Cambridge: Polity Press, 2013.

Lindahl, Hans. 'Rechtsvorming als politieke representatie: De kwestie van constitutionele toetsing'. In *De rechter als rechtsvormer*, edited by Erik-Jan Broers and Bart van Klink, 173–196. Den Haag: Boom Juridische uitgevers, 2001.

Luhmann, Niklas. *Law as a Social System*, translated by Klaus A. Ziegert. Oxford: Oxford University Press, 2004.

Marquard, Odo. *Zukunft braucht Herkunft*. Dittingen: Reklam Verlag, 2003.

Marquard, Odo. *Individuum und Gewaltenteilung*. Stuttgart: Philipp Reclam jun., 2004.

Marquard, Odo. *Skepsis in der Moderne*. Stuttgart: Philipp Reclam jun., 2007.

MacCormick, Neil. 'Time, Narratives, and Law'. In *Time, Law, and Society: Proceedings of a Nordic Symposium Held May 1994 at Sandbjerg Gods, Denmark (ARSP-Beiheft 64)*, edited by Jes Bjarup and Mogens Blegvad, 111–125. Stuttgart: Franz Steiner Verlag 1995.

Nousiainen, Kevät. 'Time of Law – Time of Experience'. In *Time, Law, and Society: Proceedings of a Nordic Symposium Held May 1994 at Sandbjerg Gods, Denmark (ARSP-Beiheft 64)*, edited by Jes Bjarup and Mogens Blegvad, 23–39. Stuttgart: Franz Steiner Verlag 1995.

Oakeshott, Michael. 'On Being Conservative'. In Michael Oakeshott, *Rationalism in Politics and Other Essays*, 168–196. London: Methuen, 1962.

Oakeshott, Michael. *On Human Conduct*. Oxford: Clarendon Press, 1975.

Oakeshott, Michael. *The Politics of Faith and the Politics of Scepticism: Selected Writings of Michael Oakeshott*, edited by Timothy Fuller. New Haven: Yale University Press, 1996.

Oakeshott, Michael. 'The Rule of Law' In Michael Oakeshott, *On History and Other Essays*, 129–178. Indianapolis: Liberty Fund, 1999.

Oakeshott, Michael. *Experience and Its Modes*. Cambridge: Cambridge University Press, 2002.

Přibáň, Jiří. *Legal Symbolism: On Law, Time and European Identity*. Aldershot: Ashgate, 2007.

Saussure, Ferdinand de. *Course in General Linguistics*, edited by Charles Bally and Albert Sechehaye, translated by Roy Harris. La Salle, Illinois: Open Court, 1983.

Sumner, William Graham. *Folkways: A Study of the Sociological Importance of Usages, Manners, Customs, Mores, and Morals*. New York: Dover Publications, Inc., 1959 (1906).

Van Klink, Bart. *De wet als symbool: Over wettelijke communicatie en de Wet gelijke behandeling van mannen en vrouwen bij de arbeid*. Deventer: W.E.J. Tjeenk Willink, 1998.

Van Klink, Bart. 'An Effective-historical View on the Symbolic Working of Law'. In *Social and Symbolic Effects of Legislation under the Rule of Law*, edited by Nicolle Zeegers, Willem Witteveen and Bart van Klink, 113–145. Lewiston: The Edwin Mellen Press, 2005.

Van Klink, Bart. *Rechtsvormen: Autonomie van recht en rechtswetenschap* (inaugural lecture, Vrije Universiteit Amsterdam). Den Haag: Boom Juridische uitgevers, 2010.

Van Klink, Bart, and Oliver W. Lembcke. 'Exploring the Boundaries of Law: On the Is-Ought Distinction in Jellinek and Kelsen'. In *Facts and Norms in Law: Interdisciplinary Reflections on Legal Method*, edited by Sanne Taekema, Bart van Klink and Wouter de Been, 201–233. Cheltenham: Edward Elgar Publishing, 2016.

Weber, Max. *The Vocation Lectures: 'Science as a Vocation' and 'Politics as a Vocation'*, edited by David Owen and Tracy B. Strong, translated by Rodney Livingstone. Indianapolis, Indiana: Hackett Publishing Company, 2004.

Weinrich, Harald. *Knappe Zeit: Kunst und Ökonomie des befristeten Lebens*. München: Beck, 2008.

Witteveen, Willem. *De wet als kunstwerk: Een andere filosofie van het recht*. Amsterdam: Boom, 2014.

Chapter 3

Law, time and inhumanity: reflections on the imprescriptible[1]

Luigi Corrias

Introduction

The crimes known as the core international crimes, such as crimes against humanity and genocide, are imprescriptible, i.e., no time bars apply for their prosecution. Ever since the atrocities of the Second World War, the notion of the imprescriptible has become synonymous with the law's dealing with the most heinous criminal acts. Not only lawyers, also philosophers have reflected on the theme and related concepts such as forgiveness and revenge. In criminal law, imprescriptible crimes form an exception. Normally, alleged criminal behaviour is subject to a so-called statute of limitations. These are 'statute(s) providing for a timeframe within which criminal proceedings must be instituted. Statutes of limitation provide for a non-exculpatory defense to a criminal defendant. Accordingly, even if the accused is allegedly culpable, a statute of limitations will bar prosecution if an action is not timely commenced. Statutes of limitation appear not only in criminal law, but in international, civil, administrative, or tax law as well.'[2] These statutes tend to 'limit two types of action: limitations to criminal actions and limitations to the enforcement of sentences.'[3] In other words, the passage of time affects the question whether or not a crime can be prosecuted. Time thus co-determines whether something is a matter of law. As said, the absence of such a statute of limitations is in contradiction with the normal situation in criminal law, in which crimes are (basically) all subjected to a statute of limitations. The especially shocking nature of international crimes is usually regarded as the justification for this exception.

In this chapter, I will concentrate on the various timelines involved in the question of imprescriptibility of international crimes. Because of its focus on the temporal dimension, this contribution is a *prolegomenon* to the debate on

1 An earlier version of this chapter was presented at the Paul Scholten Centre for Jurisprudence of the University of Amsterdam. For their valuable comments I am grateful to Lyana Francot, Roland Pierik, Bas Schotel and Marc de Wilde.

2 Ruth A. Kok, *Statutory Limitations in International Criminal Law* (The Hague: TMC Asser Press, 2007), 13.

3 Kok, *Statutory Limitations*, 14.

the desirability of imprescriptibility. The chapter is structured as follows. In the next section, I will first give a brief outline of the key legal issues concerning imprescriptibility in international criminal law. Then, I will elaborate on the relationship between imprescriptibility and the unforgiveable by revisiting the positions of Vladimir Jankélevitch, Hannah Arendt and Jacques Derrida. Within Continental philosophy, these authors are arguably the most important ones in the discussion on imprescriptibility. After that, I will distinguish four timelines involved in imprescriptibility and assess these timelines from the viewpoint of legal philosophy. Finally, I will take the perspective of the judge and spell out what is at stake in the judgment on an imprescriptible international crime.

The law of imprescriptibility

The core international crimes are the ones for which the ICC holds jurisdiction under article 5 of the Rome Statute, i.e. genocide, crimes against humanity; war crimes; and the crime of aggression. The imprescriptibility of these crimes is now uncontested from a legal point of view: 'international law, as it stands today, prohibits all states from making these core international crimes subject to prescription under domestic statutes of limitations.'[4] An individual does not possess the right to prescription, not even as part of the right to a fair trial as protected by article 6 ECHR.[5] When it comes to international documents, two treaties explicitly prohibit states from making the core international crimes prescriptible under domestic law.[6] These international treaties are the Convention on the Non-Applicability of Statutory Limitations to War Crimes and Crimes Against Humanity of 1968 of the United Nations and the European Convention on the Non-Applicability of Statutory Limitations to Crimes against Humanity and War Crimes of 1974 of the Council of Europe.[7] The problem is, however, that both treaties were ratified by very few countries. Notwithstanding the low number of ratifications, Hessbruegge points out that the 1968 Convention 'set in motion a process of gradual crystallization of the imprescriptibility principle into a customary norm as an increasing number of states introduced the principle of imprescriptibility of core international crimes into their national laws.'[8] This development culminated in the Rome Statute of the ICC of 1998. Confining ourselves to international crimes, one may say that with the adoption of the Rome Statute of the International Criminal Court (ICC) the uncertainty about the existence of a uniform state practice ceased to exist: a great number of states now acknowledge the imprescriptibility of the core

4 Jan Arno Hessbruegge, 'Justice Delayed, Not Denied: Statutory Limitations and Human Rights Crimes', *Georgetown Journal of International Law* 43, no. 4 (2012): 346.
5 Hessbruegge, 'Justice Delayed', 347.
6 Hessbruegge, 'Justice Delayed', 348.
7 Hessbruegge, 'Justice Delayed', 348.
8 Hessbruegge, 'Justice Delayed', 352.

international crimes.[9] Indeed, '[a] constant, uniform state practice to abolish statutes of limitations for genocide, crimes against humanity, and war crimes has emerged that is grounded in the sense of legal obligation (*opinio juris*) necessary to establish the "general practice accepted as law" that gives rise to a norm of customary international law according to Article 38(1) (b) of the Statute of the International Court of Justice.'[10] Directly related to their imprescriptibility, core international crimes also require specific behaviour from states. What emerged is 'an international obligation to either prosecute suspects of genocide, crimes against humanity and war crimes found on their territory or to surrender them to a third state wishing to exercise jurisdiction (*aut dedere aut judicare*). This obligation is now recognized as peremptory law (*jus cogens*) that overrides conflicting norms.'[11]

Article 29 of the Rome Statute contains the imprescriptibility of the international core crimes. It reads: 'The crimes within the jurisdiction of the Court shall not be subject to any statute of limitations.' The provision thus establishes a categorical exception to the governing rule of criminal law. From the temporal perspective I take in this contribution, it is interesting to look at the justification for this. In this regard, a hint seems to be given in the Preamble to the Rome Statute which opens as follows:

> The States Parties to this Statute,
>
> Conscious that all peoples are united by common bonds, their cultures pieced together in a shared heritage, and concerned that this delicate mosaic may be shattered at any time,
>
> Mindful that during this century millions of children, women and men have been victims of unimaginable atrocities that deeply shock the conscience of humanity,
>
> Recognizing that such grave crimes threaten the peace, security and well-being of the world,
>
> Affirming that the most serious crimes of concern to the international community as a whole must not go unpunished and that their effective prosecution must be ensured by taking measures at the national level and by enhancing international cooperation,
>
> Determined to put an end to impunity for the perpetrators of these crimes and thus to contribute to the prevention of such crimes,

While the legal value of the preamble of a treaty is disputable, it often contains important political and even moral messages. In this regard, it is my hypothesis that (the Preamble of) the Rome Statute shows how international criminal law imagines itself as law against inhumanity. In order to do so, it takes three steps: it

9 Kok, *Statutory Limitations*, 2. I follow Kok in the use of the term 'core international crimes'.
10 Hessbruegge, 'Justice Delayed', 353.
11 Hessbruegge, 'Justice Delayed', 354.

places the ICC within a specific time frame, it imagines the unimaginable atrocities and it introduces the need to attain justice in the future. I will now look at each of these steps in more detail.

The first move which is of interest in the Preamble is the way in which it places the ICC within a very specific time frame. Starting from 'common bonds' of all peoples, it seems to refer back to times immemorial, a kind of origin of mankind. In the very same consideration, however, it highlights the vulnerability of this bond mentioning a 'delicate mosaic' which may be 'shattered at any time'. The following consideration refers to a much more recent past: the terrible events of the 20th century: 'unimaginable atrocities that deeply shock the conscience of humanity'. The next two considerations seem to link the acknowledgement of these atrocities to the will to punish them and put an end to impunity. A later consideration will add that the establishment of the ICC is done 'for the sake of present and future generations'.

In this way, the establishment of the ICC is linked to a past (marked by atrocities which threaten common bonds), a present (in which the vulnerability of these bonds has moved the international community to end impunity) and a future (for the generations to come). Thus, the establishment of the ICC is placed within a specific narrative. The purpose of this narrative seems to be to legitimize the ICC: given the terrible events of the past and the need to protect future generations, the present demands the establishment of the ICC. Or, broader, given the inhumanity of which man is capable; we are in need of law to combat this inhumanity and a tribunal to ensure that the law is actually respected.

The second step is that the international community provides us with the legal image of the very atrocities it deems unimaginable. It 'imagines the unimaginable' by giving legal definitions of the crimes for which the ICC has jurisdiction.[12] Of course, it needs to do so in order for the ICC to do its job. Nevertheless, it remains remarkable how quickly the unimaginable nature of the atrocities is traded for legal definitions which are sometimes not undisputed (this mainly applies to the legal definition of genocide).

Thirdly, and here imprescriptibility enters the scene, justice is procured for the generations to come by stretching the reach of the law as far as possible. There is no loss of competence for the core crimes of international criminal law. Thus, the notion of imprescriptibility is inextricably linked with that of inhumanity. In other words: imprescriptibility seems to be the law's counter-image when it is confronted with inhumanity. The response of law when faced with inhumanity is thus that it assumes competence regardless of how much time has passed.

Imprescriptibility and the unforgiveable

From the perspective of the victims, Vladimir Jankélevitch arguably presents the most passionate case against the application of statutory limitations. In this

12 I am grateful to my colleague Wouter Werner for pointing this out to me.

section, I will discuss his views and Derrida's critical appraisal of his ideas in his work on forgiveness and the unforgiveable. For Jankélevitch, there is an unbreakable unity formed by the concepts of legal time bars, pardon and forgetting. In short, he argues that statutory limitations are not to be applied to the crimes associated with the Holocaust because this would amount to pardoning the perpetrators and forgetting about their deeds. This cannot be done for several reasons. Firstly, it is not for the survivors but for the victims to grant a pardon. Furthermore, time might have a hold on ordinary crimes; it certainly does not on the extraordinary horrors of the Holocaust. More in general, we have a duty towards the past to remember. Let me briefly explain these reasons, paying special attention to the temporal dimension of the argument.[13]

Jankélevitch holds that it is not for the survivors to pardon because the crime is unforgiveable and only the victims may pardon. He sees the application of statutory limitations as the legal and therefore official acceptance of amnesia concerning the Holocaust.[14] Jankélevitch argues that the Holocaust is of an extraordinary and unfathomable nature. To express this he uses such characterizations as unspeakable, a shameful secret, the product of pure wickedness, a metaphysical crime, immense, a truly infinite crime, inexpiable and monstrous, unmentionable, a work of hatred, incommensurable.[15] Jankélevitch qualifies the Holocaust as a crime against humanity: it targeted 'the "hominity" of human beings in general. (…) It was the very being of humanity, *esse*, that racial genocide attempted to annihilate in the suffering flesh of these millions of martyrs.'[16]

For Jankélevitch, statutory limitations are entirely beside the point, since the horror of Auschwitz only continues to grow.[17] Linking this argument directly to imprescriptibility, he states:

> The time that dulls all things, the time that uses up sorrow as it erodes mountains, the time that favors pardon and forgetfulness, the time that consoles, settling and healing time, does not diminish in the least the colossal slaughter; on the contrary, it never ceases to revive its horror. (…) Crimes against humanity are *imprescriptible*, that is, the penalties against them *cannot* lapse; time has no hold on them. (…) It is in general incomprehensible that time, a natural process without normative value, could have a diminishing effect on the unbearable horror of Auschwitz.[18]

13 For several ways of dealing with the past, see Antoine Garapon's chapter in this volume.
14 Vladimir Jankélevitch, 'Should We Pardon Them?', trans. Ann Hobart *Critical Inquiry* 22, no. 3 (Spring 1996): 566.
15 Jankélevitch, 'Should We Pardon Them?', 554–563.
16 Jankélevitch, 'Should We Pardon Them?', 555.
17 Jankélevitch, 'Should We Pardon Them?', 553.
18 Jankélevitch, 'Should We Pardon Them?', 556–557.

Against time bars, pardon and forgiveness, Jankélevitch strongly pleads for imprescriptibility, not forgiving and remembering. Legally, as we have seen, this entails the lifting of time bars and prosecution.[19] He introduces the notion of the unforgiveable:

> The extermination of the Jews was not, as was the massacre of the Armenians, a sudden outbreak of violence; it was doctrinally founded, philosophically explained, methodically prepared, and systematically perpetrated by the most pedantic dogmatists that ever existed. It fulfills an intention to exterminate that was long and deliberately matured; it is the application of a dogmatic theory that still exists and is called anti-Semitism. I would also willingly say, reversing the terms of the prayer that Jesus addresses to God in the Gospel according to Luke: Father, do not forgive them, for they know precisely what they do.[20]

This, therefore, culminates in a duty towards the past, a duty to remember.[21]

In a temporal key, the argument of Jankélevitch may thus be summarized as follows: the Holocaust is an extraordinary crime whose horror only grows and deepens with time. Hence, there is no place for legal time bars (it is an imprescriptible crime), nor for pardon or forgiveness (it is an unforgiveable crime). The application of time bars and pardoning would, Jankélevitch seems to imply, amount to forgetting. Instead, we have a duty to remember, to prosecute, not to forgive.

Jacques Derrida develops his ideas on forgiveness and the unforgiveable through a critical discussion with Jankélevitch (and Hannah Arendt). I will briefly discuss this discussion, since it brings to the fore important aspects for a philosophical understanding of imprescriptibility. Derrida distinguishes between the logic of forgiveness and the logic of exchange.[22] He juxtaposes this conditional, economic logic with the unconditional logic of forgiveness. The proper place of the latter is not so much the economic or political domain but rather 'Ethics beyond ethics'.[23] For Derrida, the central mistake of Jankélevitch is a philosophical one:

> the common or dominant axiom of the tradition, finally, and to my eyes the most problematic, is that forgiveness must have a meaning. (…) From the

19 Jankélevitch, 'Should We Pardon Them?', 562: 'The natural impulse of a person of feeling is to become indignant and to fight passionately against forgetfulness and to pursue the criminals, as the judges of the Allied Tribunal at Nuremberg promised, to the ends of the earth.'

20 Jankélevitch, 'Should We Pardon Them?', 564.

21 Jankélevitch, 'Should We Pardon Them?' ,571.

22 Jacques Derrida, 'On Forgiveness', in *On Cosmopolitanism and Forgiveness*, by Jacques Derrida, trans. Mark Dooley and Michael Hughes (London and New York: Routledge, 2001), 34.

23 Derrida, 'On Forgiveness', 36.

> inexpiable or the irreparable, Jankélévitch concludes the unforgivable. And one does not forgive, according to him, the unforgivable. This connection does not seem to me to follow.[24]

Here, Derrida submits, Jankélevitch follows Arendt. Dependent on human plurality, the faculty of forgiving is of crucial importance to her notion of action: 'Without being forgiven, released from the consequences of what we have done, our capacity to act would, as it were, be confined to one single deed from which we could never recover.'[25] There is, however, a limit to forgiveness, according to her:

> men are unable to forgive what they cannot punish and that they are unable to punish what has turned out to be unforgivable. This is the true hallmark of those offenses which, since Kant, we call 'radical evil' and about whose nature so little is known, even to us who have been exposed to one of their rare outbursts on the public scene.[26]

In his interpretation of these passages, Derrida stresses two points: '1 Forgiveness must rest on a *human possibility* (...) 2 This human possibility is the correlate to the possibility of punishment.'[27] Stressing the unconditional nature of forgiveness, Derrida seeks to keep it away from law and politics (and their economic, conditional logic of the exchange).[28] Against Jankélevitch (and Arendt), he points to the aporia of forgiveness:

> If there is something to forgive, it would be what in religious language is called mortal sin, the worst, the unforgivable crime or harm. From which comes the aporia, which can be described in its dry and implacable formality, without mercy: forgiveness forgives only the unforgivable.[29]

What does this entail for the related but ultimately separate concept of the imprescriptible? For Derrida, the imprescriptible in law gestures towards ahistoricity:

> a sort of beyond the law in the law. The imprescriptible, as a juridical notion, is certainly not the unforgivable; we have just seen why. But the imprescriptible, I come back to this, signals toward the transcendent order of the unconditional, of forgiveness and the unforgivable, toward a sort of

24 Derrida, 'On Forgiveness', 36.
25 Hannah Arendt, *The Human Condition* (Chicago and London: The University of Chicago Press, 1958), 237.
26 Arendt, *The Human Condition*, 241.
27 Derrida, 'On Forgiveness', 37.
28 Derrida, 'On Forgiveness', 39.
29 Derrida, 'On Forgiveness', 32.

> ahistoricity, even eternity and the Final Judgment, goes beyond history and the finite time of the law: for ever, 'eternally', everywhere and always, a crime against humanity will always be subject to judgment, and it will never be effaced from the judicial archive.[30]

Here, interestingly, Derrida points to the time of judgment on imprescriptible crimes as a 'beyond the law in the law'. I think that he wants us to see that imprescriptibility is a strange concept, both part of positive law and pointing beyond it. It is exactly this place of the concept, on the threshold between inside and outside the law, which makes it both fascinating and problematic. Later I will address what this place entails for the role of law and judgment in understanding imprescriptibility. In the next section, I will first discuss the different timelines implicit in the concept of imprescriptibility.

The time of imprescriptibility

In an article on the topic, Jan Arno Hessbruegge casts the debate on imprescriptibility as a clash between two legal values: justice and legal certainty. He makes it quite evident where he himself stands in this controversy: 'Justice delayed is no longer justice denied. When it comes to prosecuting crimes of the utmost gravity, considerations of material justice for the victims now prevail over formalistic notions of legal certainty.'[31] And yet, this is not the whole story. Even Hessbruegge implicitly admits that there is a connection between the two values when he links the case for time bars with the notion of procedural *justice*.[32]

A more complete view of the different interests and legal values involved in imprescriptibility may be gained when focusing on the temporal dimension of the issue. The historian Antoon De Baets distinguishes between four timelines involved in the problem of imprescriptibility. These are those of perpetrators, victims, society at large and historians.[33] Central to all four timelines is the relationship between time and justice. The first centres on the suspects and (alleged) perpetrators of international crimes. From their perspective, justice appears as the wish to receive a fair trial. Here, imprescriptibility may run counter to the presumption of innocence. With regard to this timeline, De Baets discusses two arguments against and two arguments supporting imprescriptibility.[34] First, the passing of time may influence the quality of evidence and the credibility of the witnesses. This occurred, famously, in the various cases against John Demjanjuk. Second, there is the risk of a 'memory trial': legal tribunals trying to write history by not confining themselves to (the acts of) the suspects but judging a whole regime. In

30 Derrida, 'On Forgiveness', 53.
31 Hessbruegge, 'Justice Delayed', 385.
32 Hessbruegge, 'Justice Delayed', 339.
33 Antoon De Baets, 'Historical Imprescriptibility', *Storia della Storiografia*, no. 60 (2011): 142–148.
34 De Baets, 'Historical Imprescriptibility', 142–144.

order to rebuke these arguments, De Baets points out that with the passing of time the quality of evidence may also improve, for example by the opening up of archives.[35] When it comes to the second argument, De Baets holds that the existence of legal time bars may often seriously impair constructing a complete picture of what has actually happened. Another argument against imprescriptibility concentrates on the suspect's ability to stand trial. Often, (s)he is so old that this is physically (almost) impossible.

Turning to the second timeline, De Baets stipulates that from the perspective of the victims one might argue that not prosecuting suspects of the core international crimes flies in the face of 'the laws of humanity'.[36] De Baets understands these in accordance with the famous Martens Clause, which states:

> Until a more complete code of the laws of war has been issued, the High Contracting Parties deem it expedient to declare that, in cases not included in the Regulations adopted by them, the inhabitants and the belligerents remain under the protection and the rule of the principles of the law of nations, as they result from the usages established among civilized peoples, from the laws of humanity, and the dictates of the public conscience.[37]

Thus, De Baets seems to say that since the victims are under the protection of the laws of humanity, not prosecuting suspects of these crimes would be a violation of these laws. In general, victims do feel a need for the (legal) recognition of their suffering and the trial as a stage where they can share their experiences and tell their stories.

The third timeline is the one of society as a whole. The value at stake here is that of social peace, of closure. Society may have less interest in prosecution, or, even worse, prosecution may be an obstacle in attaining reconciliation and social peace.[38] There are, De Baets tells us, 'three defenses to this powerful argument: continuity of obligations, public interest in the truth, and remembrance.'[39] In short, De Baets points to the fact that investigating gross human rights violations is a duty and may even be connected to the right to truth, which also has a social dimension with repercussions for the field of history.[40] Remembrance then ties in with what was discussed earlier under the heading of humanity but may also be linked to the desire 'never again':

> the rights to mourn and to remember are essential for the symbolic reparation of historical injustice, and as such, for restoring the dignity of deceased victims

35 Kok also points to the beneficial role of technology in this regard: Kok, *Statutory Limitations*, 243–245.
36 De Baets, 'Historical Imprescriptibility', 144.
37 Convention (II) with Respect to the Laws and Customs of War on Land (The Hague, 29 July 1899), preamble.
38 De Baets, 'Historical Imprescriptibility', 145.
39 De Baets, 'Historical Imprescriptibility', 145.
40 De Baets, 'Historical Imprescriptibility', 146.

> and for dealing appropriately with the past. Dignified commemoration is also a confirmation of humanitarian norms and in doing so it helps prevent the repetition of repression in the future.[41]

Finally, De Baets points to the timeline of historians who have an epistemological stake. Here, the danger is that of anachronism and the solution may be found in retrospection. Whatever one chooses, De Baets points out the political stakes involved. Victims have a right to the truth, entailing that they have a right to know what has happened in case of gross human rights violations.[42] Hence, 'failing to deal properly with historical injustice is an injustice *in itself*.'[43]

In the legal philosophy of Gustav Radbruch the idea of law, justice, is of a multifaceted nature.[44] It consists of the following three values: distributive justice, legal certainty and expediency. If we try to connect the four timelines of De Baets with these ideas, we can see that the interest of the suspects in a fair trial is basically an interest in a just criminal procedure, i.e. one in which their rights (as they are summarized in article 6 ECHR) are respected. In this timeline, legal certainty takes precedence over the two other values. The humanity of the victims, their need for legal recognition of their suffering, corresponds with the value of justice which asks of a legal order that it gives each his own ('suum cuique tribuere'). Finally, the interest of society as a whole is captured under the value of expediency, which stipulates that law always has a social purpose. It thus asks attention for the political origins of law. Politics assigns law its goals. Hence, these can change depending on the political colour of the ruling party. This makes the purpose of law dependent on political and social circumstances. In order to move on, a society might need to close the books and could decide to grant amnesty, to forget what has happened. However, there might also be political reasons to make crimes imprescriptible, e.g. when the new regime (thinks it) needs to bring members of the old regime to trial in order to start a new chapter. Here, in cases of dealing with historical injustice politics takes the guise of a politics of memory.[45]

41 De Baets, 'Historical Imprescriptibility', 146.
42 This right was developed in the context of the UN. A 2006 study on the subject concludes that 'the right to the truth about gross human rights violations and serious violations of human rights law is an inalienable and autonomous right, linked to the duty and obligation of the State to protect and guarantee human rights, to conduct effective investigations and to guarantee effective remedy and reparations. This right is closely linked with other rights and has both an individual and a societal dimension and should be considered as a non-derogable right and not be subject to limitations.' See E/CN.4/2006/91 of 8 February 2006, *Study on the right to the truth. Report of the Office of the United Nations High Commissioner for Human Rights*, 2.
43 De Baets, 'Historical Imprescriptibility', 149.
44 See also the introduction to this volume.
45 Wouter Veraart has taken up the thought of Radbruch in the context of dealing with historical injustice. Radbruch points to the so-called antinomic character of the three components of the idea of law, meaning that they presuppose and reject one another. Veraart has taken this dynamic relationship as the starting point from which to

As the reader will have noticed, I have refrained from assigning a place to the timeline of the professional historian within the philosophy of Radbruch. The reason for this is that he does not seem to have a proper place for it within his philosophy, which is a philosophy of *law*. Recall that De Baets linked the timeline of the historian with an interest in truth. This is the truth from a historical perspective. The historian, looking at past events from a certain distance and detached from the need to pass (moral) judgment, may take her time to take into account all the relevant sources in order to reach the highest possible level of objectivity. Writing history might thus be seen as the preliminary endpoint in an ongoing discussion. One may state that the truth of law and a legal trial is of a different nature. In a criminal trial only that which may be legally proven may count as evidence and thus play a role in the construction of a legal truth. It might, as Arendt and Koskenniemi amongst others have pointed out, even be dangerous to make a trial into a quest for the historical truth for this may transform it into a 'show trial'.[46] Furthermore, and this is a matter I will return to, the legal discussion – unlike the one on (the interpretation of) history – does have an endpoint.

Importantly, Radbruch denies the possibility of a perfect solution.[47] Whatever route one takes, one is forced to give precedence to one of the three components of law. *Mutatis mutandis*, one cannot but give more weight to one of the timelines of De Baets. This entails that any solution may be criticized from the perspective of the remaining components, or timelines and corresponding interests. There is no higher point where all tensions may be *aufgehoben* and every way of dealing with past injustice remains contingent and contestable. What might work at one time and/or place might not be the best solution for another time and/or place.

The time of judgment

Let us retrace our steps. In the second section above, I have sketched the legal and institutional framework of the imprescriptibility of international core crimes. In particular, I have shown how the ICC's jurisdiction of these crimes is legitimized through a very specific narrative in which past, present and future converge in the establishment of the ICC. Then, in the third section of this chapter, I have discussed Jankélevitch's and Derrida's views on the (im)possibility of forgiving the most heinous crimes. In the previous section, drawing on De Baets's work, I

understand different ways to deal with historical injustice. See Wouter Veraart, *De passie voor een alledaagse rechtsorde. Over vergeten, herinneren en vergeven als reacties op historisch onrecht* (Den Haag: Boom Juridische uitgevers, 2010).

46 On the topic of show trials and political trials, see: Hannah Arendt, *Eichmann in Jerusalem: A Report on the Banality of Evil* (New York: Viking Press, 1963) and Martti Koskenniemi, 'Between Impunity and Show Trials', *Max Planck Yearbook of United Nations Law* 6 (2002): 1–35.

47 Gustav Radbruch, 'Legal Philosophy', in *The Legal Philosophies of Lask, Radbruch, and Dabin*, trans. by Kurt Wilk, (Cambridge: Harvard University Press, 1950), 109–112.

distinguished between four timelines involved in the notion of imprescriptibility and analysed them with the help of Radbruch's philosophy. Now, I would like to turn to the perspective of the judge.[48] For imprescriptibility entails that law is called upon to judge, that a judgment remains possible and is even asked for. Which temporalities are involved in this possibility of judgment? In this section, I will distinguish between finality and finitude.

Drawing on the work of Paul Ricoeur, we can make more sense of the *finality* involved in the act of judging. Conceiving of the judgment as the intervention in a deliberation, the ending of a social conflict, Ricoeur submits that

> it is a characteristic of judgment on the judicial plane to interrupt the back-and-forth play of arguments by giving them an endpoint, even if this latter is provisory, at least so long as the ways of appeal remain open. But there will ultimately be a place or moment where a final ruling is sanctioned by public force.[49]

Now, interestingly, Ricoeur draws a distinction between two kinds of finality. Short-term finality concerns the particular conflict and the parties involved: it ends their uncertainty and 'expresses the force of law; what is more, it states the law in terms of a singular situation.'[50]

Yet, this type of finality does not exhaust the act of judging

> [b]ecause the trial process itself is only the codified form of a broader phenomenon, namely that of conflict. It is a question therefore of replacing the trial process, with its precise procedures, against the background of the broader social phenomenon inherent in the functioning of civil society and situated at the origin of public discussion.[51]

This background, Ricoeur argues, is ultimately formed by the specific way in which a society deals with conflict, namely through discourse and the institution of a trial instead of through violence in the guise of vengeance. Hence, judging should be understood within the framework of distributive justice.[52] As the German *Ur-teil* still expresses, there is a direct link between judging and giving each his own (*suum cuique tribuere*).[53] The ultimate or long-term finality of judging is thus 'the contribution of a judgment to public peace.'[54]

48 This perspective is also taken by Lyana Francot in her contribution to this volume. She focuses on the question of the authority of the judge in times of (social) acceleration.
49 Paul Ricoeur, *The Just*, trans. David Pellauer (Chicago and London: The University of Chicago Press, 2000), 128.
50 Ricoeur, *The Just*, 129.
51 Ricoeur, *The Just*, 130.
52 Ricoeur, *The Just*, 129.
53 Ricoeur, *The Just*, 130
54 Ricoeur, *The Just*, 127

In a move typical for his work, Ricoeur puts this goal in the key of mutual recognition:

> I think that the act of judging reaches its goal when someone who has, as we say, won his case still feels able to say: my adversary, the one who lost, remains like me a subject of right, his cause should have been heard, he made plausible arguments and these were heard. However, such recognition will not be complete unless the same thing can also be said by the loser, the one who did wrong, who has been condemned. He should be able to declare that the sentence that condemns him was not an act of violence but rather one of recognition.'[55]

This leads to a vision of society in which shared values take central stage and in which there is an intrinsic connection between judging and sharing:

> the act of judging has as its horizon a fragile equilibrium of these two elements of sharing: that which separates my share or part from yours and that which, on the other hand, means that each of us shares in, takes part in society.[56]

In order to evaluate what we can learn from Ricoeur, it is useful to consider what he said about finality by using Radbruch's terms. With Ricoeur we may thus grasp the relationship between what in the terminology of Radbruch are called legal certainty and expediency. Both these values have to do with the finality of the act of judging. The former with short-term, the latter with long-term finality. Legal certainty seems first and foremost pointed to particular legal conflicts. It asks of law to bring these conflicts to an end by an authoritative decision. Expediency has many guises, depending on the specific political goal pursued through the means of law. It is connected to long-term finality, since what is taken into account in this type of finality is the broader societal interest in a peaceful ending of conflicts, namely the avoidance of violence.

Furthermore, the act of judging is also understood by Ricoeur against the broader background of distributive justice. Also here, Ricoeur and Radbruch seem to concur. Yet, the connection Ricoeur seems to stipulate between distributive justice and mutual recognition is not altogether convincing. Mutual recognition is recognition between equals. This entails that we are dealing here with a horizontal relationship. Distributive justice, however, is justice done from the viewpoint of a third instance (e.g. the State). Hence, distributive justice implies a vertical relationship. In short, distributive justice precedes mutual recognition because the verticality involved in the former determines the horizontality of the latter. It – the third – distributes by giving each his own. But before the sharing can begin,

55 Ricoeur, *The Just*, 131–132.
56 Ricoeur, *The Just*, 132.

one needs to determine among whom to share, i.e. who is equal to whom. Since equality is never a given but results from an abstraction of given inequalities, it always rests on a political decision.[57] *Pace* Ricoeur, distributive justice is thus not only about sharing. Deciding precedes sharing, inclusion and exclusion precede distribution. Assuming an immediate link between distributive justice and mutual recognition begs the question.

How can this question be formulated within the context of our inquiry into imprescriptibility? It is the question of the self of a society, the question of the We.[58] This is not simply a normative but a reflexive question. In his famous book *Oneself as Another*, Ricoeur discusses this reflexive question on the level of the individual.[59] With regard to the plural level, Ricoeur also seems aware of it. However, he immediately links it to national reconciliation, amnesty and forgetting – notions which he rejects: 'What is at issue here? Certainly, national reconciliation. And in this regard, it is perfectly legitimate to seek to mend things by forgetting the tears in the social fabric. But we may worry about the price of this reaffirmation (which I have called magical and desperate) of the indivisible character of the sovereign political body.'[60] His main problem with amnesty seems to be that he regards it as a politically motivated command for amnesia with the aim 'to wipe away the traces of public discord.'[61]

Ricoeur juxtaposes amnesty with pardon. For the latter, memory constitutes a precondition. In one sense, Ricoeur argues, pardon is of an extra-legal nature both in terms of its logic and in terms of its end.[62] Indeed, '[p]ardon is a kind of healing of memory, the end of mourning. Delivered from the weight of debt, memory is freed for great projects. Pardon gives memory a future.'[63] And yet, pardon may – indirectly – have an effect on the legal order. It calls to mind the equity or fairness demanded from judgment: 'pardon constitutes a permanent reminder that justice is the justice of human beings and that it must not set itself up as the final judgment.'[64] Ultimately, its meaning should be placed on the symbolic level: 'On the deepest symbolic plane, what is at stake is the separation between *Dike*, the justice of the humans, and *Themis*, the ultimate and shadowy refuge of the equation of Vengeance (with a capital V) and Justice (with a capital J).'[65]

57 Radbruch, 'Legal Philosophy', 75.
58 On this topic – the importance of the first person plural in political discourse – see: Hans Lindahl, *Fault Lines of Globalization: Legal Order and a Politics of A-Legality* (Oxford: Oxford University Press, 2013) and Bert van Roermund, *Legal Thought and Philosophy: What Legal Scholarship is About* (Cheltenham: Edward Elgar Publishing, 2013).
59 Paul Ricoeur, *Oneself as Another*, trans. Kathleen Blamey (Chicago and London: The University of Chicago Press, 1992).
60 Ricoeur, *The Just*, 143.
61 Ricoeur, *The Just*, 143–144.
62 Ricoeur, *The Just*, 144.
63 Ricoeur, *The Just*, 144.
64 Ricoeur, *The Just*, 145.
65 Ricoeur, *The Just*, 145.

In this respect, I would like to draw a distinction between finality and finitude. Whereas the finality of the judgment may be linked to legal certainty and to social peace, the finitude of the act of judgment reflects the act as an administration of human justice. The finitude of the act of judgment thus reflects the contingency of the legal order it speaks for and the relativity of the rightness of the community it represents. Ricoeur comments that pardon may only be carried out by the victim and therefore 'pardon is never owed. Not only can it not be expected, but such an expectation can be legitimately refused. To this extent, pardon must first have run into the unpardonable, that is, the infinite debt, the irreparable wrong.'[66] The judgment of an infinite debt can only be finite – it can never exhaust the debt, never do absolute justice to the wrong suffered. As the reflection of pardon in the act of judgment, its finitude does not directly give us an argument in the normative debate regarding the desirability of imprescriptibility. Rather, it forms a constant reminder of the nature of the trial as the administration of *human* justice. It thus not only relativizes the extent to which justice may be obtained, it also points to the limits of law, to the boundaries of what law may achieve.

When does this Final Judgment which Ricoeur rejects take place? Not on the last day but on the day after the last day. In his 'comments on Ricoeur', Bert van Roermund – using a formulation reminiscent of Derrida – speaks of a 'time beyond time'.[67] Interestingly, these comments address Ricoeur's reflections on forgiveness:

> forgiveness can only be thought in a time beyond time, in the optative mode of wish and hope rather than in the indicative mode of description or the imperative mode of prescription. For this anticipation of a memory that will once turn out be unequivocally 'blessed', Ricoeur uses the theological term 'eschatology', though in a radically philosophical (rather than a theological) sense.[68]

Note thus that both the Final Judgment performed by human beings and the act of forgiveness as performed by human beings are connected to one and the same narrative about the end of time.

It is Van Roermund's aim to complement this narrative with a second one. This second narrative tells about the beginning of time and the coming into being of the human condition: 'why would we be interested in forgiveness in the first place? (…) Answering these and similar questions amounts to narrating a beginning of time that is unimaginable and yet undeniable; a story of how the human condition came about.'[69] In doing this, he also takes issue with Ricoeur's and

66 Ricoeur, *The Just*, 144.
67 Bert van Roermund, 'Time Beyond Time – Time Before Time: Comments on Ricoeur', in *Public Forgiveness in Post-Conflict Contexts*, ed. Bas van Stokkom, Neelke Doorn and Paul van Tongeren (Cambridge and Antwerp: Intersentia, 2012): 91–92.
68 Van Roermund, 'Time Beyond Time', 92.
69 Van Roermund, 'Time Beyond Time', 97.

Derrida's rejection of public forgiveness and reconciliation. In this respect, Van Roermund points to the political (or in his terms: proto-political) origins of reconciliation in the Arendtian notion of natality:

> Even if Arendt is too quick in finding a parallel between promising and forgiving, her concept of 'natality' points to the kind of dissociation that Ricoeur is (rightly) demanding. (…) For Arendt it is part of a political anthropology or protology, one might say – while Ricoeur refers it to a realm beyond the political, to a time beyond time that is the ultimate perspective of morality. But note that natality as a protological concept is as much about dissociation as the eschatological account of forgiveness can be.[70]

With natality, Van Roermund argues, we are at the very heart of politics – and of the human condition, one may add:

> Something new can be expected from individual men, precisely because they are held to account not only by those who are present (their fellow human beings), not only by one who remains absent (a transcendental God), but also, and even primarily, by those who are present in their absence (those who gave them birth and those to whom they will give birth). Again, this makes natality more rather than less political.[71]

In the political sphere, the power of beginning comes quintessentially to the fore in the phenomenon of revolutions. Just like public forgiveness and reconciliation, revolutions are about the re-constitution of the polity.[72] They are about saying 'We' again.[73]

But what role is there for law to play? Legal finitude as I understand it is the supplement to natality in the political sphere. For law not to freeze into a final word of power, it needs to remain open for an interruption by the unexpected. The judge should always leave room for the unexpected event of reconciliation and forgiveness by taking finitude into account. There seems to be no right time for the judgment. It hovers between a time before time and a time beyond time. And yet, between these two unattainable moments, the judge might find time and make space for the possibility of reconciliation and new beginnings. The Dutch word for adjudication is *rechtsvinding*, literally 'finding law'. In this case, finding law may be a question of finding time: the time of our lives, together within a space where one can expect the impossible.

70 Van Roermund, 'Time Beyond Time', 100–101.
71 Van Roermund, 'Time Beyond Tme', 101.
72 For this interpretation of revolutions, see Luigi Corrias, 'Revolution, Authority and the Institution of Legal Order: Phenomenological Reflections', *Archiv für Rechts- und Sozialphilosphie* 100, no. 3 (July 2014): 295–307.
73 Van Roermund, 'Time beyond time', 103.

Conclusion

In this chapter, the (legal) imprescriptibility of the core international crimes has been analysed from a philosophical point of view and with a special focus on the temporal dimensions. Several timelines have been discerned both in the justificatory narrative in the preamble of the Rome Statute of the ICC and in the academic debate on imprescriptibility. Whether or not one finds imprescriptibility desirable and/or defensible depends on which timeline is given precedence. Since these timelines correspond to irreconcilable legal values, no ultimate answer is available. Having to grapple with imprescriptibility in the light of the task to procure finality and attaining justice – such is the ordeal of a finite legal order.

Bibliography

Arendt, Hannah. *The Human Condition*. Chicago and London: The University of Chicago Press, 1958.

Arendt, Hannah. *Eichmann in Jerusalem: A Report on the Banality of Evil*. New York: Viking Press, 1963.

Corrias, Luigi. 'Revolution, Authority and the Institution of Legal Order: Phenomenological Reflections'. *Archiv für Rechts- und Sozialphilosphie* 100, no. 3 (July 2014): 295–307.

De Baets, Antoon. 'Historical Imprescriptibility'. *Storia della Storiografia* no. 60 (2011): 128–149.

Convention (II) with Respect to the Laws and Customs of War on Land. The Hague, 29 July 1899.

Derrida, Jacques. 'On Forgiveness'. In *On Cosmopolitanism and Forgiveness*, by Jacques Derrida. Translated by Mark Dooley and Michael Hughes, 25–60. London and New York: Routledge, 2001.

Hessbruegge, Jan Arno. 'Justice Delayed, Not Denied: Statutory Limitations and Human Rights Crimes'. *Georgetown Journal of International Law* 43, no. 4 (2012): 335–385.

Jankélevitch, Vladimir. 'Should We Pardon Them?'. Translated by Ann Hobart. *Critical Inquiry* 22, no. 3 (Spring 1996): 552–572.

Kok, Ruth A. *Statutory Limitations in International Criminal Law*. The Hague: TMC Asser Press, 2007.

Koskenniemi, Martti. 'Between Impunity and Show Trials'. *Max Planck Yearbook of United Nations Law* 6 (2002): 1–35.

Lindahl, Hans. *Fault Lines of Globalization: Legal Order and a Politics of A-Legality*. Oxford: Oxford University Press, 2013.

Radbruch, Gustav. 'Legal Philosophy'. In *The Legal Philosophies of Lask, Radbruch, and Dabin*. Translated by Kurt Wilk, 45–224. Cambridge: Harvard University Press, 1950.

Ricoeur, Paul. *Oneself as Another*. Translated by Kathleen Blamey. Chicago and London: The University of Chicago Press, 1992.

Ricoeur, Paul. *The Just*. Translated by David Pellauer. Chicago and London: The University of Chicago Press, 2000.

Study on the right to the truth. Report of the Office of the United Nations High Commissioner for Human Rights. E/CN.4/2006/91 of 8 February 2006.

Van Roermund, Bert. 'Time Beyond Time – Time Before Time: Comments on Ricoeur'. In *Public Forgiveness in Post-Conflict Contexts*, edited by Bas van Stokkom, Neelke Doorn and Paul van Tongeren, 91–105. Cambridge and Antwerp: Intersentia, 2012.

Van Roermund, Bert. *Legal Thought and Philosophy: What Legal Scholarship is About.* Cheltenham: Edward Elgar Publishing, 2013.

Veraart, Wouter. *De passie voor een alledaagse rechtsorde. Over vergeten, herinneren en vergeven als reacties op historisch onrecht.* Den Haag: Boom Juridische uitgevers, 2010.

Part 2

Legal certainty

Chapter 4

Airports built on shifting grounds?

Social acceleration and the temporal dimension of law

Hartmut Rosa

Introduction

Modern societies are characterized by a progressive transformation in their temporal fabric which can be understood as a consistent trend towards dynamization and social acceleration.[1] This trend implies that there is not just an ongoing technological acceleration in the speed of transport, communication and the production of goods and services, but also a progressive decrease in the stability of social arrangements and practices; that is, a change in the rates of change themselves. In other words, the social, technological and economic world transforms itself at an ever increasing pace. If one accepts this as a defining feature of modernity and hence as an adequate description of modern society, the interesting question for the role of law in this process arises almost as an enigma. On the one hand, law is supposed to ensure stability and calculability in a dynamic world. So this would mean that the rule of law is a prerequisite and even a safeguard for the dynamism of the socioeconomic world, but is not itself accelerated in the process. On the other hand, of course, laws need to be adapted to changing needs, values and environments, so lawmaking itself has become a perennial task in the modern world. And furthermore, of course, law itself can be the source of considerable social dynamics, as every historian can tell from the introduction of welfare, educational or gender legislation. In this contribution, I will try to sort out the role and function of law in the process of social acceleration in a systematic fashion. In the first step, I will briefly sketch out the logics and workings of social acceleration as a consequence of modernity's core principle: dynamic stabilization, and I will point out how this leads to escalatory processes of speed-up, increase and innovation. In the second step, I will scrutinize the argument that law can be understood as a functional and indispensable 'stabilizer', even a decelerator, in the acceleration-game. However, not all aspects or spheres of social life can be dynamized to the same extent and at the same speed. This systematically raises the danger of desynchronization, for example, between the speed of market developments and

1 Hartmut Rosa, *Social Acceleration: A New Theory of Modernity* (New York: Columbia University Press, 2013).

the pace of democratic decision-making. Therefore, as I will try to point out in the third step, law serves a vital function in 're-synchronizing' the pace of social life. This explains why law-making and applying, in some cases, actually is a tool to accelerate or dynamize certain social spheres or populations. Nevertheless, there is something like a natural speed-limit for law to be capable to fulfil this function. Beyond it, the rule of law itself is in danger of becoming anachronistic, of being too slow for the pace of social dynamics and hence of being eroded by the escalatory tides of acceleration. It might well be that late-modern societies are approaching this state of affairs quickly. It might mean, however, that the system of dynamic stabilization and social acceleration is finally undermining itself. This will be the topic of my concluding remarks in the fourth part of this paper.

Social acceleration and dynamic stabilization

Obviously, the question of what makes a society a *modern* society, is notoriously difficult to answer. In a way, it has been the foundational question for sociology altogether, and it has never been answered without concerns about normative or ethnocentric biases such that some social scientists think the concept of modernity should be given up altogether. Others, however, feel that there is something specific about the way modern society functions and reproduces itself that actually makes it distinct from other socio-cultural formations we know of, such as the Greeks or the Romans, the Babylonians or the ancient Chinese, Indians or Incas, for example. Here is my straightforward definition of what this difference might consist of: *A society should be called modern, I suggest, when its mode of stabilization is dynamic, that is to say, when it systematically requires growth, acceleration and (increasing) innovation in order to reproduce its structures and to maintain its institutional status quo.* Of course, no social formation ever could stabilize and reproduce itself in a merely *static* way. All societies occasionally need change and development. However, in non-modern social formations, the mode of stabilization is *adaptive*: growth, acceleration or innovations can and do occur, but they are either accidental or adaptive, i.e., they are reactions to changes in the environment (e.g., climate changes or natural disasters such as droughts, fires, earthquakes, or the appearance of new enemies, etc). Dynamic stabilization as I use it here, by contrast, is defined by the systematic requirement for *increase, augmentation and acceleration* as an internal, endogenous requirement.

When we look at it historically, it turns out that the shift from an adaptive to a dynamic mode of stabilization can be observed as a systematic transformation in all cardinal spheres of social life that occurs, despite some historic predecessors, mainly from the 18th century onwards. Most obviously, of course, it can be found in the realm of the economy. The accounts of both Max Weber and Karl Marx vividly focus on this transformation. In a capitalist economy, virtually all economic activity depends on the expectation and promise of an *increase* in the sense of profit of one sort or another. Money – Commodity – Money (m-c-m), is the short formula for this, where the prime signifies the increased return. It is realized, of course, through innovation (of product or process) and through acceleration, mostly in the form of increased productivity: the latter can be defined as an increase in output (or value production) per unit of time, i.e., as acceleration. I do not want to go into the details of economic theory here, which can show that the need for innovation, acceleration and growth really is intrinsic to the logic of production, to the logic of competition and even to the logic of the monetary and the credit systems. The net result of it is that without permanent growth, acceleration and innovation, at least under late-modern conditions of globalized economic and financial markets, capitalist economies cannot maintain their institutional structures: jobs are lost, companies close down, tax revenues decrease, while state-expenditure (for welfare and infrastructural programmes) increases, which in turn tends to cause a severe budget-deficit at first and then a delegitimation of the political system; all of this can be seen in the present crisis in Southern Europe, particularly in Greece. Thus, not just the economic system in a narrow sense depends on the logic of escalation which is the consequence of a mode dynamic stabilization, but also the welfare-state and the system of democratic politics. As Niklas Luhmann showed more than 30 years ago, the latter is based on the logic of dynamic stabilization, too; not only has the rather static monarchic order – where kings or queens rule for a lifetime and then are simply replaced by a dynastic succession that preserves order in an identical fashion – given way to a democratic system that require dynamic stabilization through repeated voting every four or five years, but, much more dramatically: elections can only be won on the basis of political programmes that promise an *increase* – an increase in income, or in jobs, or in universities, high school diplomas, hospital beds etc.[2]

Yet, quite independent of the escalatory logic of capitalist reproduction, the modern conception of *science* and knowledge display a quite similar shift from and adaptive to a dynamic mode of stabilization which transforms its institutional order; in non-modern social formations, knowledge quite regularly is considered and treated as a social possession, or a treasure, that carefully needs to be handed down from one generation to the next. This knowledge in most cultures is traced back to some ancient or sacred source, for example to 'holy scriptures', or 'the wisdom of the ancient', and there always is an attempt to preserve this knowledge in a 'pure' form. It is knowledge about *how things are done* – how one builds a home, or produces clothing and food, for example, when to sow or to reap or how and when to hunt game, and, not least, how to perform the sacred rituals. Knowledge is transferred from one generation to the next either simply by doing and performing, or in some form of *schola*. By contrast, modern societies shift from *Wissen* (knowledge) in this sense to Wissen*schaft* (science). As the second part in the German word indicates quite nicely, the central form and art of knowledge in modernity is not about preservation and schooling, is no longer about treasuring, but it is about systematically pushing the borders, increasing the

2 Niklas Luhmann, *Politische Theorie im Wohlfahrtsstaat* (München: Olzoc, 1981).

volume of the known, transgressing into the yet unknown. Science is about looking further into the universe than ever before, deeper into the micro-structures and particles of matter, closer into the workings of life etc. The sacred spaces of knowledge have moved from the schola to the laboratory: Science is reproduced dynamically, through growth, increase and transgression. Just as the propelling dynamics of m-c-m lies at the heart of modern economy, a similar process of knowledge-research-increased knowledge (k-r-k) provides the basis for modern science.

In *Science as a Vocation*, Max Weber[3] has formulated this point quite forcefully:

> In science, each of us knows that what he has accomplished will be antiquated in ten, twenty, fifty years. That is the fate to which science is subjected; it is the very meaning of scientific work, to which it is devoted [...] Every scientific 'fulfilment' raises new 'questions'; it asks to be 'surpassed' and outdated. Whoever wishes to serve science has to resign himself to this fact. Scientific works [...] will be surpassed scientifically – let that be repeated – for it is our common fate and, more, our common goal. We cannot work without hoping that others will advance further than we have. In principle, this progress goes on ad infinitum.

Finally, in the arts, the situation looks quite the same, too; after millennia of a predominantly mimetic art, for which the goal of artistic creation is the emulation either of nature or of some traditional style or ancient mastery, there is a shift in literature and poetry as well as in painting, dancing and music that puts the onus on innovation and originality; as in science – and quite contrary to what Weber thought – going beyond what others have done before becomes the central challenge in the arts as well.[4]

In this way, the logic of dynamic stabilization has become the hallmark of modern society in toto. It is translated into individual subjects' lives via the logic of competition: In the end, it is us humans who have to achieve growth, acceleration and innovation through incessant optimization, and we play this escalatory game through the endless accumulation of economic, cultural, social and bodily capital. As with Weber's capitalist entrepreneur, modern subjects find themselves unavoidably 'on their way down', like on a downward escalator or on a slippery slope, if they do not run uphill to improve their standings and keep track with the changes around them.[5] So in the end, the acceleration-cycle between technological acceleration, the acceleration of social change and the corresponding acceleration of the pace of life that results from dynamic stabilization has become a

3 Max Weber, *Essays in Sociology*, trans. H. H. Gerth and C. Wright Mills (New York: Oxford University Press, 1946).

4 Boris Groys, *On The New* (London: Verso, 2014).

5 Hartmut Rosa, 'De-Synchronization, Dynamic Stabilization, Dispositional Squeeze', in *The Sociology of Speed*, ed. Judy Wajcman and Nigel Dodd (Oxford: Oxford University Press, 2017), 25–41.

self-propelling mechanism in modernity. It maintains the socioeconomic status quo as well as the institutional structure of the market system, of the welfare-state as well as of science, art and education via a substantive escalation of its productive power and substantive output. Needless to stay, the stability achieved thereby is robust enough to keep the machines going for more than 250 years already, but nevertheless increasingly fragile, too; it can be undermined anytime either because of its externalities, e.g. in ecological costs, because of a failure of social integration despite growth and acceleration (as e.g. in phenomena of 'jobless growth' and increased social precarization), or because of problems created by desynchronization, to which I will turn in the fourth section below. At this point, perhaps, it is sufficient to see that dynamic stabilization resembles a ride on a bicycle: The faster the bike wheels, the more robust it is in its course (a slow bike can be made to tumble at the slightest push from the side, not so a fast one) – but the higher the risk of severe accidents, too. Thus, certainly, the faster the ride on the bike goes, the more foresight is required: the road needs to be even and predictable. This foresight, I want to claim, is provided by modern law.

Law as a functional decelerator

For Max Weber, rationalization, as the key-process of modernity, means making the world, or the conditions of action, calculable and controllable. When it comes to the social conditions of action, there is no doubt that modern law plays a key-role in achieving and guaranteeing just that: stability and predictability in the background conditions of action and of planning. Dynamic stabilization to a large extent rests on the logic of (long-term) investments: money, energy and other resources are invested, for example, to yield profits in the long run, but the prospects for these investments needs to be calculable. Similarly, no one enrolls on a long-term educational or research-programme if the payoffs cannot be expected with a certain degree of predictability. And inventions can only become social innovations when there are predictable and calculable pathways for introducing them. Hence, the faster and more dynamic a social formation becomes, the more it requires a solid, stable infrastructure to keep the cycle of acceleration and dynamization going. In fact, the same relationship between dynamics and stability can be observed with respect to the requirements of traffic: the faster the vehicles of transport become, the vaster the requirements for stable and inert infrastructural requirements 'on the ground'. Train stations already take an extensive amount of space when compared to what was needed for horse-carts, but airports multiply that size considerably – let alone spaceports.

In the same way, the economic, technological and cultural dynamization of society needs a corresponding institutional 'grounding', or stabilization, of societal background conditions; and this stability is provided and secured by law in its quite extensive ramifications. Just as aeroplanes need vast, solid, inert airports, economic transactions and technological developments need stable horizons of calculability for planning and investment, and hence the security of legal regulations. Without them, social acceleration in the sense of technological progress and economic growth would be impossible. Thus, just as civil law ensures the stability needed for trade and business, constitutional law provides predictability and stability for the conditions of politics and political law-making itself. Hence, the vast extension of legal regulations over most if not all aspects of social life in modernity can be seen as a reaction and an answer to the emerging processes of acceleration and dynamization since the 18th century. They provide, so to speak, the 'airports' for the take-off of the m-c-m and k-r-k machines.

As it turns out, therefore, the relationship between law and acceleration is quite complex, it is almost dialectical in fact. If, as I have argued above, modernization signifies the acceleration or dynamization of the social world, this implies the contingency and malleability of social institutions and arrangements as well. Modern law appears to be a reaction to this very experience; it does not put an end to this contingency and malleability, but it ensures that institutional change and development ensue along predictable 'tracks' and calculable pathways. The rules of the acceleration-game, so to speak, can be changed themselves in due process, but only at a slow and steady pace.[6] In this sense, I want to suggest, law serves at least sometimes as a functional 'decelerator' in the process of social acceleration. It slows down and 'tames' (chaotic) dynamicity in some segments of social life in order to unleash the powers of dynamization and to allow for unprecedented speeds in other spheres.

Law as a re-synchronizer

However, not all of those other spheres, and not all aspects of social life or all social groups are 'speedable' to the same extent. By consequence, a basic problem caused by endemic and escalating dynamization consists in the fact that accelerated systems or actors systematically put pressure on the slower ones – and risk de-synchronization and friction at the points of intersection. Whenever there is a temporal juncture or 'fit' between two systems, actors or processes, and one of them increases its velocity, the other one appears to be too slow, it figures as a brake or hindrance, and synchronization is impaired. This, on the one hand, helps to explain the deepening of social stratification. In fact, those who are well-equipped with economic, social and cultural capital successfully use these as resources in the competitive struggle for acceleration: they enter the accumulative race for their children before they are even born, while those who lack such resources are 'left behind', resulting in a further widening of the social gap.

But de-synchronization also lies at the heart of the four major crises of late modern societies in the 21st century. If we loosely follow a 'systems-theoretical'

6 Holger Bonus, 'Die Langsamkeit der Spielregeln', in Die Beschleunigungsfalle oder der Triumph der Schildkröte (3rd ed.), edited by Klaus Backhaus and Holger Bonus (Stuttgart: Schäffer/Pöschel, 1998), 41–56.

approach,[7] we can envision the 'social system' as being located between the over-arching ecological system(s) and the individuals' psychosomatic systems. The acceleration of society places stress and pressures of de-synchronization on both these other systems. Furthermore, even within society in a narrow sense, some processes or subsystems are more 'accelerable' than others. For example, economic transactions, scientific progress, media-processing and technological innovations can be accelerated relatively easily, while the processes of political democracy and cultural reproduction cannot – thus, democracy in particular (and perhaps education as well) is in increasing danger of being 'de-synchronized'. Finally, the problem of de-synchronization reappears even *within* separate social *sub*systems. Thus, while the financial markets in their interaction and transfer systems and algorithms can be accelerated to almost the speed of light, thereby altering how transactions are conducted and profits can be made, the 'real economy' of material production and consumption remains to be much slower. This causes frictions between economic production and financial transaction. Hence, potentially harmful de-synchronization lurks even within the economic realm itself. Now the claim I want to explore in the following is that in societies operating in a mode of dynamic stabilization, law serves the basic function of bridging the ensuing temporal gaps and thus of iteratively re-synchronizing social spheres and processes. Let us take a closer look at those processes one by one.

Macro-level: environmental law

Virtually all aspects of what we call 'the ecological crisis' can be re-interpreted as a problem of de-synchronization. The temporality of many natural processes – or nature's proper times[8] – obviously is out of sync with our sociotechnical and socioeconomic temporalities. For example, it is not a problem for nature per se if we cut down trees and catch fish – but it becomes a problem if we cut down the trees in the rainforest and catch the fish in the oceans at rates too high for the pace of natural reproduction. Obviously, the discrepancy vastly increases when we look at the rate at which we deplete oil and carbon-based energy supplies and the time needed for nature to reproduce *them*. Similarly, most of what is considered to be a 'poisoning' of the environment is only a problem because we produce these substances and emissions at speeds that are higher than nature's capability to dispose of them. Finally, even the problem of 'global warming' can be read as a form of physical and material de-synchronization: *heating up the atmosphere* literally means making the molecules in these layers of air *move faster*; thus, the physical heat produced through technological acceleration on the ground leads to atmospheric acceleration in the skies. In other words, the process of material dynamization

7 Fritz Reheis, *Kreativität der Langsamkeit: Neuer Wohlstand durch Entschleunigung* (Darmstadt: Wissenschaftliche Buchgesellschaft, 1996).

8 Helga Nowotny, *Time: The Modern and Postmodern Experience* (Cambridge/Malden: Polity, 1996).

driven by the consumption of physical energy leads to a 'de-synchronization' in earth's atmosphere that results in its warming.

Now, interestingly, as soon as these phenomena of 'de-synchronization' have entered social awareness and political discourse, the idea and then the institutions of *environmental law* pop up. Environmental law actually serves the main, if not the sole, purpose of protecting nature's proper times against the assaults of social acceleration. It regulates the amount of emissions that can be released into the atmosphere per unit of time, or the amount of toxic waste that can be dumped, but also the speed of wood cutting, hunting or fishing, or it limits the purposes and speeds of the consumption of scarce material resources. Hence, environmental law is an attempt to re-synchronize nature's and society's temporal patterns in order to guarantee at least some degree of sustainability

Micro-level: burnout and labour law

If the mode of dynamic stabilization entails the incessant acceleration of material, social and cultural reproduction of society, this cannot leave the structures of the individual psyche (and body) and the character of the human subject untouched. Thus, the question arises as to how much acceleration and dynamization individuals can take before they 'break', so to speak. Here the evidence for pathological forms of de-synchronization appears to be overwhelming as well. Thus, while the use of drugs that slow people down ('downers' like heroine, LSD, alcohol) are on the decline, 'speed', amphetamines and other drugs that promise 'synchronization' (like Ritalin, Taurin, Focus Factor etc.) are on the rise.[9] In fact, most forms of 'human enhancement' have to do with increasing the accelerability of human bodies and minds – from 'fixing' those who are viewed as 'disabled' to transhumanist fantasies of reconciling the speed of digital technology with the speed of social actors. Signs of growing pathological de-synchronization in the form of burnout and depression are alarming. In fact, even the WHO now realizes that – alongside other pathological stress-reactions like eating and sleeping disorders and chronic anxieties – depression and burnout are the fastest-growing health problem on a worldwide scale.[10] One of the most striking features of both burnout and depression is the resulting lack of dynamics: for those who fall into the trap of a burnout or depression, time stands still, the world and/or the self appear to be 'frozen', void of motion and significance. This has led researchers like Alain Ehrenberg[11] to suppose that depression is a stress-induced reaction of a de-synchronized psyche to the speed requirements of modern life. The fact that journals and magazines all over the world regularly double their sales by reporting on

9 United Nations Office on Drugs and Crime, *World Drug Report 2015* (New York: United Nations Publications, 2015).

10 Gabriela Stoppe and Anke Bramesfeld and Friedrich-Wilhelm Schwartz, *Volkskrankheit Depression? Bestandsaufnahme und Perspektiven* (Heidelberg: Springer, 2006).

11 Alain Ehrenberg, *The Weariness of the Self: Diagnosing the History of Depression in the Contemporary Age* (Montreal: McGill-Queens University Press, 2010).

stress, burnout, depression and exhausted selves on their cover-page should serve as a warning against an impending state of de-synchronization, even for those who are sceptical of the diagnostic practices of our medical services.

However, the problem of 'de-synchronization' between workers and their families on the one hand and the 'proper-times' of capitalist production on the other is not a new phenomenon at all. Since the evolution of modern labour law in the early industrial age, the length of the work day and of working hours as well as legal provisions for the protection of recreational 'proper times' such as week-ends or holidays,[12] but also of educational periods, have built the focus of legisla-tion not just in industrial relations but also in the struggle for many if not all welfare-provisions: protecting the temporal requirements of pregnancy and par-enthood, of education, disease and old-age is perhaps the central challenge of social and welfare legislation writ large. Contemporary struggles over labour laws (such as the ones erupting violently in France in 2016) express the attempt to balance or synchronize the temporal needs of workers and employees against the logic of 24/7 availability in the age of digital technologies and against neoliberal regimes of accelerated hiring and firing. Thus, as in the case of environmental law, it turns out that a central function of law-making in the realms of labour regulations as well as welfare institutions lies in the synchronization of social and industrial or capitalist time

Intra-social: the speed of finance and the real economy

Yet, this is not all there is to de-synchronization. In addition to acceleration pro-ducing temporal problems between natural and socio-technical processes and between the human fabric and capitalist requirements, it turns out that even within social subsystems such as the economy there are different speeds at work which can cause pathological frictions. For even after two hundred years of tech-nological acceleration, producing cars or houses is still a time-consuming process, and so is, to some extent at least, the production (and designing) of clothes or computers. Furthermore, it is not just the production, but even more so the *con-sumption* of these commodities that is time-consuming. Compared to its quickly crumbling price, it takes ages to really 'consume', i.e. *read*, a book, or *listen* to an album (to give just two examples), and the ratio for the other consumer goods mentioned is not much better either. Yet, the need for growth and speed in global competitive markets is insatiable. Hence, it is a small wonder that the financial industries discovered ways and means to dynamize the speed of the flows of capital and the creation of profits way beyond these material speed barriers. By buying and selling 'financial products', and thus by 'virtualizing' production and con-sumption, transactions could be accelerated to an extent approaching the speed of light. In fact, in many ways the speed of financial transactions has become too

12 Edward P. Thompson, 'Time, Work-Discipline and Industrial Capitalism', *Past & Present* 38 (1967): 56–97.

high for human agents to understand or steer any more: it is left to computer algorithms that harvest surplus profits by exploiting fluctuations in the market within micro-seconds. Alas, this inevitably led to a serious de-synchronization between the financial markets and the 'real' or material economy, up to a point where these two had little connection with one another at all. In this way, 'the bubble' that splashed in 2008 was a temporal bubble, too, and its bursting had dramatic consequences that are yet to be resolved. Re-synchronization seems to be an economic necessity, even to economists, but it comes at a high price: it seems that the world-economy is still seeking a temporal balance not just between the financial industry on the one hand and the 'real industries' on the other, but also between markets and governments or politics. And it may very well be that such a re-synchronization is only possible at the price of a significant slow-down of the (financial) economy.

In any case, legal regulations are the main, if not the sole instrument through which re-synchronization can be achieved. In fact, it was changes in national and international financial laws and economic regulations that unleashed the unprecedented speed of financial capitalism in the first place, and it is legal instruments such as a '*tobin tax*' or new requirements for banking – e.g. the separation of investment- and commercial banking – that are discussed or introduced now to slow down the speed of trading and speculation and to secure the proper times of the 'real economy'.

Inter-social de-synchronization: constitutional law, markets and legislation

Finally, a potentially most severe form of social desynchronization affects the logic and temporality of law itself.[13] It is the widening temporal gap between the speed of proper democratic legislation and the temporal requirements made on this very legislation by faster social spheres or systems such as the markets, the media or techno-scientific progress.

As I have argued at length elsewhere,[14] the current weakness of western democracy – as can be seen from both its unattractiveness for non-western states in Africa or Asia as well as the decline in support and credibility it receives in its core countries, where populists and demagoguery are on the rise[15] – basically arises from the fact that the democratic processes of political will-formation, decision-making and implementation are, by their very nature, inevitably time-consuming. In fact, the more pluralistic and post-conventionalist society gets, and the more complex its networks, chains of interaction and contexts of action and

13 Lyana Francot and Sophie Mommers, 'Picking up the Pace: Legal Slowness and the Authority of the Judiciary in the Acceleration Society (A Dutch Case Study)', *International Journal of the Legal Profession* 23 (2016): 1–19.

14 Rosa, *Social Acceleration*, 251–276.

15 Cf. Colin Crouch, *Post-Democracy* (Cambridge: Polity 2004).

decision-making become, the slower democracy – and hence legislation – proceeds. Thus, while the speed of cultural and economic life and technological change increases, the pace of democracy slows down – and hence, we can observe a frightening extent of de-synchronization between politics on the one side and the social systems it tries to control or steer on the other.

It is important to notice at this point that this has not always been the state of affairs, though. Legislation is not intrinsically slower than the rest of society – quite the contrary: when society shifted to a mode of dynamic stabilization in the 18th century, and in many respects for a long time even through the 20th century, legislation was the prime political instrument through which this shift was achieved, and hence, it was the prime instrument to dynamize or speed-up social developments; the prime tool of social engineering. This holds for economic laws just as for educational laws, family law, welfare laws, laws regulating the use and responsibility for infrastructures, gender-laws, human rights legislation or environmental law etc. In this way, legislation and, (if we think of Supreme Court decisions e.g. in the United States), adjudication, too, for a long time have been the pacemakers of social change und thus an engine of social acceleration.[16]

By the 21st century, however, democracy no longer appears to be a pace-maker of social change; rather, it has shifted to a role of 'fire-extinguisher' and to a mode of 'muddling through', at best reacting to the pressures created elsewhere rather than shaping our shared world.[17] It is not just that new rules and regulations often take too long to be forged, for even worse than this, when, possibly after years of deliberation and negotiation, a new law (for example on internet-traffic or protection of intellectual property rights or genetic engineering) is finally passed, chances are high that it is already anachronistic, that it has been outpaced and overtaken by new developments in that very sector. Nowhere could this be seen more clearly than in the recent financial crisis, when political decisions always came too late and too slow for the markets – and yet too fast for legislatures to even have a say. Parliaments, it seems, are reduced to *ex post facto* yes or nay-sayers, and this leads to increasing frustration or alienation on the part of the voters, who (at least in some cases) tend to elect xenophobic or populist parties (or to adopt completely 'de-synchronized' propositions such as the *Brexit Referendum* by the British electorate in 2016) in response, or to abstain from voting altogether. The de-synchronization between democratic politics through parliamentary legislation and the economy, or its markets, thus results in a state of affairs where citizens have lost faith in political self-efficacy; for them, political institutions no longer respond to their needs and aspirations.

With this, the most interesting question arises: How, if at all, can law protect itself from de-synchronization? If we look more closely, it turns out that there are in fact (legal) provisions against legal desynchronization in the modern political

16 Francot and Mommers, 'Picking up the Pace'.

17 Hartmut Rosa, *High-Speed Society: Social Acceleration, Power and Modernity*, ed. William E. Scheuerman (Pennsylvania: Pennsylvania State University Press, 2009): 65–75.

system. For this system actually allows for three distinct temporalities in the legal order.[18] In most countries, constitutional law (and the corresponding courts) serves as the infrastructural 'airport' so to speak, to safeguard against the eroding pressures of high-speed dynamics: It guarantees that law-making follows stable, predictable patterns and pathways even in turbulent times, and thus provides long-term stability, calculability and predictability. It is extremely hard and time-consuming to change constitutional provisions. Parliamentary legislation, by contrast, also takes its time and includes a whole array of temporal regulations that ensure democratic deliberation and consultation on many levels and between different actors – with the notorious filibuster being just the most folkloristic element of it. Nevertheless, as I have pointed out, legislation is the instrument that turns democracies into dynamic societies, and it can well serve as a tool for comprehensive social acceleration. Finally, emergency laws and executive regulations allow for an additional speed-up in legislation in times of crises, when speed is vital. Executive orders and decrees can be forged on short notice and within hours, they are the tools that allow for high-speed political action and reaction. Little wonder, therefore, that authors like Bill Scheuerman[19] observe a shift from legislative to executive policy making. Yet, they obviously come at a price that resembles the destruction of the airport: once they become a regular element of politics, the calculability and predictability of the background conditions of action are on the decline – and thus, the speed game starts to undermine itself.

Law under pressure

So far, I have presented law as a functional prerequisite for dynamic stabilization in that it provides both the secure background conditions for socioeconomic and technological acceleration and the tools for re-synchronization between social systems, groups and processes. This seems to suggest that law itself is not accelerated, or has not switched to an escalatory mode of dynamic stabilization. However, this is not the whole story. In fact, what is true for the shift from 'knowledge' to 'science' can be said about the structural reproduction of law, too. As with knowledge, 'laws' are for most if not all non-modern sociocultural formations a treasure to be guarded, too. Very often, they come in the form of a 'holy law', which either represents the will of some divine power or the heritage of some mythical ancestors, and it is codified in some sacred scripture, perhaps guarded in some holy shrine or so. Therefore, more often than not, this kind of law is supposed to be 'eternal' or 'timeless law'. Even when, as for Plato, there is no assumption of the pre-existence of such eternal law, the task was to seek the best

18 Gisela Riescher, *Zeit und Politik: Zur Institutionellen Bedeutung von Zeitstrukturen in Parlamentarischen und Präsidentiellen Regierungssystemen.* (Baden-Baden: Nomos, 1994). William E. Scheuerman, *Liberal Democracy and the Social Acceleration of Time* (Baltimore and London: Johns Hopkins University Press, 2004).

19 William E. Scheuerman, 'Liberal Democracy and the Empire of Speed',' *Polity* 34, no.1 (2001): 41–67.

possible law for human beings, i.e. to find and codify the 'golden rules' for human social existence once and for all.

Contrary to this, the basic premises of modern law have changed radically. Legislation has become a permanent, iterative task for the institutional body which carries the highest social authority. With the shift from 'natural law' to modern positive law, law itself shifts to the mode of dynamic stabilization – it is stabilized by an institution (the legislative body, i.e. parliament) which is itself constituted dynamically, that is, through the never ending cycle of elections. Today, basically no law is made or intended for eternity: all legislators know that it is not just the social, economic and technological conditions which change fast, but also the ever-changing will of the people to which laws need to be adapted. If laws are the instrument by which social processes are coordinated and synchronized, and if these processes speed up on an escalatory pace, then law itself needs to increase its pace of adaptation. The decay-rate of law increases, too. This very observation has led Carl Schmitt to speak of the 'motorized legislator'.[20] It reveals an insurmountable calamity of acceleration-society: As the logic of law is the logic of an institution (from Latin, *instituere*), i.e., it is geared towards stability and permanence, the processes of acceleration and dynamization set it under mounting pressures of liquefaction and dissolution. Basically, there are two ways to respond to this: Either laws are made in an increasingly less substantial and more abstract, procedural, formal way such that the same laws can be used to manage evolutionary processes at the cost of diminishing substantive content or 'bite', or the substance of law has to be adapted at an accelerated pace itself. This latter course leads to a loss of diligence and prudence in the formulation of laws: international treaties, labour laws, family law: no matter what the substance matter is, legislators, much to the grief of jurists and lawyers, know that the new rules they make will not last for very long, hence they do not overtly care for the exactness and coherence of regulations and formulations.[21] This certainly leads to a decrease in predictability and calculability of the background conditions of action, and it sometimes leads to severe uncertainty and confusion, as at the time of this writing, when politicians find out that Article 50 of the EU Lisbon Treaty contains such loose provisions that no one seems to know how the 'Brexit' can actually be administered. In other words: legal certainty, as one of the core values of modern law and as a precondition for social stability in acceleration society, is about to be sacrificed to the speed-game.

The conclusion of this train of thinking is that law – the very logic of law – itself is in danger of becoming de-synchronized and anachronistic. In a world of high-speed, digital and global transactions, it might not only take too long to *make* laws and to decide which law applies in which case of conflict, but it also seems to

20 Carl Schmitt, 'The Motorized Legislator' in *High-Speed Society: Social Acceleration, Power and Modernity* (Philadelphia: Pennsylvania State University Press, 2009): 65–75

21 Rosa, *Social Acceleration*, 251–255. Scheuerman, *Liberal Democracy and the Social Acceleration of Time.*

become too painstaking to follow legal procedures all the way through. Therefore, new forms of legal pluralism and of extra-legal conflict mediation and arbitration seem to prop up all over the place.[22] This, however, is bad news for societies operating in a mode of dynamic stabilization, for it indicates that the infra-structural 'airport' of the acceleration regime is built on unstable and shifting grounds. While the kinetic energy in the sense of speed and dynamics still increases, predictability and calculability of the background conditions of action – i.e. legal certainty – decrease. As the British referendum on leaving the EU in June 2016 has made apparent in quite drastic terms, we are back to a point where the future legal conditions of social and economic life can become almost wholly unpredictable from one day to the next. As the bicycle moves faster than ever, legal myopia might set the path towards ultimate dynamic de-stabilization.

Bibliography

Bonus, Holger. 'Die Langsamkeit der Spielregeln', in *Die Beschleunigungsfalle oder der Triumph der Schildkröte* (3rd ed.), edited by Klaus Backhaus and Holger Bonus, 41–56. Stuttgart: Schäffer/Pöschel, 1998.

Crouch, Colin. *Post-Democracy*, Cambridge: Polity 2004.

Ehrenberg, Alain. *The Weariness of the Self: Diagnosing the History of Depression in the Contemporary Age*. Montreal: McGill-Queens University Press, 2010.

Francot, Lyana, and Sophie Mommers. 'Picking up the Pace – Legal Slowness and the Authority of the Judiciary in the Acceleration Society (a Dutch Case Study)'. *International Journal of the Legal Profession* 23 (2016): 1–19.

Groys, Boris. *On the New*, London: Verso, 2014.

Günther, Klaus. 'Rechtspluralismus und universaler Code der Legalität: Globalisierung als rechtstheoretisches Problem', in *Die Öffentlichkeit der Vernunft und die Vernunft der Öffentlichkeit* (Festschrift für Jürgen Habermas), edited by Lutz Wingert and Klaus Günther , 539–567. Frankfurt am Main: Suhrkamp, 2001.

Luhmann, Niklas. *Politische Theorie im Wohlfahrtsstaat*. München: Olzoc, 1981

Nowotny, Helga. *Time: The Modern and Postmodern Experience*. Cambridge/Malden: Polity, 1996.

Reheis, Fritz. *Kreativität der Langsamkeit. Neuer Wohlstand durch Entschleunigung*. Darmstadt: Wissenschaftliche Buchgesellschaft, 1996.

Riescher, Gisela. *Zeit und Politik. Zur institutionellen Bedeutung von Zeitstrukturen in parlamentarischen und präsidentiellen Regierungssystemen*. Baden-Baden: Nomos, 1994.

Rosa, Hartmut. *Social Acceleration: A New Theory of Modernity*. New York: Columbia University Press, 2013.

22 Klaus Günther, 'Rechtspluralismus und Universaler Code der Legalität: Globalisierung als rechtstheoretisches Problem' in *Die Öffentlichkeit der Vernunft und die Vernunft der Öffentlichkeit*, ed. Lutz Wingert and Klaus Günther (Frankfurt am Main: Suhrkamp, 2001): 539–567. Günther Teubner, 'Privatregimes: Neo-Spontanes Recht und Duale Sozialverfassung in der Weltgesellschaft?', in *Zur Antonomie des Individuums – Liber Amicorum für Spiros Simitis* ed. Dieter Simon and Manfred Weiss (Baden-Baden: Nomos, 2000): 437–453.

Rosa, Hartmut. 'De-Synchronization, Dynamic Stabilization, Dispositional Squeeze: The Problem of Temporal Mismatch' in *The Sociology of Speed*, edited by Judy Wajcman and Nigel Dodd, 25–41. Oxford: Oxford University Press, 2017.

Rosa, Hartmut. *High-speed Society. Social Acceleration, Power and Modernity*, edited by William E. Scheuerman. University Park, Philadelphia: Pennsylvania State University Press, 2009.

Scheuerman, William. 'Liberal Democracy and the Empire of Speed'. *Polity* 34, no.1 (2001): 41–67.

Scheuerman, William. *Liberal Democracy and the Social Acceleration of Time*. Baltimore and London: Johns Hopkins University Press, 2004.

Schmitt, Carl. 'The Motorized Legislator', in Hartmut Rosa, *High-speed Society: Social Acceleration, Power and Modernity*, edited by William Scheuerman, 65–75. University Park, Philadelphia: Pennsylvania State University Press, 2009.

Stoppe, Gabriela, Bramesfeld, Anke, and Friedrich-Wilhelm Schwartz. *Volkskrankheit Depression? Bestandsaufnahme und Perspektiven*. Heidelberg: Springer, 2006.

Teubner, Günther. 'Privatregimes: Neo-Spontanes Recht und duale Sozialverfassung in der Weltgesellschaft?' In *Zur Autonomie des Individuums – Liber amicorum für Spiros Simitis* edited by Dieter Simon and Manfred Weiss, 437–453. Baden-Baden: Nomos, 2000.

Thompson, Edward P. 'Time, Work-discipline and Industrial Capitalism'. *Past & Present* 38 (1967): 56–97.

Weber, Max. *Essays in Sociology*, translated and edited by H. H. Gerth and C. Wright Mills. New York: Oxford University Press, 1946.

UNODC, United Nations Office on Drugs and Crime. *World Drug Report 2015*, New York: United Nations Publication, 2015.

Chapter 5

Suspended in Gaffa: legal slowness in the acceleration society[1]

Lyana Francot

Souviens toi que le Temps est un joueur avide
Qui gagne sans tricher, à tout coup! C'est la loi
Charles Baudelaire, *L'Horloge*

Introduction

In our era, we are highly aware of time in its multiple appearances and especially of the scarcity of time. Even though almost everything is moving faster due to technical and technological innovations, it seems that there is less and less time left. The fact that social order is changing at an ever-faster pace, and all the more so when it comes to power and authority constellations, triggers this inquiry into a possible connection between authority and time.

Authority, in particular political authority, never really went without critics.[2] Its justification and legitimation are often under scrutiny – not only in a scholarly way – as is its locus. Traditionally, authority is personified by a ruler, a head of state as a representative of God or the people, or a combination. Of course, there are also other forms of authority, such as the religious one, the legal one, the in our time rather dominant economic one and so on. These forms are vested in specific institutions and organizations, represented by more or less well-known authority figures. However, nowadays, traditional loci of authority seem to be under siege. This may well be understood as the outcome of the process of modernization, rendering individuals autonomous and empowered but traditional authority has, in general, lost its self-evidence. Authority needs to be earned, so to speak.

Time is of the essence in all societies, as one of the dimensions that contributes to shaping and shifting social order.[3] Time also appears in different forms, and a variety of conceptualizations attest to that.[4] A first look into contemporary

1 I would like to thank Luigi Corrias for his comments on an earlier draft.
2 Most obviously: anarchism.
3 Also see the chapter of Nomi Claire Lazar in this volume.
4 Carol J. Greenhouse, "Just in Time: Temporality and the Cultural Legitimation of Time", *The Yale Law Journal*, 98 (1989): 163.3

literature reveals a variety of (sometimes overlapping) concepts of time such as chronological time, clock time, standardized time, social time, cultural times and so on.[5] In modernity, time is thought of as being predominantly linear.[6] This is closely related to the modern idea of change as progress and to finality.

In this chapter, I seek to make a first inquiry into the probable relationship between time and authority. More so, this contribution starts from the idea that the dominant manifestation of time in a society influences – at the very least partially – the observation and experience of authority in that particular society. This implies that our experience of time is subject to change. Moreover, it suggests that this experience is not without consequences for the way we perceive authority.

An in depth, detailed analysis and reconstruction of the relationship between time and authority is a substantial undertaking and cannot be covered in one chapter. Rather I will be testing the water, elaborating a set of points in order to illustrate the possible relationship between authority and time. Hence, I will not entertain a general concept of time. For now, it suffices to maintain that time as such cannot be observed, unless in terms of change. Changes can be observed in a sequential order, so what we are actually able to observe are courses of events.[7] Instead of deploying a general concept of time, I will turn to a specific modality of time, i.e. speed, and its manifestation in society in terms of social acceleration. For this, I will draw upon the work of German sociologist Hartmut Rosa.

Time is all-pervasive and penetrates all domains and dimensions of sociality and in this vein, acceleration is also ubiquitous. Authority however is limited in the sense that it is related to a certain locus, so to speak. In this contribution, I will inquire into the authority of the judiciary in order to draw a sketch of the changing perception of authority. In order to map out this development, I will draw upon systems theory. Systems theory offers the possibility to elucidate the various time-lines and tempi of the legal system. I will argue that the time gap between law and society is both a necessity and a risk when it comes to the authority of the judiciary.

Late modern times: social acceleration

The ubiquity of time as a social phenomenon resonates in scholarly inquiries and publications as much as it does in popular culture.[8] In our contemporary society,

5 See for example: Roberto Cipriani (2013), "The Many Faces of Social Time: A Sociological Approach", *Time & Society* 22 (2013): 5–30. Also see Greenhouse, "Just in Time", 1631–1651.
6 Greenhouse, "Just in Time", 1633.
7 This is not to say that time and change are one and the same phenomenon but that they are correlated in the sense that change can be observed, whereas time cannot. Of course we can observe that change in the hands of the clock and so on, but time remains intangible. Also see Liaquat Ali Khan, "Temporality of Law", *McGeorge Law Review* 40, no. 1 (2009): 69.
8 In music and literature. Famous is of course Proust's À *la recherche du temps perdu* (1913–1927). Also: Milan Kundera, *Slowness* (1996). Just to mention a few in pop music: Molokko, *The time is now* (2000), the Steve Miller Band in their *Fly like an*

the product of modernization, time is predominantly observed as linear time.[9] Linear time connects the past to present and the present to the future in a straight line, so to speak, one time-unit follows upon another. There is no turning back the time nor will it repeat itself. We can reflect upon the past, remember or forget, forgive of resent. We can anticipate the future, in utopian or dystopian images, but whatever happens, happens in the present. More in particular, modern (linear) time takes the shape of speed, of acceleration. Acceleration has become more and more central to our perception of the temporal dimension of social order. It also intensifies the experience of an increasingly shorter presence and a future that starts now rather than tomorrow.

The most comprehensive work about social acceleration has been written by Hartmut Rosa. In *Beschleunigung – Die Veränderung der Zeitstrukturen in der Moderne*, he analyses the phenomenon of acceleration as one of the essential pillars of the late modern society.[10] Indeed, according to Rosa acceleration is no longer only an incidental phenomenon but has become a structural feature of contemporary society. If this is so, acceleration cannot but have substantial consequences for primary systems such as the economy, politics, law and institutions.

In his book, Rosa seeks to unravel the logic of social acceleration, as he considers this the fundamental principle of the modern society: the experience of modernization is essentially an experience of acceleration.[11] Consistently, Rosa unfolds a theory of modernization, wherein the process of modernization is also conceived as a structural and fundamental transformation of temporal structures. The key characteristic of this transformation is most aptly described by the notion of social acceleration.[12] One of the general assumptions in our society is that acceleration is accompanied by an overall increase of our options and possibilities: educational possibilities, life choices, a wide variety of consumer goods and so on.[13] While such an increase is mostly considered a positive development, there is a downside to it as well. The more options and possibilities we have, the higher the risk to miss out on chances will become. In the end, it is impossible to realize all options, at least at the same time. Selections and choices – hence decisions – are unavoidable.

eagle (1976), The Rolling Stones, *Time is on my side* (1964), Foo Fighters, *Times like this* (2002). Movies: *X-men: Days of Future Past* (2014), *Groundhog Days* (1993), *Twelve Monkeys* (1995).

9 Linear time is dominant but by no means the only modality. See Greenhouse who observes that the public domain is ruled by linear time and the private domain moves in temporal cycles: Greenhouse, "Just in Time", 1637. In the same line, see Helga Nowotny, *Time. The Modern and Postmodern Experience* (Cambridge: Polity Press, 2005), 72 and further.

10 Hartmut Rosa, *Beschleunigung. Die Veränderung der Zeitstrukturen in der Moderne* (Frankfurt/Main: Suhrkamp: 2005). Translation: Hartmut Rosa, *Social Acceleration. A New Theory of Modernity* (New York: Columbia University Press, 2013).

11 Rosa, *Beschleunigung*, 11, 14–15, 51.

12 Rosa, *Beschleunigung*, 24, 52.

13 Obviously and sadly, this is not the case for everyone and everywhere.

To be clear, the experience of speed and acceleration as a core characteristic of our era may prevail but does not exclude other perspectives. Rosa refers to the perspective of crystallization that conceives our society as immobile and motionless: nothing really changes, nothing really new happens.[14] Notably, not 'everything' in modern societies accelerates, or does so at the same rate or in the same way. There are also counter-movements such as Slow Food, Slow Fashion, Slow Science and so on. So, if not everything accelerates and one wants to analyse social acceleration, then the analysis requires the exact identification of the specific categories and/or processes that are speeding up.[15]

To this end, Rosa analyses three dimensions of social acceleration: technical acceleration, the acceleration of the pace of life and, last but not least, the acceleration of the tempo of social and cultural change.[16] Illustrative for technical acceleration are the speeding up of transport, communication and production. This type of acceleration is relatively easy to observe and to quantify. The manifestations of technical acceleration and its effects are well-known. Examples are abundant. For instance, we can travel by plane to places that by horse or carriage or even by train would have been out of reach or would have taken weeks. Goods and services are produced, distributed and even consumed in a unprecedented speed.[17] The acceleration of the pace of life pertains to the speed and compression of action and experience on a daily basis: we do more of everything in shorter time-spans. Finally, the acceleration of social change refers to the speeding-up of society itself, i.e. the rate at which societal changes take place. These three dimensions interact in a complex way with each other and create, according to Rosa, a state of time-emergency, a *Zeitnotstand*.[18] This time-crisis challenges the way we shape our lives and society. It also exacerbates our experience of living in a time of crisis.

The notion of *Zeitnotstand* reveals that a predominantly negative connotation accompanies the phenomenon of social acceleration.[19] One of the negative aspects is denoted by Rosa as de-synchronization, whereby for example societal processes proceed too fast for individuals, hindering them to keep up with new developments. For instance, elderly people that are not capable of managing all the ongoing technological innovations. Another level of de-synchronization – the one that is relevant for this contribution – concerns a differentiation of timelines of

14 Rosa, *Beschleunigung*, 41

15 Rosa, *Beschleunigung*, 53–54. An interesting argument for slowness is offered by Paul Cilliers, "On the Importance of a Certain Slowness", *Emergence: Complexity and Organization* 8 (2006): 106–112.

16 These categories or dimensions are factually closely intertwined and their connection cannot be reduced to simple causal relations. Rosa, *Beschleunigung*, 129–130.

17 Cheap mass production is still the norm even though humanitarian and environmental concerns necessitate reconsideration and action. Beside those costs, mass production has also almost eradicated (slow) craftsmanship.

18 Rosa, *Beschleunigung*, 16

19 Even though Rosa carefully words that a negative or positive qualification of acceleration as such a qualification is related to its effects. Rosa, *Beschleunigung*, 44.

function systems. A commonly shared observation is for example that the development of the economy, technology and science and social changes in their slipstream have become too fast to be regulated politically and legally.[20] The political and legal systems lag behind. Consequently, and due to the structural coupling between systems, the continuous acceleration of even one system, for example the economy, causes problematic effects for all other systems. The worldwide financial crisis is illustrative.

The focus of this chapter is on the interaction between social acceleration, law and the judiciary. Even though all three categories of acceleration have their bearings upon the law and its organizations, the most interesting is the speeding up of the rate of social change. The acceleration of processes of social change is non-intentional, unlike for example technical acceleration. The latter is goal oriented and is aiming at achieving a higher pace. Well known examples are transport, technology but also production and communication.[21] Technical acceleration contributes substantially to contemporary experience of the shrinking of space: because we are able to move around faster and to communicate real-time with people all over the globe, space seems to shrink and faster to bridge.[22] The acceleration of communication is essentially both a speeding-up of information transferal and an increase of the quantity of information per time unit.[23] Furthermore, modern communication technologies, such as the internet and mobile phones, enable real-time interaction without the necessity of our actual presence in one space. It is not even required for a person to remain in one place anymore. Communication has become hyperdynamic. It goes without saying that these intentional processes of acceleration have a deep impact on the law and the judiciary as well. For example, the speedy rate of technical innovations requires the law to act fast and pro-actively, or it must face the consequences such as the loss of privacy. Communication between professionals and clients has been speeding up and increasing in quantity as well. The resulting increase of workload and pressure illustrates Rosa's category of the acceleration of the pace of life.[24]

Nevertheless, I consider the acceleration of social change to be the most interesting category when it comes to its effects on the legal system and its organizations, precisely because it is un-intentional and hence unpredictable for a better part of its consequences regarding social chance. After all, the function of law is to stabilize normative expectations, a function that takes its actual shape also in the performances of the judiciary. In this sense, law is traditionally seen as a coordinator of social change. Law, in a modern society, makes a substantial contribution to the

20 Rosa, *Beschleunigung*, 46, also see 48.
21 Rosa, *Beschleunigung*, 113, 124, 128–129.
22 Rosa, *Beschleunigung*, 125.
23 Rosa, *Beschleunigung*, 126.
24 I have discussed this elsewhere. See: Lyana Francot and Sophie Mommers, "Picking up the Pace – Legal Slowness and the Authority of the Judiciary in the Acceleration Society (a Dutch Case Study)", *International Journal of the Legal Profession*, 23 (2016): 1–19.

dynamic stabilization of that society.[25] Law enables dynamic stabilization – growth and change with the aim of maintenance – precisely because stabilizing normative expectations enables change. The market could not properly function without commonly acknowledged and stable rules: who would for example engage in a multi-million deal if it is not certain whether the other party is going to meet their end of the deal, without the safeguard of law? This is not to say that the law guarantees a successful deal but that it serves as a safety net 'just in case': if expectations are not met, parties can hold on to those expectations and employ the law to do so. The same goes for normative expectations regarding property. Well-defined property law is a prerequisite for trade and hence for a successful capitalist society. In its turn, capitalism is a motor of acceleration.[26] As a consequence law, by enabling (controlled) social change, also has to deal at one point with the effects of that social change.

But what is social change? And if we know what is changing, how can we grasp its pace? In a first description, Rosa refers to social acceleration in terms of a change of practices, orientations for actions, structures for association, relationship patterns.[27] Societal changes manifest themselves as alterations of lifestyles, fashions, attitudes, values, social languages and so on.[28] Subsequently, to determine the pace of social change, Rosa suggests introducing the concept of *Gegenwartsschrümpfung*, the shrinking of the present.[29]

The present is actually a time period of stability. Note that 'the present' has a different meaning in a variety of settings: the present in a stock market is (usually) shorter than the present in a marriage, a fashion fad lasts shorter than a judicial ruling.[30] In this situation of stability, past experiences allow for conclusions guiding decisions about the future and only in this case can these decisions serve as orientation for action. This is so because stability refers to a known and relatively high degree of certainty regarding expectations. In this line of thought, the past refers to all that no longer holds and the future to that which does not apply yet.[31] Luhmann understands the present as differentiating the past and the future, whereby the past is determined and future is undetermined. In the present the temporal horizons of past and future remain stable, hence constituting a stable basis for new expectations and decisions remains. According to Rosa, both Luhmann and Lübbe observe a progressive shrinking of this period of time we call the present.[32] Consequently the period of stability becomes shorter and shorter. In Luhmann, the focus is on increasing instability or contingency, and less on social

25 In his chapter in this volume, Rosa elaborates on dynamic stabilization.
26 Rosa, *Beschleunigung*, 257 and following.
27 Hartmut Rosa, "Social Acceleration: Ethical and Political Consequences of a Desynchronized High-Speed Society", *Constellations* 10, no. 1 (2003): 129.
28 Rosa, "Social Acceleration", 7. Rosa, *Beschleunigung*, 129–134.
29 For this, he draws on the work of Lübbe and Luhmann. Rosa, *Beschleunigung*, 131.
30 Rosa, *Beschleunigung*, 186.
31 Rosa, *Beschleunigung*, 131.
32 Rosa, *Beschleunigung*, 134.

change. Luhmann terms the current temporal state of affairs as scarcity of time rather than as social acceleration.[33] Social acceleration is, within the Luhmannian framework, one way of dealing with the scarcity of time.

Rosa subsequently defines the acceleration of social changes as an increase in the decay rates of expectations and experiences guiding action and as a shrinking of the present – whatever the time period of that present in a specific social domain may be.[34] To formulate it somewhat differently: there is sufficient stability to make decisions and to act upon them only if and when experiences and expectations remain stable within a certain period of time, i.e. the present. But it becomes increasingly difficult to make informed decisions pertaining to a course of action based on experiences and expectations and the period of time to do so – the present – becomes shorter and shorter. This goes for almost every domain of sociality: politics, science, art, economy – no domain is immune, no system is left untouched by acceleration, the shrinking of the present is present in society in its entirety.[35] As a consequence, Rosa holds that the speeding up of social change entails the acceleration *of* society whereas the other two categories, technical acceleration and an increasingly higher pace of life, pertain to acceleration *within* society.[36]

In line with the foregoing, Rosa pinpoints the transformation – the erosion even – of structural and cultural certainties. Those certainties are rooted in the basic institutions of society. The basic institutions of society are those institutions that organize the fundamental processes of production and reproduction.[37] Instead of analysing social change by means of an analysis of the basic institutions, one could also turn to a perspective that takes the primary societal differentiation as the fundamental shape of society. In Luhmann, for example, this would pertain to a functionally differentiated society. However, Rosa considers an acceleration of a change in this primary differentiation unconceivable because from this perspective Luhmann's own diagnosis of time (an ongoing shrinking of the period of stability of time horizons) remains out of sight.[38] May that as it may, it is very probable that while functional differentiation *per se* does not accelerate, systems do – each in their own speed – and this speeding up is often a sheer necessity for their autopoietic reproduction as well.

Whether it is possible to observe an acceleration *of* society depends, I suggest, on the employed notion of society – an issue Rosa's theory does not address. From a systems theoretical perspective, it is not entirely satisfactory to argue that

33 Niklas Luhmann, "Die Knappheit der Zeit und die Vordringlichkeit des Befristeten", in: Niklas Luhmann, *Politische Planung. Aufsätze zur Soziologie von Politik und Verwaltung* (Opladen: Westdeutscher Verlag 1971), 143–164

34 Rosa, "Social Acceleration", 7.

35 This is even so when it comes to all the counter-movements: they exist in and through their resistance to acceleration.

36 Rosa, *Beschleunigung*, 133.

37 Rosa, *Beschleunigung*, 178–179.

38 Rosa, *Beschleunigung*, 179, footnote 8.

acceleration of social change can be diagnosed by observing the basic institutions of society. It implies that the total of all basic institutions equals society. Society as a social system is however more than the sum of all its basic institutions, it is constituted by a differentiation between all actual and possible communications and the non-communicative environment. Hence, the acceleration *of* society would imply the acceleration of all that communication. Clearly from this theoretical perspective it would not make sense to speak about the acceleration *of* society, only of acceleration *within* society as there are still communicative processes that do not accelerate or even resist speeding up. Rather than lingering upon the differentiation of acceleration *of* and *within* society, I would like to suggest to inquire into the acceleration of social systems. More in particular I will focus on the legal system and the judiciary. Both are types of social systems, more specifically a function system and an organization.

So Rosa, not considering functional differentiation as the subject of social change and hence of its acceleration turns to the traditional approach and takes family and work as a point of departure.[39] I will not entertain this argument in detail and for now, it must suffice to say that Rosa observes that social change no longer takes place over a span of generations but within one generation. This illustrates the speeding up of the rate of social change: it transitions from *intergenerational* into *intragenerational*, changes take place within one generation. We do not stick with one and same employer and receive a gold watch with retirement. Job security is an exception, job-hopping has become the rule – be it by choice or necessity. A marriage rarely still is a bond for life but covers one period in our personal development.[40] Decisions concerning life (style) choices are conditional, and change with the ever faster changing social circumstances. This instability or uncertainty is symptomatic for the acceleration of social change. The present as a period of stability or *Stabilitätsraum* shrinks.[41] Fundamental decisions do not last forever but need to be made over and over again, within one's lifespan: where to live, with whom, where to move to, where to work and is there any work available at all, which political party to vote for. All options and possibilities available in late modern society do not only contribute to freedom but also to uncertainty and the necessity of choice: but what to choose, how to obtain all the necessary information to make the right choice? What is the 'right' decision any way and how long will it be right? Taking into account that everything could be different by our own choice or not, uncertainty has become a constant companion of late modern life.[42]

Rosa adds to this phenomenon of late modern contingency the temporal dimension of acceleration: the time-period wherein we have to decide is shrinking

39 Rosa does however consider functional differentiation to be one of the driving forces, a motor, of social acceleration. Rosa, "Social Acceleration", 14.

40 Rosa, *Beschleunigung*, 179, 184.

41 Rosa, *Beschleunigung*, 185, 186.

42 Lyana Francot, "Dealing with Complexity, Facing Uncertainty: Morality and Ethics in a Complex Society", *Archiv für Rechts- und Sozialphilosophie* 2 (2014): 201–218.

faster and faster, tomorrow turns into today in the blink of eye – or so it seems. This all leads to a general increase of a *Kontingenzbewußtsein*, of contingency awareness: we are increasingly aware that everything could be different and that nothing lasts forever, not even cold November rain.[43] None the less, the experience of acceleration, as a raging stream of relentless change into the future, is and remains constitutive of our society. And in general, change is deemed positive and faster is usually better. The short term rules supreme in late modern society. Even so, movements like Slow Food, Slow Fashion and publications like the Slow Professor[44] illustrate how not everybody submits to the speed-rage of late modernity. But then this reluctance or even resistance to acceleration requires justification.[45]

Rosa conceptualizes the consequences of acceleration in terms of de-synchronization.[46] De-synchronization affects sociality in all its aspects, function systems as well as social groups. Illustrative is the changed perception of the elderly. Once deemed as a source of wisdom, old age now stands for slowness, for not being able to keep up with progress and change and lagging behind. This state of affairs implies that consolidated knowledge and wisdom seems to become outdated and is surpassed by a stream of new data, of information, that is flexible, and in need of constant updating. It is all about flexibility instead of stability, the capacity to gather new information, to be innovative rather than to provide consolidated knowledge and wisdom.[47] If this is so, it triggers the question for the state of the legal system. The legal system seeks to provide a high degree of stability, by means of consolidated rules. Law is only flexible within a small margin since changing legal rules is a slow process. This is on the one hand a necessary pre-condition for the dynamics of change. On the other hand, the legal system might be too slow for its rapidly changing environment, causing it to become dysfunctional. One might even conjecture if its slowness endangers its authority: if law cannot keep up, why follow its rules and rulings – they are yesterday's news so to speak.

Overall, the late modern society is depicted as unstable: the prerequisites for decisions and actions are continuously changing at a rapid pace. This in itself stable uncertainty causes actors – individuals, groups, organizations, institutions – to adapt their expectations constantly, to reconsider what is relevant and what not. To stop, by not deciding and acting, seems no longer a viable course if one wants to stay connected with future options.[48] There is no rest for late modern mankind:

43 Rosa, *Beschleunigung*, 181. Guns N' Roses, *November Rain*, album: Use Your Illusion I, 1992.
44 Also see Cilliers, "On the Importance", 106–112.
45 Maggie Berg and Barbara K. Seeber, *The Slow Professor: Challenging the Culture of Speed in the Academy* (Toronto: University of Toronto Press, 2016). Rosa, *Beschleunigung*, 72.
46 Also see Hartmut Rosa's chapter in this volume.
47 Rosa, *Beschleunigung*, 188–189.
48 Rosa, *Beschleunigung*, 190.

act today or be obsolete and outdated tomorrow. Every current IPhone is already old fashioned.

The result of the acceleration of social change is a *Entscheidungslandschaft*, a decisionscape that is under permanent construction. The erosion of experiences and knowledge is a relentless ongoing process. Hence it becomes next to impossible to foretell what future options and possibilities will become relevant. If and when such an assessment becomes difficult, it seems rational to keep open as many as possible options. And to hope that the future will tell which ones to realize.

The *Eigenzeit* of law

If Rosa's analysis of the ever increasing pace of social change is accurate then this inevitably has its bearings upon the legal system. Law is not just a passive bystander in the process of social acceleration but contributes to and is confronted with the consequences of that process. More so, when the question arises what accelerates, a closer look at the legal system might be informative. My suggestion is to relate the acceleration of social change to the pace of change of function systems and their organizations rather than to the basic institutions of society. This might offer a more distinctive point of departure for the analysis. As said before, social systems such as function systems and organizations have their own temporalities, their own 'present' and hence their own typical past and future. Those system specific timelines constitute their particular decisionscape. To put it somewhat differently, social systems operate – produce and reproduce their operations– in their own pace. The (re)production of legal operations requires a different amount of time than those of the economy, or of politics, and so on. This *Eigenzeit*, the temporality inherent in the systemic processes, is in fact the manifestation of the temporal autonomy of a system.

The law also has its temporal autonomy, as a dimension of its operational autonomy.[49] Within the systems theoretical context, operational autonomy refers to the fact that only law determines what law is: only law produces and reproduces law. The notion of operational closure denotes this state of affairs. It is not an expression of autarchy but pertains to self-sufficiency on its *operational* level, that is, its communications and hence its communicative structures, processes and finally, its own unity and identity. And (re)production of all this takes place in its own time, the *Eigenzeit* of law.[50] Eventually, it is law itself that determines how long processes of (re)production take. The legal system is of course not the only system using time to differentiate itself nor is it the only way to bring about operational autonomy. All systems have their own timelines, and operational autonomy is brought about in a complex dynamic between factual, social and temporal dimensions.

49 Cf. Luigi Corrias' chapter in this volume.

50 Niklas Luhmann, *Gesellschaftsstruktur und Semantik. Studien zur Wissenssoziologie der modernen Gesellschaft – Band 1* (Frankfurt am Main: Suhrkamp, 1993), 240–241.

What is striking, and well-known, about the legal tempo is its notorious slowness.[51] Processing conflicts through courts may take years and not seldom does. Relevant aspects are the complexity of the case, the bureaucracy involved, strategic delays by parties and so on. The law is usually also slow in its response to social changes such as for example the legalization of euthanasia. It is clear that the legal timelines differ from those in its societal environment. The creation of such a time differential is one of the modi the legal system deploys to bring about a demarcation between itself and its environment. Even more so, the typical timelines and legal tempi are essential for the realization of the autonomy of law.

The temporal dimension also resonates in the function of the legal system. Indeed, Luhmann argues that law seeks to solve a *Zeitproblem*, a problem of time.[52] Like all function systems, law contributes in its very own way to the reduction and transformation of social complexity. Law constitutes a second order normativity by generalizing and stabilizing normative expectations. Expectations are essentially references to a future in which something might happen or not, an event might occur or not. The future is both complex and contingent and, as a consequence, uncertain. I understand uncertainty to refer to an experience of a situation at a certain point of time: a moment wherein it is difficult or even impossible to make a selection between options. This can be so because the options per se are unknown or unclear, or the consequences are unforeseeable. It concerns a lack of information, and this is often perceived as a lack of certainty – not knowing how the selection or decisions will turn out in the (nearby) future. Some relief is offered by framing and delimiting options and decisions, not only factual and social but also in a temporal sense. This is part and parcel of the function and performances of functions systems, and hence of law. In this sense, law contributes to our quest for certainty and usually this contribution appears as an offer of legal certainty. It cumulates in the function of law, that is what the legal system provides the entire society with, i.e. the stabilization and generalization of expectations facing disappointment. To be clear, this is not another way to say that the legal system is all about avoiding conflicts. But what the law does, is offer a possibility to deal with conflicts in a specific, canalizing way: that is, the possibility to continue communication but in different circumstances. In order to enable this continuation, the law stabilizes expectations that can be maintained even in case of rejection and disappointment. Stabilization here refers, to put it briefly, to the fact that the law regulates expectations by casting them into norms, which attributes durability to those expectations over time. Time passes by, sometimes quickly but these expectations reformulated as legal norms cannot be changed overnight.

51 See for example David Nelken, "Normalising Time: European Integration and Court Delays in Italy" in *Paradoxes of European Legal Integration*, edited by Hanne Petersen, Helle Krunke, Anne-Lise Kjaer & Mikale Rask Madsen (Aldershot: Ashgate, 2008), 299–323.

52 Niklas Luhmann, *Das Recht der Gesellschaft* (Frankfurt am Main: Suhrkamp Verlag, 1993), 125. Luhmann also speaks of the time binding character of law, ibid., 126 and further.

The foregoing also implies that if and when an expectation is disappointed there are two main ways of dealing with this disappointment: a cognitive and a normative mode. The former refers to the possibility to react upon rejection or disappointment by adjusting the expectation at stake. Here, the disappointment is an incentive to learn. The latter, the normative mode, pertains to the possibility to maintain the expectation and to demand satisfaction from the one who has not met the expectation, for example an apology. Obviously, by 'fixating' a selection of expectations, the uncertainty related to these specific expectations will decrease or at least change in nature as normative expectations or norms can be maintained counterfactually, that is to say, in view of and despite of their possible disappointment. Through the differentiation of normative expectations from cognitive ones, the legal system demarcates its boundary *vis-à-vis* society and other social systems. This is however not the only differentiation characterizing law. The legal system is also internally differentiated into centre and periphery, that is adjudication and legislation.[53] This internal differentiation is in fact the organizational backup of the differentiation of the legal system in society. Both the centre and the periphery have their own system-internal timelines, such as the tempi of the formal procedures in court, times to draft and issue laws, the entry into force of law, and so on. All these legal tempi and timelines contribute to social order as we know it and do so by temporalizing complexity.

All in all, law is a time machine that is geared towards absorbing uncertainty thus reducing or at least transforming complexity and contingency. To this aim, law reshuffles time so that it becomes legal time. And by means of legal time, law contributes on its own terms to the temporal order of society.[54] Significantly, the central organizations of the legal system, i.e. the judiciary, represent this ordering through time. They utilize a strict temporal regime, wherein the beginning, the different stages and the end are fixed moments in legal time, that allow for very little room to manoeuvre. These strict timelines of the judiciary do not necessarily nor mostly will they concur with the social and professional timelines of parties, lawyers and so on. Parties mostly want a speedy ruling, lawyers may sometimes consider it felicitous to stall, etc. This strict time regime and the fact that the judiciary maintains its own pace and timelines is also part of their autonomy and their authority.

53 Luhmann, *Das Recht der Gesellschaft*, 297–338. The relationship between adjudication and legislation is a circular one, in the sense of a mutual limitation of *Entscheidungsspielräume* see Luhmann, *Das Recht der Gesellschaft*, 305, also see 323. This internal differentiation is the primary one, and does not exclude that within the centre, other differentiations are also manifest, in terms of specialism or hierarchy between the different instances, see: Luhmann, *Das Recht der Gesellschaft*, 324.

54 The relation between law and time was and is subject to enquiry. To name a few, with ample illustrations and examples of the ubiquity of time in law: Khan, "Temporality of Law", 55–106; Andrew J. Wistrich, "The evolving Temporality of Lawmaking", *Connecticut Law Review* 44, no. 3 (2012): 737–826; François Ost, *Le Temps du Droit*, (Paris: Odile Jacob, 1999).

Legal slowness

What becomes apparent, is that by differentiating normative expectations from cognitive ones, law provides stability and hence certainty over time: normative expectations 'last' longer and are usually not subjected to fast change, whereas cognitive expectations are typically geared towards change. This stability turns into slowness if and when the rest of society keeps on speeding up. Even though one has come to expect the law to be slow to some extent, its slowness is notwithstanding that expectation, a source of frustration and complaints. But as such, the discrepancy between the expectation towards the legal system and the actual experience of legal slowness is nothing new.[55] In its function, modern law may be geared to the future as it generalizes expectations in to stabilizing norms but in its operations and especially in its core, i.e. the judiciary, it is a *nachgeschaltetes* system.[56] It operates after the facts and is for the better part focused on the past rather than on the future. Consequently, from the perspective of an external observer law always moves at a slower pace than its societal environment, be it politics or the economy, public opinion, and so on.

The time differential, between slow law and its fast(er) societal environment, denotes the nature of the relationship between law and the rest of society in terms of legal slowness. And as society keeps speeding up, the time differential increases. This increase instigates public demands to step it up, to shake and rattle internal timelines, and these demands especially target the tempi of the organizations. To put it somewhat differently, slowness pertains to the performances of law, to its output so to speak, rather than to its function.[57] The central location of that output is the judiciary, the formal organization of the legal system. More in particular and unsurprisingly, the output is cast in judicial decisions. The judiciary is under the obligation to decide due to the *Verbot der Justizverweigerung*.[58] In the acceleration society, the judiciary is not only legally obliged to decide but also has to do so faster than before. The judiciary finds itself confronted with the request to speed up, by both the societal environment (society, consumers of legal services, politics, public opinion) not only from an but also by what could be considered as an 'internal' actor, its own management.[59] Often the necessity of speeding up is corroborated by the argument that, in order not to widen the so-called gap

55 See for example: Remco van Rhee, "De traagheid van de civiele procedure: een eeuwenoud fenomeen" (The slowness of the civil procedure: an ancient phenomenon) in: *De rechtspraktijk in beeld. Van Justinianus tot de Duitse bezetting*, edited by Beatrix Jacobs, (Tilburg: Tilburg University, 1997), 57–67. Also Luhmann, *Das Recht der Gesellschaft*, 319.

56 Luhmann, *Das Recht der Gesellschaft*, 197.

57 Also see Bart van Klink's chapter in this volume.

58 Luhmann, *Das Recht der Gesellschaft*, 310 and further. In the Netherlands, for example, this can be found in article 13, Wet Algemene Bepalingen.

59 Francot and Mommers, "Picking up the Pace", 3. All examples pertaining to the Dutch judiciary stem from this article. I am grateful to Sophie Mommers for her contribution.

between the judiciary and society, and to re-enforce the trust of the citizens in the adjudication, that it is of the utmost importance that the judicial tempo is in line with society's pace.[60]

To the judiciary, the demand for fast administration of justice, presents itself primarily as an organizational problem. This is no surprise since it translates into an expected increase in output – more rulings – in less time than before.[61] The judiciary does however not only respond with projects that speed-up procedures but there is also resistance and a plea for slowing down.[62] Acceleration does not come natural to law and its organizations. The nature of the legal system seems to reject the up-beat tempo of our contemporary society. This is so, according to Khan, because

> [T]emporal inertia is law's core attribute. It ensures the systemic stability of law because one primary purpose of law is to provide stable rules that do not change over a period of time. [...] Systemically, law is the opposite of arbitrariness because arbitrariness carries no temporal inertia. Without temporal inertia, law is an arbitrary and fickle order that can change without timely notice.[63]

Moreover, it can be argued that law's inertia does not only secure its own stability but is also constitutive of the societal stability as such. Rosa puts forward that processes of acceleration became possible and still are because of the stability provided for by for example law and democracy.[64] But whereas acceleration first signalled progress it might now turn into acceleration for the sake of preventing decline. A consequence might be, according to Rosa, that the success of social acceleration becomes a threat to the very pre-conditions that enable future

60 Illustrative are the Agendas of the Judiciary in the Netherlands wherein acceleration in terms of timeliness is a necessity rather than an option. See for example *Agenda voor de Rechtspraak* 2011–2014, 14, also see 11, accessed on 16 June, 2016. https://www.rechtspraak.nl/Zoeken/Pages/default.aspx?k=duplicates:%22http%3A%2F%2Fwww.rechtspraak.nl%2FOrganisatie%2FPublicaties-En-Brochures%2FAgenda-voor-de-Rechtspraak%2FDocuments%2FAgenda-van-de-Rechtspraak-2011-2014.pdf%22%20

61 As a consequence, and unsurprisingly, the Dutch judiciary for example seek solution also on the organizational level. Exemplary are projects with the aim to shorten time-consuming procedures. For instance, the Public Prosecution Service presented its new approach called "ZSM", which translates as ASAP. See: https://www.om.nl/algemeen/english/; https://www.om.nl/actueel/nieuwsberichten/@24445/factsheet-zsm/, accessed on 16 June, 2016.

62 For example, the so-called "Leeuwarder Manifest", a statement of the Court of Appeal Leeuwarden, wherein judges warn about a decline in quality now that the focus is on fast justice and quantity. Published in 2012, accessed on 16 June, 2016 https://www.rechtspraak.nl/actualiteiten/nieuws/pages/reactie-raad-voor-de-rechtspraak-op-kritisch-manifest-raadsheren.aspx

63 Khan, "Temporality of Law", 81. Also see Bart van Klink's chapter in this volume.

64 Rosa, "Social Acceleration", 16.

acceleration or even a status quo. This observation might well hold true for the acceleration of the judiciary and the legal system, if even partially so. Khan:

> (…) the principle of temporal inertia that law exemplifies, creates, and enforces in various forms. Law maintains temporal inertia by resisting or refusing to acknowledge changes. […] This inertia is as much a human need as is change. Perpetual change, particularly when disorderly, devolves into chaos. Even well-structured change can cause disorientation when it occurs at a rapid speed. […] although law is an instrument of change, it is also an anchor for stability. Laws fortify the status quo.[65]

Khan attributes the feature of temporal inertia to the entire legal system but I think that a differentiation into several temporalities reflects the actual state of legal slowness more adequately. Luhmann offers a helpful start with the internal differentiation of the legal system into legislation and the courts. Notably Luhmann does not refer to a semantical differentiation like distinctions between different fields of law such as penal or labour law, or statutory law and judge-made law since these do not inform us, according to Luhmann, about the organizational back up of the legal system.[66] This perspective on the organizational backup is complemented by Wistrich's suggestion to distinguish between methods of 'lawmaking' with each their own temporality:

> Law is made by several methods. Those methods include written constitutions, judicial decisions, statutes, treaties, administrative rulemaking, and administrative rulemaking. Each of those methods possess its own distinctive temporality.[67]

He distinguishes between methods that are predominantly future-oriented, like for example legislation, and those that are predominantly past-oriented. And adjudication is first and foremost past-oriented. It is of course not a new insight that adjudication 'is inherently backward-looking' nor does it represent the whole story.[68] What is however (relatively) new are the changed societal circumstances in terms of acceleration, that not only triggers a greater focus on the future but also a demand to step it up.[69]

One of the most prominently voiced expectations is the one for fast justice, shorter and quicker procedures, and timely court rulings. Not meeting this expectation seems to contribute to a loss of authority, the 'clients' become dissatisfied and impatient. This is also because authority refers to a certain status or

65 Khan, "Temporality of Law", 80.
66 Luhmann, *Das Recht der Gesellschaft*, 298.
67 Wistrich, "The Evolving Temporality of Lawmaking", 750.
68 Wistrich, "The Evolving Temporality of Lawmaking", 750, 773.
69 Wistrich, "The Evolving Temporality of Lawmaking", 746.

prestige ascribed to the judiciary, and how we – as a society – judge the judges. It is connected to the practical authority of the judiciary, based on their legal expertise as well as a long institutional tradition.

As observed above, complaints about the slowness of the judiciary are nothing new. Hence, it is also not a very surprising state of affairs that these complaints persist in the acceleration society. Parties turn to the judge mostly because of conflicts and a speedy solution is wanted because of financial interests, or emotional ones or because matters of security are at stake. At the heart of a complaint about slowness is an expectation, that is the expectation of a speedy solution, an end to the problem preferably as soon as possible but at the very least within a reasonable period of time. Essentially, a complaint about slowness is nothing but the expression of a disappointed expectation. This expectation of a timely ruling increasingly gains momentum in the acceleration society. And not only that, because in a society wherein speed and acceleration have become structural features, the expectation of justice here and especially now also becomes structural and seems to acquire a normative quality. That is to say that the expectation is not altered in case of disappointment but is, to the contrary, maintained.

The question that comes to the fore is whether not meeting this expectation of accelerated adjudication affects the authority of the judiciary.[70] This suggests that there is a relationship between (not) meeting (cognitive) expectations and the authority of an institution. In a general sense, authority has a stabilizing quality or at least pretends to offer some stability over time. Stability as certainty, opposed to contingency and uncertainty, pertains to expectations: knowing what to expect in the future, based on past experiences and hence on acquired or shared knowledge about how a particular kind of authority functions. The allure of authority lies in a promise of stability and certainty, two features that are considered part and parcel of most types of social order that are deemed desirable.

Authority functions, that is contributes to stability over time, as long as it is not questioned. It requires trust: to trust that this was the right decision, even without considering the arguments if necessary, because those arguments were delivered by professionals and should carry the decision.

To be clear, expectations concerning the acceleration of the judiciary are basically cognitive expectations. But as social acceleration has become structural and the new 'normal', this cognitive expectation settles so to speak, it becomes a general and stable expectation. The slowness of the law and its organizations does no longer provoke the adaptation or adjustment of the expectation but the latter turns into a normative expectation of the first order. If, subsequently, the legal system triggered by the ongoing communication about these cognitive turned normative expectations, selects these expectations to be generalized and stabilized, acceleration becomes a part of the system – albeit an inconvenient part. Something remarkable happens at this point. The legal system, while producing these

70 In the Netherlands this seems to be the case, or so it suggested by the Council of the Judiciary in its Agendas, see Francot and Mommers, 'Picking up the Pace', 8–9.

'acceleration norms' itself, loses somewhat of its autonomy and authority by adapting to the societal timelines. On the other hand, considering it operational autonomy, this is the only way in which the legal system can deal with what are essentially cognitive expectations: by turning them into second order norms.

The relationship between the authority of the judiciary and social acceleration basically seems to be a negative one. It is not the process of acceleration *per se* that erodes or at least changes the authority of the judiciary but a complex interplay of expectations induced by acceleration and how these expectations are met, or not. A memo of the Dutch Council of the Judiciary is illustrative as it states that authority, even in times of an increasing demand for impartial authority,[71] needs to be earned as it is no longer self-evident. In order to earn its authority, the judiciary has to fully focus on its 'clients' and their expectations *vis-à-vis* the organization.[72] In a sense, this entails a shift from judicial decision to persuasion by judges which is a game-changer for the authority of the judiciary.

Concluding remarks

Times are changing and social acceleration, as is extensively theorized by Hartmut Rosa, has become a *structural* feature of contemporary society. In order to analyse social acceleration, Rosa discerns three dimensions, i.e. technical acceleration, the acceleration of the pace of life and the acceleration of social change. All three dimensions affect the legal system and its organizations but my focus was on the third category, the speeding-up of social change.

As a consequence of *structural* acceleration, the legal system is no longer only occasionally confronted with the request of its social environment to pick up its pace but has to face this issue on both its organizational level and on a fundamental level. At the organizational level, the legal system needs to reconsider the ways – its procedures, its processes – in which the law deals with time. This pertains especially to the central *formal* organizations of the legal system, the courts. The courts are the loci where the legal system communicates directly with its societal environment and where it is confronted in an unabridged way with the demand for fast justice, preferably here and now.

71 In the Dutch debate, most scholars also argue that there is an increased demand for authority in our era. Paradoxically this demand goes together with a rejection of or at least a very critical attitude towards authority. This is called the authority-paradox. Thijs Jansen, Gabriël van den Brink & René Kneyber (Eds.), *Gezagsdragers. De publieke zaak op zoek naar haar verdedigers* (Amsterdam: Boom, 2012). My suggestion would be that in an era of uncertainty, people expect authority to provide for certainty but that this does not necessarily imply that they want more of the same. On the contrary, given the dissatisfaction with 'traditional' authorities or loci of authority, it might well be a demand for a different type of authority.

72 https://www.rechtspraak.nl/Organisatie/Raad-Voor-De-Rechtspraak/Visie-op-de-rechtspraak/Pages/Beeldenover2020.aspx accessed on 16 June, 2017.

The discrepancy between the moderate tempo of law and the accelerating tempo of society urges an inquiry into the state of the authority and autonomy of the judiciary and the legal system. There was and always has been a difference between legal time and social time, a temporal differential. Moreover, this differential was and to a certain degree still is constitutive of the demarcation of the legal system vis-à-vis society and other social systems. In this sense, the considerable gap between legal time and societal time serves a goal. However, this gap might be widened by social acceleration up to the point that it actually threatens the autonomy of the law and hence the authority of the judiciary. Nowadays, it seems that social acceleration widens the gap even further and the question becomes if law is not left behind to the extent that it becomes irrelevant, a residue of modern times within late modernity.

Both meeting and not subjugating to the demand of fast justice might put a strain on the law's autonomy and the authority of the judiciary. In a sense, it is a catch 22. If the legal system does not speed up, it might become irrelevant as it fails to deliver in conformity with contemporary expectations. However, if the judiciary does accelerate, this might at its turn cause 'system overload' as it clashes with the characteristic and traditional legal timelines, or to put it somewhat differently, its typical inertia.

Bibliography

Berg, Maggie, and Barbara K. Seeber. *The Slow Professor: Challenging the Culture of Speed in the Academy.* Toronto: University of Toronto Press, 2016.

Cilliers, Paul. 'On the Importance of a Certain Slowness'. *Emergence: Complexity and Organization* 8 (2006): 106–112.

Cipriani, Roberto, 'The Many Faces of Social Time: A Sociological Approach'. *Time & Society* 22 (2013): 5–30.

Francot, Lyana, 'Dealing with Complexity, Facing Uncertainty: Morality and Ethics in a Complex Society'. *Archiv für Rechts- und Sozialphilosophie* 2 (2014): 201–218.

Francot, Lyana, and Sophie Mommers. 'Picking up the Pace – Legal Slowness and the Authority of the Judiciary in the Acceleration Society (a Dutch Case Study)'. *International Journal of the Legal Profession* 23 (2016): 1–19.

Greenhouse, Carol J. 'Just in Time: Temporality and the Cultural Legitimation of Time'. *The Yale Law Journal* 98 (1989): 1631–1651.

Jansen, Thijs, Gabriël van den Brink and René Kneyber, eds. *Gezagsdragers. De publieke zaak op zoek naar haar verdedigers.* Amsterdam: Boom, 2012.

Khan, Liaquat Ali. 'Temporality of Law'. *McGeorge Law Review* 40 (2009): 55–106.

Luhmann, Niklas. 'Die Knappheit der Zeit und die Vordringlichkeit des Befristeten'. In Niklas Luhmann, *Politische Planung. Aufsätze zur Soziologie von Politik und Verwaltung*, 143–164. Opladen: Westdeutscher Verlag, 1971.

Luhmann, Niklas. *Gesellschaftsstruktur und Semantik. Studien zur Wissenssoziologie der modernen Gesellschaft – Band 1.* Frankfurt am Main: Suhrkamp, 1993.

Luhmann, Niklas. *Das Recht der Gesellschaft.* Frankfurt am Main: Suhrkamp, 1993.

Nelken, David. 'Normalising Time: European Integration and Court Delays in Italy'. In *Paradoxes of European Legal Integration*, edited by Hanne Petersen, Helle Krunke, Anne-Lise Kjaer and Mikale Rask Madse, 299–323. Aldershot: Ashgate, 2008.

Nowotny, Helga. *Time: The Modern and Postmodern Experience*. Cambridge/Malden: Polity, 2005.

Ost, François. *Le Temps du Droit*. Paris: Odile Jacob, 1999.

Van Rhee, Remco. 'De traagheid van de civiele procedure: een eeuwenoud fenomeen'. In *De rechtspraktijk in beeld. Van Justinianus tot de Duitse bezetting*, edited by Beatrix Jacobs, 57–67. Tilburg: Tilburg University, 1997.

Rosa, Hartmut. 'Social Acceleration: Ethical and Political Consequences of a Desynchronized High-speed Society'. *Constellations* 10, no. 1 (2003): 3–33.

Rosa, Hartmut. *Beschleunigung. Die Veränderung der Zeitstrukturen in der Moderne*. Frankfurt am Main: Suhrkamp, 2005.

Rosa, Hartmut. *Social Acceleration. A New Theory of Modernity*. New York: Columbia University Press, 2013.

Wistrich, Andrew J. 'The Evolving Temporality of Lawmaking'. *Connecticut Law Review* 44, no. 3 (2012): 737–826.

Chapter 6

Uncertain futures and the problem of constraining emergency powers: temporal dimensions of Carl Schmitt's theory of the state of exception

Marc de Wilde

Introduction

In the past decade or so, a succession of crises has led governments across the globe to take refuge in their emergency powers. Examples include the use of emergency powers in the so-called 'war on terror' and the emergency measures taken in response to the recent financial crisis. As these examples suggest, it has proved to be difficult to effectively constrain executive uses of emergency powers and to prevent their abuse. Indeed, in several cases, uses of emergency powers have led to arbitrary exercises of power that undermined democracy and the rule of law. A notorious example is the practice of indefinite detention and enhanced interrogation of suspects of terrorism adopted by the United States and other countries after 9/11, which largely escaped judicial and parliamentary control.[1] More recent examples include the way in which American and British intelligence agencies used their emergency powers to justify practices of enhanced surveillance as well as massive and systematic interception of phone and e-mail communication.[2]

In the literature, the failure to effectively constrain executive uses of emergency powers has been explained by various causes. For instance, it has been pointed out that there has generally been wide democratic support for the use of emergency powers, even in spite of frequent violations of the rights of individuals and minorities. This has been explained by the fact that in emergencies, when vital interests

1 Judicial control was gradually restored in a series of landmark decisions by the US Supreme Court, in which it held that suspects of terrorism detained at Guantánamo Bay had the right to challenge their detention before an impartial court under *habeas corpus*. The first of these decisions was *Rasul v. Bush*, 542 US 466 (2004).

2 On 7 June 2013, *The Guardian* and *The Washington Post* published documents from Edward Snowden which revealed that the American and British intelligence agencies NSA and GCHQ had systematically intercepted phone, e-mail and video communications. Barton Gellmann and Laura Poitras, 'US and British Intelligence Mining Data From Nine US Internet Companies in Broad Secret Program', *The Washington Post*, June 7, 2013; Glenn Greenwald and Ewan MacAskill, 'NSA PRISM Program Taps into User Data of Apple, Google, and Others', *The Guardian*, June 7, 2013.

of the nation are at stake, there is a tendency to 'rally behind the flag' and to unconditionally support executive emergency measures.[3] In those instances, it may be difficult for majorities to identify with the interests of individuals and minorities whose rights are violated, especially if a rhetoric of fear frames these others as an existential threat to the majority's way of life. For instance, it is striking that in the United States, it is Congress, not the President, which prevents the closing down of Guantánamo Bay, arguing that the detention of suspects of terrorism on American soil would constitute a major threat to the people's vital security interests.

Others have explained the failure to effectively constrain executive exercises of emergency powers by pointing at structural causes. It has thus been argued that the need for secrecy in matters of national security, the complexity of policy problems especially in the economic domain, and the sheer speed of responses required in emergencies combine to make meaningful legislative and judicial oversight virtually impossible.[4] This explains why it is generally left to the executive to decide whether there is an emergency at all, because, contrary to parliament and judges, only the executive is believed to have the means and expertise necessary to adequately assess the crisis as well as the emergency measures it requires. This is especially true if the identification of the crisis depends on information that is secret because of national security interests. Here, claims to secrecy and national security may prevent parliaments and judges from effectively controlling executive exercises of emergency powers.

Although these structural causes are certainly important, I believe they are not sufficient for explaining the failure to effectively constrain executive uses of emergency powers. In brief, what I will argue in this chapter is that the failure to constrain emergency powers can only be adequately explained if its *temporal* assumptions are taken into account. Emergencies are thus often believed to be inherently *unpredictable*. They are believed to unexpectedly disrupt the normal legal order and its regular temporality, putting the law out of joint. Therefore, the legislator cannot determine in advance what the nature of future crises will be, nor what measures they will require. Hence, the legislator cannot set strict *ex ante* limitations to emergency powers, for it may cause these powers to become insufficiently flexible to cope with the crisis. Instead, it is largely left to the executive to decide whether there is an emergency at all and what measures it requires. It is thus the belief that future emergencies are inherently unpredictable which explains why legislators have generally produced very broad delegations of emergency powers: in an emergency, the executive may take all the measures he deems necessary, and even act without prior legal authorization, because it is impossible to determine in advance what the nature of the crisis will be and what measures it requires.

3 Compare, for instance, Mark Tushnet, 'Controlling Executive Power in the War on Terrorism', *Harvard Law Review* 118, no. 8 (2005), 2678.

4 Eric Posner and Adrian Vermeule, *The Executive Unbound: After the Madisonian Republic* (Oxford: Oxford University Press, 2010), 11.

The belief in the unpredictability of emergencies – the belief that they occur in an *exceptional time* which cannot be anticipated – is expressed in contemporary discourses of emergency powers. Current crises are thus often claimed to be 'unprecedented' and in need of unprecedented emergency responses. These crises are said to be unique and unforeseen, without history or precedent. They are believed to arrive unannounced, disrupting the existing legal order unexpectedly. Thus, after 9/11, it was claimed that the threat of terrorism was 'unprecedented' and that the existing laws were insufficient to understand and cope with this threat. More specifically, it was claimed that the laws of war and criminal law did not apply to suspects of terrorism, as the legislator had not foreseen, and could not have foreseen, this unprecedented threat.[5] Likewise, the 2008 financial crisis was said to be 'unprecedented' and in need of 'unprecedented' emergency responses.[6] More particularly, it was emphasized that the sudden failure of banks could not have been foreseen or anticipated by the legislator. Hence, governments were tacitly allowed to act without prior legal authorization and nationalize banks and financial institutions which were considered too big to fail.

From a rule of law perspective it is important to tackle the general belief that emergencies are inherently unpredictable, such that emergency responses cannot be subject to *ex ante* legal constraints. This belief is based on the assumption that in emergencies, the regularity of law, i.e., the temporal continuity between *ex ante* legislation and *ex post* adjudication, has been interrupted and become disfunctional. In the literature, this belief is often attributed to the German constitutional lawyer Carl Schmitt. In the 1920s and 30s, Schmitt advocated exceptionally wide and, indeed, extra-legal emergency powers. He justified these powers by pointing at the inherent unpredictability of emergencies. He thus claimed that each crisis could unexpectedly develop into an extreme emergency, a threat to the state and its constitution. In view of these existential threats, it was justified to proclaim a 'state of exception', which led to the temporary suspension of the laws. For Schmitt, it was the very exceptional and inherently unpredictable nature of emergencies that justified the categorical suspension of the laws. If the state itself was imperiled, there could be no legal obstacles to executive emergency responses. After 1933, Schmitt would collaborate with the National Socialists and use his theory of emergency powers, amongst other things, to justify the extra-legal

5 In speeches and press statements, members of the US government often referred to the 'unprecedented threat of terrorism' to justify exemptions from the law. Compare, for instance, President George Bush's speech on terrorism of 6 September 2006: 'We had to wage an *unprecedented* war against an enemy *unlike any we had fought before*. We had to find the terrorists hiding in America and across the world before they were able to strike our country again' (italics MdW). A transcript of this speech can be found at http://www.nytimes.com/2006/09/06/washington/06bush_transcript.html?pagewanted=all.

6 Compare, for instance, the press release of the President of the European Commission José Manuel Barroso issued on 14 October 2008: 'This is an *unprecedented* crisis. This is precisely why it requires *unprecedented* EU action' (italics MdW). The statement can be found at http://europa.eu/rapid/press-release_SPEECH-08-524_en.htm?locale=en.

execution of Hitler's political opponents.[7] Indeed, by advocating a theory of extra-legal emergency powers Schmitt actively contributed to legitimizing the transition towards Hitler's dictatorship.

Notwithstanding Schmitt's collaboration with the Nazis, his theory has proved to be immensely influential in the contemporary debate on emergency powers.[8] This is especially true of his claim that emergencies are inherently unpredictable, so that emergency powers cannot be subject to *ex ante* legislative constraints. It is invoked by scholars like Oren Gross, Eric Posner and Adrian Vermeule, who advocate extra-legal responses to emergencies,[9] but also by David Dyzenhaus and Mark Tushnet, who propose rule of law restrictions on emergency powers, while rejecting the possibility of *ex ante* legislative constraints.[10] Although these scholars are very critical about the illiberal implications of Schmitt's theory, they share his assumption that executive emergency powers cannot be subject to *ex ante* legislative constraints, as neither the nature of the emergency itself, nor the measures it requires can be anticipated by the legislator.

In what follows, I will try to tackle the general belief that there can be no *ex ante* legislative restrictions on executive emergency powers by tracing it back to its source. More particularly, I will offer a genealogical critique of Schmitt's theory of extra-legal emergency powers and its underlying temporal assumptions. I will demonstrate that Schmitt's claim that emergency powers are essentially extra-legal depends on a notion of *exceptional time*, which is highly problematic from a rule of law perspective. More particularly, I will contest Schmitt's thesis about the extra-legality of emergency powers by criticizing its underlying assumption that emergencies are inherently exceptional and unpredictable, such that they cannot be anticipated by the legislator, nor subjected to *ex ante* rule of law-constraints.

7 See, in particular, Carl Schmitt, 'Der Führer schützt das Recht', *Deutsche Juristen-Zeitung* 39, no. 15 (August 1, 1934), 945–950. Schmitt's collaboration with National Socialism is discussed in Dirk Blasius, *Carl Schmitt: Preussischer Staatsrat in Hitlers Reich* (Göttingen: Vandenhoeck und Ruprecht, 2001). For an analysis of Schmitt's Anti-Semitism: Raphael Gross, *Carl Schmitt und die Juden: Eine deutsche Rechtslehre* (Frankfurt am Main: Suhrkamp, 2005).

8 For an overview of Schmitt's influence on the contemporary debate about emergency powers see: William E. Scheuermann, 'Emergency Powers and the Rule of Law after 9/11', *The Journal of Political Philosophy* 14, no. 1 (2006), 61–84.

9 Oren Gross, 'Chaos and Rules: Should Responses to Violent Crises Always Be Constitutional?', *The Yale Law Journal* 112, no. 5 (2003), 1120–1121 and Posner and Vermeule, *The Executive Unbound*, 4–5, 32–34, 42.

10 Mark Tushnet, 'Emergencies and the Idea of Constitutionalism', in *The Constitution in Wartime: Beyond Alarmism and Complacency*, ed. M. Tushnet (Durham: Duke University Press, 2005), 39–54 and David Dyzenhaus, *The Constitution of Law: Legality in a Time of Emergency* (Cambridge: Cambridge University Press, 2006), 34–54. Compare also Dyzenhaus's excellent analysis of Schmitt's legal theory in *Legality and Legitimacy: Carl Schmitt, Hans Kelsen and Hermann Heller in Weimar* (Oxford: Oxford University Press, 2003), 38–101.

Coping with an uncertain future: Carl Schmitt in Weimar

To grasp the stakes of Schmitt's theory of emergency powers we need to understand it in its historical context. Schmitt first developed his ideas about emergency powers in the early 1920s, during the so-called Weimar Republic. This was a time when the future seemed highly uncertain. World War I had resulted in the sudden collapse not only of states and empires, but of an entire world order with its traditional ways of life and horizons of meaning. Thus, the world in which Schmitt's generation had grown up, in which emperor, church and nation had embodied shared values, no longer existed. In the course of a single generation, this world had disappeared. In the Weimar Republic, this led to feelings of cultural and political disorientation.[11] Expectations with regard to the future could no longer be predicted on the basis of past experiences. Indeed, the gap between present and past seemed to have become unbridgeable.[12] In a world, in which the tradition had suddenly lost its normative force, everything seemed to have become possible: the future appeared to be radically open, and nobody could predict what it held in store.

This was also true of the Republic itself: in the early 1920s, the future of the young Republic was still highly uncertain. The Republic had literally been founded on the ruins of the Great War: it was thus narrowly associated with Germany's military defeat and many considered it an illegitimate, foreign imposition. More importantly, in spite of its modern, democratic constitution, a genuinely democratic tradition and culture were lacking.[13] As Eric Weitz observes in a recent

11 These feelings of disorientation are, for instance, expressed by Walter Benjamin: '[a] generation that had gone to school on a horse-drawn street car now stood under the open sky in a countryside in which nothing had remained unchanged but the clouds, and beneath these clouds, in a field of force of destructive torrents and explosions, was the tiny, fragile human body.' Walter Benjamin, 'The Storyteller', in *Illuminations*, trans. Harry Zohn (New York: Schocken, 2007), 84.

12 Reinhart Kosseleck argues that modernity, in the sense of *Neuzeit*, can be defined as the condition in which 'expectations have distanced themselves evermore from all previous experience.' However, in this modern condition, the concept of 'progress' could still bridge the gap between expectations with regard to the future and experiences from the past. By contrast, we may add, the catastrophic experience of the Great War undermined the belief in progress itself, causing the gap between expectations and experience to become unbridgeable. Reinhard Kosseleck, *Futures Past: On the Semantics of Historical Time*, trans. Keith Tribe (New York: Columbia University Press, 2004), 263.

13 In her contribution to this volume, Nomi Claire Lazar argues that modern constitutions seek to establish a radical rupture with the past. The promulgation of these constitutions is framed as a turning point, joining past event series to a projected future and thereby changing expectations of a state's trajectory. According to Lazar, these constitutional time frames serve to control an otherwise uncertain future. However, as Lazar rightly emphasizes, the capacity of modern constitutions to effectively control uncertain futures is dependent on the continuity of the political climate. The constitution of the Weimar Republic failed in this respect, because it depended on an unstable

study of the Weimar Republic, '[d]emocracy needs democratic convictions and a democratic culture that ripple through all the institutions of a society, not just the formal political ones. That was hard to find in many of the key institutions of the [R]epublic.'[14] More particularly, the legitimacy of the Republic was continuously contested by political movements at both the radical left and extreme right. Thus, from the outset, the Republic faced a succession of grave political crises, which caused its government to take refuge in emergency powers on an almost daily basis. In the first five years of its existence, a state of emergency was proclaimed on no less than 135 occasions.[15] Especially in 1919 and 1920, emergency powers were frequently deployed to put down a series of communist uprisings and right wing putsch attempts. At one of these occasions, Carl Schmitt, who at the time worked as a legal councilor at the Bavarian Ministry of Defence, witnessed the summary execution of one of his colleagues by revolutionaries: his colleague was shot through the head behind the desk opposite to him.[16]

Schmitt's theory about the necessity of extra-legal responses to emergencies should be seen against this historical background: it is haunted by the spectre of revolutionary violence. At the time Schmitt first developed his theory, the threat to the Republic was real and, indeed, existential: it was far from certain whether the Republic would survive. Moreover, the revolutionary violence Schmitt had witnessed in Bavaria did indeed seem to call for strong governmental responses. Hence, in a series of books and articles, published between 1922 and 1932, Schmitt rejected the limited, rule of law responses to emergencies proposed by liberal lawyers. He criticized these liberal lawyers for failing to understand the political dilemmas inherent in emergencies. Thus, in his view, in an extreme emergency, when the survival of the political community was at stake, the laws could not be an obstacle to governmental emergency responses. In such cases, formal legal restrictions could not prevent the executive from effectively protecting the Republic. Instead, the executive was allowed to do everything in its power to prevent the collapse of the existing order, even if it required a transgression of the laws. By contrast, liberal lawyers wished to maintain the rule of law even in emergencies. According to Schmitt, they did not realize that by doing so, they jeopardized the very constitutional order which made the rule of law possible in the first place.

and polarized political climate: even among the governing elites, there were very few willing to actively support its liberal values.

14 Eric D. Weitz, *Weimar Germany: Promises and Tragedy* (Princeton: Princeton University Press, 2007), 366. For an extensive analysis of the 'antidemocratic spirit' of Weimar's political elites, see: Kurt Sontheimer, *Antidemokratisches Denken in der Weimarer Republik* (München: Deutscher Taschenbuch Verlag, 1994).

15 Fritz Poetzsch-Heffter, 'Vom Staatsleben unter der Weimarer Verfassung: Erster Bericht, vom 1. Januar 1920 bis zum 31. Dezember 1924', *Jahrbuch des öffentlichen Rechts* 13 (1925), 141ff.

16 Joseph Bendersky, *Carl Schmitt: Theorist for the Reich* (Princeton: Princeton University Press, 1983), 22.

Emergency, unpredictability, sovereignty: legal dimensions

Schmitt first presented his theory of emergency powers in his influential 1922 essay *Political Theology.* Here he distinguishes between the 'state of necessity [*Notstand*]' and the 'state of exception [*Ausnahmezustand*]'.[17] The concept of the 'state of necessity' refers to more or less regular emergencies, such as local disturbances of public order or natural disasters, which occur every once in a while and can thus be foreseen by the legislator. As Schmitt explains, executive responses to such emergencies can be subjected to rule of law restrictions. By contrast, the concept of the 'state of exception' refers to more extreme and exceptional emergencies, in which the survival of the political community itself is at stake. In Schmitt's view, such exceptional situations cannot be anticipated by the legislator. Indeed, if the legislator would set strict *ex ante* limitations to executive emergency responses, these would be ignored at the very first occasion, because the community's survival depends on it. Hence, Schmitt argues that in a 'state of exception', when the survival of the political community is at stake, there can be no legal restrictions whatsoever on executive emergency powers.

In Schmitt's theory, there is a direct link between the claim that emergency powers must remain legally unlimited and the belief that emergencies are inherently exceptional and unpredictable. Thus Schmitt emphatically claims that it is impossible for the legislator to specify in advance what kinds of emergencies constitute a 'state of exception': 'The precise details of an emergency cannot be anticipated, nor can one spell out what may take place in such a case, especially when it is truly a matter of an extreme emergency and of how it is to be eliminated.'[18] As the actual manifestation of future emergencies cannot be anticipated, 'the precondition as well as the content of the competence in such a case must necessarily be unlimited.'[19] The legislator can define the state of exception only in the most general terms, as a 'case of extreme peril, a danger to the existence of the state, or the like.'[20] Yet, he cannot specify in advance what cases constitute a 'state of exception'; due to its exceptional nature, the emergency itself must remain legally unspecified. Nor is it possible to predict what kinds of responses these future emergencies will require. This implies that it is ultimately left to the executive to decide whether there is an emergency at all and what measures should be taken to respond to it. This competence – if it can still be called a competence[21] – must necessarily be unlimited, as neither the emergency itself, nor the measures it requires, can be specified in advance.

17 Carl Schmitt, *Politische Theologie: Vier Kapitel zur Lehre von der Souveränität* (Berlin: Duncker und Humblot, 1996 [1922]), 13–14 and 18. Translated as Carl Schmitt, *Political Theology: Four Chapters on the Concept of Sovereignty*, trans. Georg Schwab (Chicago: Chicago University Press, 2005), 6 and 12.
18 Schmitt, *Politische Theologie,* 13; trans., 6–7.
19 Schmitt, *Politische Theologie,* 13; trans., 6–7 (trans. modified).
20 Schmitt, *Politische Theologie,* 13; trans., 6.
21 Cf. Schmitt, *Politische Theologie,* 14; trans., 7: 'From the liberal constitutional point of view, there would be no competence at all' (trans. modified).

The unpredictability of emergencies and the unlimited competence that follows from it allow Schmitt to relate the state of exception to the concept of sovereignty. As we have seen, the legislator cannot anticipate the emergency or the measures it requires. At best, Schmitt argues, the legislator can determine who has the authority to act: 'The most guidance the constitution may provide is to indicate who can act in such a case.'[22] This is important, for, as the emergency powers must remain legally unlimited, the authority invested with those powers can be identified as the sovereign ruler. It is the sovereign who determines whether a particular emergency constitutes an existential threat to the state that justifies the suspension of the laws. Indeed, in Schmitt's view, by proclaiming a 'state of exception', the sovereign may potentially suspend the entire legal order: he may decide whether 'the constitution needs to be suspended in its entirety.'[23] Thus, the belief in the exceptionality and unpredictability of extreme emergencies leads Schmitt to conclude that the authority invested with emergency powers must be sovereign, that is, no longer bound by the laws.

However, Schmitt does not claim that the sovereign may use his emergency powers arbitrarily: the right to sovereign discretion is not a licence to arbitrary decision. Instead, the sovereign remains bound by his task: to protect the existing order and restore the situation of normality, in which the laws can once again be applied. As Schmitt explains: 'there exists no norm that is applicable to chaos. For a legal order to make sense, a normal situation must exist.'[24] In Schmitt's view, it is this situation of normality which makes the application of the laws possible in the first place. The normal situation is suddenly disrupted by the emergency: it is interrupted by the threat of anarchy and chaos that the extreme emergency embodies. Hence, in the state of exception, it is the sovereign's task to effectively respond to the emergency and *restore* the situation of normality, so that legal norms can once again be applied. Although no longer bound by rule of law restrictions, the sovereign remains bound by his task, i.e., he remains responsible for restoring the situation of normality on which the applicability of the laws and, indeed, the rule of law itself depends.[25]

It is at this point that Schmitt blames his liberal colleagues for advocating a naïve and even dangerous understanding of emergency powers. He criticizes liberal scholars like Hugo Krabbe and Hans Kelsen for denying the reality of the exception and stressing the importance of maintaining rule of law restrictions even

22 Schmitt, *Politische Theologie*, 14; trans., 7.
23 Schmitt, *Politische Theologie*, 14; trans., 7.
24 Schmitt, *Politische Theologie*, 19; trans., 13.
25 As Ellen Kennedy points out, hostile readers have criticized Schmitt for his 'determination to destroy the normative and with it the rule of law'. However, Kennedy criticizes this 'misreading': she argues that, on Schmitt's view, the rule of law presupposes a normal situation, which the sovereign decision first produces and guarantees. Hence, the sovereign decision is not independent of legal norms, even if they do not determine its outcome. Ellen Kennedy, *Constitutional Failure: Carl Schmitt in Weimar* (Durham: Duke University Press, 2004), 85–86.

in extreme emergencies. By binding the sovereign to legal restrictions, they prevent him from responding quickly and effectively to the threat. They do not realize that by doing so, they prevent him from restoring the very situation of normality on which the validity of the laws and the rule of law itself depends. For if the sovereign proves incapable of restoring the normal situation, chaos and anarchy will rule, and the preconditions for the law's validity and for the rule of law will no longer be fulfilled. In other words: by subjecting the sovereign in the state of exception to rule of law restrictions, liberal layers risk jeopardizing the very conditions of the rule of law, for they hamper the sovereign's capability to restore the situation of normality which makes the application of the laws possible in the first place.

For Schmitt, the question of sovereignty and the state of exception is related to what we may call the 'life of the law.' Indeed, as Schmitt himself suggests, it is in the exception that the 'power of real life' suddenly and unexpectedly announces itself:

> [t]he exception is more interesting than the rule. The rule proves nothing; the exception proves everything: It confirms not only the rule but also its existence, which derives only from the exception. In the exception the power of real life breaks through the crust of a mechanism that has become torpid by repetition [*In der Ausnahme durchbricht die Kraft des wirklichen Lebens die Kruste einer in Wiederholung erstarrten Mechanik*].'[26]

Schmitt's existentialist rhetoric is problematic as it tends to overemphasize the importance of the exception at the expense of the rule. In doing so, it risks denying the very conditions of normality (i.e., the self-evident, everyday application of legal rules), on which the effectiveness of the laws and the rule of law depend. However, Schmitt's main concern appears to be that the liberal conception of the legal order which denies the reality of both sovereign decisions and extreme exceptions risks making that legal order defenceless in the face of existential threats. It is this aspect of his theory that Schmitt develops in his later texts, notably in his famous essay on *The Concept of the Political* (1927/1932), to which we will now turn.

Emergency powers and the substance of the constitution: political dimensions

In his later texts Schmitt adopts an anti-positivist approach to the state of exception and emergency powers by highlighting their political and existential dimensions. Contrary to the view of legal positivists like Kelsen, Schmitt emphasizes that the question of how to respond to emergencies should not be considered as a merely technical juristic question. Instead, he believes it is an intensely political question. In his *Concept of the Political*, Schmitt famously defines the political as being

26 Schmitt, *Politische Theologie*, 21; trans., 15.

constituted by the friend/enemy distinction. It is this friend/enemy distinction which allows us to identify a certain human practice as a *political* practice.[27] Schmitt understands the friend/enemy distinction in existential terms: the enemy is defined by the fact that he constitutes a threat to our existence, to our way of life. This implies that a violent conflict with the enemy is a 'real possibility.' By relating his notion of the political to the 'exceptional case' of violent conflict, Schmitt suggests that a state of exception may only be proclaimed if a nation is facing an enemy that constitutes a direct threat to its way of life, that is, if violent conflict with the enemy has become a 'real possibility'.[28] According to Schmitt, it is only in this extreme situation that the state of exception and the suspension of the laws it entails are justified.

By highlighting the political and existential dimensions of the state of exception and emergency powers Schmitt turns against the positivist tendency to *neutralize* the domain of the state and constitutional law. In his view, legal positivists fail to see that emergencies involve existential struggles which are in fact highly political. Here, Schmitt probably had in mind contemporary examples. Thus, at the time he wrote his essay, even outright anti-constitutional parties such as the Communists and National Socialists were permitted to use their constitutional rights and to participate actively in the parliamentary system. These parties strategically used the neutrality of constitutional rights and procedures to gain power for the very purpose of destroying that same constitution. By contrast, Schmitt believes that a state cannot afford to remain neutral *vis-à-vis* parties that deny its legitimacy and reject its constitutional values. In this existential struggle, the state and, more particularly, the President, needs to be prepared to temporarily suspend the laws and limit the rights of anti-constitutional parties. Hence, in Schmitt's view, the President is authorized, and indeed has the duty, to temporarily suspend the laws to protect the constitution itself.

However, in the early 1930s, Schmitt's position towards National Socialism becomes more ambivalent. He still argues that the President may use his emergency powers to limit the rights of anti-constitutional parties and prevent such parties from obtaining a position of power that allows them to 'close the door behind [themselves], thus shoving aside the principle of legality by legal means.'[29]

27 Carl Schmitt, *Der Begriff des Politischen: Text von 1932 mit einem Vorwort und drei Corollarien* (Berlin: Duncker und Humblot, 2002 [1932]), 26. Translated as: Carl Schmitt, *The Concept of the Political*, trans. George Schwab (Chicago: Chicago University Press, 2007), 26.

28 Schmitt, *Der Begriff des Politischen*, 35; trans., 35.

29 Carl Schmitt, *Legalität und Legitimität* (Berlin: Duncker und Humblot, 2005 [1932]), 35. Interestingly, the prepublication of this essay contained an editorial remark stating that 'Whoever grants the National Socialists a majority on 31 July [1932, the day of the Reichstag elections], leaves Germany entirely at the mercy of this group.' Carl Schmitt, 'Der Missbrauch der Legalität', in *Tägliche Rundschau* 167 (July 19, 1932), 2. Whether this editorial remark had been proposed by, or discussed with, Schmitt himself remains unclear. Reinhard Mehring, *Carl Schmitt: Aufstieg und Fall: Eine Biographie* (Munich: Beck, 2009), 650, n. 36.

Yet, he also protests against the manner in which, in the summer of 1932, the Prussian government had prevented the National Socialists from taking power by changing the rules of parliamentary elections. His main argument seems to be that it is the President's prerogative, rather than the right of state governments, to declare anti-constitutional parties 'illegal':

> [i]t belongs to the dangers of a pluralist party state that all the means of the state and all the possibilities of interpreting the constitution and law become tactical instruments in the hands of parties. The enemy of the[se] parties will then be declared 'illegal' to deprive him of an equal chance. The foundation of every parliamentary state, which grants all parties an equal chance, is thereby undermined. However, on the other hand, it would of course be completely impossible to grant parties truly inimical to the state an equal chance, and to hand over to them the legal possibilities of the state's will formation as weapons.[30]

In this context, Schmitt argues that the President as an 'authority standing above the parties' has the exclusive right to declare anti-constitutional parties 'illegal'. He may thus use his emergency powers to intervene in a state like Prussia and protect its constitutional integrity.

In his *Constitutional Theory* (1928), Schmitt attempts to specify in more detail the nature and scope of Presidential emergency powers. He claims that in the state of exception, the President's task is to protect the *political* substance of the constitution. In this context, he distinguishes between 'the constitutional law [*der Verfassungsgesetz*]' and 'the constitution [*die Verfassung*]' itself.[31] The concept of the constitutional law refers to the law, in which the specific tasks and competences of state institutions and the rights of citizens are laid down. By contrast, the concept of the constitution itself refers to the fundamental *political* decisions on which the constitutional law is founded. According to Schmitt, it consists of the decisions by which a people defines itself as a particular political community. Thus, in Schmitt's view, the constitution of the Weimar Republic consists of the fundamental political decisions of the German people for a democracy, a republic, a federally structured state, a parliamentary-representative form of legislative authority and government, and a *bourgeois Rechtsstaat* with its principles, fundamental rights and the separation of powers.[32] Schmitt believes that, compared to these fundamental political decisions, the 'constitutional law' of the Republic is of secondary importance.

30 Carl Schmitt, 'Die Verfassungsmässigkeit der Bestellung eines Reichskommissars für das Land Preussen', *Deutsche Juristen-Zeitung* 37, no. 15 (1 August 1932), 958.

31 Carl Schmitt, *Verfassungslehre* (Berlin: Duncker und Humblot, 1993 [1928]), 22. Translated as: Carl Schmitt, *Constitutional Theory*, trans. and ed. Jeffrey Seitzer, foreword by Ellen Kennedy (Durham: Duke University Press, 2008), 76.

32 Schmitt, *Verfassungslehre*, 23–24; trans., 77–78.

Schmitt's distinction between the constitutional law and the constitution itself turns out to be of decisive importance for determining the nature and scope of executive emergency powers: Schmitt argues that in a state of exception, the *constitutional law* is temporarily suspended, while the executive remains bound by the *constitution* itself. For instance, Article 48 of the Weimar Constitution authorizes the President to proclaim a state of exception and to temporarily suspend several rights of citizens, including the inviolability of person, domicile and property, and the freedom of speech, association and assembly. Yet, in doing so, the President remains bound by the constitution itself: in suspending these rights, he must respect the political decisions underlying the constitution, including the decision for a *Rechtsstaat* based on fundamental rights. Indeed, as Schmitt explains, the temporary suspension of these rights 'stands precisely in the service of the constitution's preservation and restoration.'[33] In other words: it is to protect the *political* substance of the constitution, that the President is authorized to temporarily suspend the constitutional law and its individual provisions.[34]

More particularly, Schmitt argues that in the state of exception, the President is temporarily allowed to derogate from the 'rule of law-provisions of the constitution' to protect the constitution itself.[35] Schmitt seems to associate the rule of law-provisions of the constitution with a negative form of freedom; they serve as 'limits to the state's political action'.[36] However, in a public emergency, these rule of law-provisions threaten to become obstacles to the effective defence of the state. Hence, in a public emergency, when quick and resolute emergency responses are required, the President is temporarily released from the rule of law-restrictions on his power. According to Schmitt, these restrictions are temporarily suspended to enable the executive to effectively protect the constitution itself: 'In instances of the endangerment of the *political* form of existence, they must appear as a hindrance to state self-defense. During disturbances of public safety and order, in dangerous times like war and domestic unrest, constitutional limitations such as these are suspended.'[37] On Schmitt's understanding, even the rule of law can only be effectively protected by temporarily releasing the President from the individual rule of law-restrictions on his power, so that he can respond to the emergency

33 Schmitt, *Verfassungslehre*, 27; trans., 80 (trans. modified).

34 Schmitt, *Verfassungslehre*, 109; trans., 156: 'The temporal setting aside of individual or of all constitutional provisions is often imprecisely designated as the putting out of force or suspension of "the constitution." The constitution in the actual sense, the fundamental political decisions over a people's form of existence, obviously cannot be set aside temporarily, but certainly the general constitutional norms established for their execution can be precisely when it is in the interest of the preservation of these political decisions.'

35 Schmitt refers to 'the norms for the protection of *bourgeois* freedom which are typical for the *Rechtsstaat* [*die typisch rechtsstaatlichen Normierungen zum Schutz der bürgerlichen Freiheit*].' Schmitt, *Verfassungslehre*, 109–110; trans., 156 (trans. modified).

36 Schmitt, *Verfassungslehre*, 110; trans., 156.

37 Schmitt, *Verfassungslehre*, 110; trans., 156 (italics in the original).

quickly and effectively and restore the conditions of normality on which the rule of law depends.

By contrast, Schmitt criticizes liberal lawyers for advocating rule of law-responses to emergencies and claiming that the constitution must remain 'inviolable' even in extreme emergencies.[38] According to Schmitt, this 'doctrine of inviolability' is not only theoretically problematic, but politically dangerous. It is theoretically problematic, because it fails to distinguish between the political substance of 'the constitution' and 'the constitutional law' in which it is laid down.[39] It thus implies that 'every single constitutional law' must remain inviolable in public emergencies. This implication is politically dangerous, for it hampers the President's ability to effectively respond to public emergencies. On Schmitt's understanding, the liberal argument implies that in an emergency, 'every single constitutional provision' must become an 'insurmountable obstacle to the protection of the constitution in general'.[40] This rule of law-approach to the state of exception is politically dangerous, for it boils down to sacrificing the substance of the constitution to its individual provisions, which are declared 'inviolable'. In Schmitt's view, this would mean 'nothing other than placing the individual statute above the entirety of the political form of existence and to twist the meaning and purpose of the state of exception into its opposite.'[41]

Schmitt first developed his critique of the doctrine of inviolability in 1924, in a lecture presented at a meeting of the Association of German Constitutional Lawyers in Jena.[42] Here he analysed in detail the scope of the President's emergency powers. He argued that, under Article 48 of the Constitution, the President had in fact two different competences: a general competence to take all the 'measures necessary for restoring public security and order' and a specific competence to suspend certain fundamental rights. While his specific competence was limited to the rights mentioned in Article 48: 2, Schmitt argued that this limitation did not apply to his general competence: hence, on Schmitt's interpretation, the President was allowed to *derogate* from other constitutional provisions than those enumerated in Article 48, as long as he did not *suspend* those provisions.[43] At the same time, however, he suggested that there were several limitations to the President's emergency powers. Most importantly, the President was not allowed to violate the 'organizational minimum' that was presupposed by Article 48 itself. Among other things, this implied that his emergency measures should not prevent the 'normal

38 Schmitt, *Verfassungslehre*, 111–112; trans., 158.
39 Schmitt, *Verfassungslehre*, 112; trans., 158.
40 Schmitt, *Verfassungslehre*, 27; trans., 80.
41 Schmitt, *Verfassungslehre*, 27; trans., 80.
42 Carl Schmitt, 'Die Diktatur des Reichspräsidenten nach Artikel 48 der Weimarer Verfassung' [1924], in Schmitt, *Die Diktatur* (Berlin: Duncker und Humblot, 1994 [1921]), 209–257. On this debate see my 'The State of Emergency in the Weimar Republic: Legal Disputes over Article 48 of the Weimar Constitution', *The Legal History Review* 78 (2010), 135–158.
43 Schmitt, *Die Diktatur*, 227.

functioning' of the presidency, the government and the Reichstag. Moreover, the concept of emergency 'measures' (as opposed to laws) implied that the President's emergency competences were limited to regulating specific cases, such that he was not allowed to issue legal norms that were generally binding (which had to remain a prerogative of the Reichtstag).[44]

In spite of these limitations, Schmitt's criticism of the doctrine of inviolability in effect contributed to justifying exceptionally wide grants of emergency power. In the Spring of 1930, Weimar's last majority government (a broad coalition led by the Social Democrats) resigned due to internal disagreements about how to cope with the effects of the financial crisis which had broken out in the previous year. Thereupon, the President of the Republic, Paul von Hindenburg, appointed a minority cabinet under the Catholic politician Heinrich Brüning. It soon became clear that Brüning lacked the necessary political support in the Reichstag. This led Hindenburg to take a decision with far-reaching consequences: instead of dismissing Brüning and his cabinet, he proclaimed a state of exception and dissolved the Reichstag.[45] In the following elections, the National Socialists surged ahead, winning 18.3 per cent of the vote. Together with other antidemocratic parties, such as the Communists and *Völkischer* Nationalists, they obtained almost half of the seats of the Reichstag. In the next two and a half years, the President's emergency powers gradually became a regular means of governance as the Reichstag was paralysed by political polarization and no longer able to agree on anything substantial. This normalization of emergency powers contributed to the gradual erosion of Weimar's parliamentary system. The Republic remained a parliamentary democracy in name only, and had essentially become a Presidential dictatorship.[46]

As a legal advisor to President Hindenburg's staff, Schmitt publically endorsed the practice of Presidential emergency government. In 1931, he published an essay in which he defended Hindenburg's decision, arguing that the President had acted as a 'guardian of the constitution' by preventing the constitutional order from falling prey to narrow and conflicting party interests.[47] Applying the criteria of his Jena lecture, he claimed that the President's emergency powers were limited by the constitution's organizational minimum, which implied that they remained subject to parliamentary control, rather than by 'legally formed barriers'. However, now that the Reichstag was politically divided and failed to take its legislative responsibilities, the President had to take his own responsibility and govern without parliament instead.[48] Indeed, in the following year, Schmitt published an essay in which he openly acknowledged that in practice, Presidential emergency

44 Schmitt, *Die Diktatur*, 243–244 and 247.

45 Heinrich August Winkler, *Weimar, 1918–1933: Die Geschichte der ersten deutschen Demokratie* (CH Beck, 1993), 379–80.

46 See my 'Just Trust Us: A Short History of Emergency Powers and Constitutional Change', *Comparative Legal History* 3, no. 1 (2015), 14.

47 Carl Schmitt, *Der Hüter der Verfassung* (Berlin: Duncker und Humblot, 1969 [1931]), 131.

48 Schmitt, *Der Hüter der Verfassung*, 131.

measures had violated even the organizational provisions of the constitution (notably, the competences of the Reichstag and the Länder). Moreover, he now suggested that the very distinction between emergency measures and laws had become obsolete, as the President had been tacitly allowed by the Reichstag and Courts to issue generally binding norms. Instead of criticizing these developments, Schmitt suggested they had to be accepted as practical realities.[49]

It was essentially Schmitt's anti-positivist approach that allowed him to downplay the importance of legal limitations to the President's emergency powers. In this unprecedented crisis, Schmitt claimed, the President's first responsibility was to protect the *political* substance of the Constitution. There could thus be no *formal* limitations to his emergency powers. Instead, the President was allowed to derogate from the rule of law provisions of the Constitution and even from its organizational provisions, if other organs of the state such as the Reichstag and the Länder failed to take their responsibility. However, by downplaying the importance of these constitutional restrictions on Presidential emergency powers Schmitt in effect contributed to justifying the transition towards a more authoritarian form of government. If the President was allowed to use his emergency powers to derogate from the rule of law provisions of the Constitution, if he was allowed to govern without the Reichstag and issue generally binding norms, and if he had the authority to intervene in the Länder by depositing state governments,[50] then it no longer made sense to speak of a constitutional system based on parliamentary democracy, the rule of law, federalism and the separation of powers. Indeed, then the practice of Presidential emergency government had implicitly transformed the political substance of the constitution itself. In the end, then, it was Schmitt's anti-positivist approach, his focus on extreme, unprecedented and exceptional emergencies to which formal rules could no longer apply, that led him to justifying the transition towards a Presidential dictatorship.

49 Schmitt, *Legalität und Legitimität*, 73.

50 On 20 July 1932, Chancellor Franz von Papen forced the Prussian State government to resign, installing himself as a Reich Commissioner for Prussia on the basis of a Presidential emergency decree. By doing so, the Chancellor not only destroyed one of the last bastions of democratic opposition in the Weimar Republic, but also acquired control over the powerful Prussian police force. In the following trial, Schmitt led the defence of the Reich. In his opening statement, he reaffirmed his anti-positivist interpretation of Article 48: he argued that Article 48 granted the President the authority to directly intervene in the Länder if the state government had failed in its responsibility for maintaining public order. More particularly, he claimed that under conditions of threatening civil war, the President had the duty to protect the constitution against a violent take-over by 'illegal' political parties. Moreover, he argued that in a state of exception, 'illegal' meant not merely the lack of correspondence to positive legal norms, but the factual condition of being an enemy of the state. *Preussen contra Reich: Stenogrammbericht der Verhandlungen vor dem Staatsgerichtshof in Leipzig vom 10 bis 14 Oktober 1932* (Berlin, 1933), 39–40. Cf. Peter Caldwell, *Popular Sovereignty and the Crisis of German Constitutional Law: Theory and Practice of Weimar Constitutionalism* (Durham: Duke University Press, 1997), 171–172 and Blasius, *Carl Schmitt*, 40–50.

Evaluating Schmitt's theory

As we have seen, Schmitt's theory about the extra-legality of emergency responses is based on temporal assumptions that are in fact deeply problematic. First, Schmitt assumes that emergencies are inherently exceptional and unpredictable, such that executive emergency responses cannot be subject to *ex ante* legal constraints. As we have seen, this interpretation depends on particular historical experiences and, more specifically, experiences of cultural and political disorientation in the wake of World War I. Hence, we should be careful not to uncritically project Schmitt's theory about the extra-legality of emergency powers onto our own present-day context, and keep in mind that Schmitt's theory was informed by fears and concerns that were specifically related to the crisis of Weimar. This is especially true of Schmitt's claim that emergencies are inherently exceptional and unpredictable: it expresses a temporal experience that was characteristic of the post-WWI generation, for whom the gap between present and past had become unbridgeable and traditional sources of legitimacy had lost their meaning. For this generation, it no longer seemed possible to predict what the future held in store, and it was therefore understandable (if not excusable) that Schmitt emphasized the belief that emergencies were inherently unpredictable, such that they could not be anticipated by the legislator.

By contrast, in our own present-day context, it is not self-evident that emergencies are inherently unpredictable. Instead, even extreme emergencies have their histories: they are preceded by similar ones and can be explained by historical causes. For instance, the 2008 financial crisis has been called 'unprecedented', yet there have been similar and even worse crises before – the financial crisis of 1929 comes to mind (which heralded the end of the Weimar Republic). There is thus no reason to assume that the legislator cannot anticipate such crises. Hence, Schmitt's claim that emergency responses cannot be subject to *ex ante* legal constraints is based on the incorrect assumption that emergencies cannot be anticipated: though unusual, emergencies are historical events, the effect of historical causes that can be recognized and explained. There is thus no reason to assume that emergency responses cannot be anticipated by the legislator and subjected to *ex ante* legal constraints.

A similar criticism applies to Schmitt's claim that extreme emergencies necessarily involve an existential threat to the survival of the state. As we have seen, Schmitt believes that emergency powers cannot be subject to legal restrictions, because in extreme emergencies, when the survival of the state is at stake, there can be no legal obstacles to executive emergency responses. More particularly, Schmitt claims that in such exceptional cases, those invested with emergency powers cannot be bound by the rule of law-provisions of the constitution, for their task is to protect the constitution's political substance, on which the rule of law depends. As we have seen, in the early 1920s, when Schmitt first developed this theory of extra-legal emergency powers, the threat to the Weimar Republic was real and, indeed, existential: the legitimacy of the Republic was contested by parties of both the radical left and the extreme right. It was far from certain whether the Republic would survive the many violent uprisings of communist revolutionaries and right wing putsch attempts. A decade later, when Schmitt developed his theory about the President as a 'guardian of the constitution', the Republic had once again plunged into a deep political crisis, with the National Socialists threatening to take to power and overturn the republican constitution. In this context, it was understandable that Schmitt claimed that the President had to do anything in his power to protect the existing constitution, even if it required a violation of the rule of law restrictions on his power.

However, although it is certainly true that in the 1930s, the Weimar Republic was facing an existential crisis, as it was confronted with the rise of anti-constitutional parties that openly called for its destruction, we should be careful not to project Schmitt's existentialist discourses onto our present-day context. For instance, the 9/11 terrorist attacks have been called an 'attack on the American way of life'. Indeed, this rhetoric was actively used by the US government to justify the indefinite suspension of the laws and the enhanced interrogation – or to put it more straightforwardly: torture – of suspects of terrorism. Yet, at no point did these attacks constitute a real threat to the survival of the American republic. Of course, they threatened the life of the population, which was a sufficient justification for temporarily restricting the rights of suspects of terrorism. But, it is important to distinguish the physical threat to the population from a political threat to the existing constitution: terrorism threatened the lives of thousands, but it did not pose an existential threat to the state or its republican constitution.[51] Indeed, ultimately, the suspension of habeas corpus and other constitutional rights of suspects of terrorism (including the right not to be tortured) did more damage to the constitution than the threat of terrorism itself. There is thus no reason to assume that the prolonged, categorical suspension of rule of law-provisions of the constitution was necessary at all.

As we have seen, Schmitt's theory of extra-legal emergency responses appears to be premised on the notion of *exceptional time*: it tends to frame emergencies as 'unprecedented' events which arrive suddenly and unexpectedly, such that they cannot be anticipated by the legislator, nor subjected to *ex ante* rule of law constraints. On Schmitt's view, emergencies are essentially without history: they interrupt the normal course of events and are therefore unsuitable to be governed by law. The temporal continuity of law – connecting *ex ante* legislation and *ex post* adjudication – is suddenly disconnected by an exceptional event, which cannot be foreseen and therefore cannot be adjudicated on the basis of pre-existing norms. This implies that in emergencies, the laws are temporarily suspended: the executive

51 Bruce Ackerman argues that it is crucial to distinguish between 'two different dangers posed by terrorism: the physical threat to the population and the political threat to the existing regime. Future attacks undoubtedly pose a severe physical threat: The next major strike may kill hundreds of thousands, or even millions. But they do not pose a clear and present danger to the existing regime.' Bruce Ackerman, 'The Emergency Constitution', *The Yale Law Journal* 113 (2004), 1039.

is temporarily exempted from rule of law-constraints on his power. According to Schmitt, in the exceptional time of emergency, the logic of law can no longer be valid: it is replaced by the logic of the political, an existential struggle to save the existing constitutional order at any price. This temporality of the exception serves as the tacit assumption of Schmitt's theory of extra-legal emergency responses. However, as I have tried to show, we should be careful not to uncritically project Schmitt's theory onto our own present-day context, because present-day emergencies – whether they be terrorist attacks or financial melt-downs – are rarely existential in the Schmittian sense: they rarely involve a threat to the state or the existing constitution (even if they may involve a threat to life). Indeed, as I have suggested, extra-legal emergency responses may constitute a more direct threat to the existing constitution than the emergencies they are intended to meet. Hence, there is no reason to assume with Schmitt that executive emergency responses cannot be subject to *ex ante* rule of law-constraints.

Bibliography

Ackerman, Bruce. 'The Emergency Constitution'. *The Yale Law Journal* 113, no. 5 (2004): 1029–1091.

Bendersky, Joseph. *Carl Schmitt: Theorist for the Reich*. Princeton: Princeton University Press, 1983.

Benjamin, Walter. 'The Storyteller.' In *Illuminations*. Translated by Harry Zohn. New York: Schocken, 2007, 83–111.

Blasius, Dirk. *Carl Schmitt: Preussischer Staatsrat in Hitlers Reich*. Göttingen: Vandenhoeck und Ruprecht, 2001.

Caldwell, Peter. *Popular Sovereignty and the Crisis of German Constitutional Law: Theory and Practice of Weimar Constitutionalism*. Durham: Duke University Press, 1997.

Dyzenhaus, David. *Legality and Legitimacy: Carl Schmitt, Hans Kelsen and Hermann Heller in Weimar*. Oxford: Oxford University Press, 2003.

Dyzenhaus, David. *The Constitution of Law: Legality in a Time of Emergency*. Cambridge: Cambridge University Press, 2006.

Gellmann, Barton, and Laura Poitras. 'US and British Intelligence Mining Data From Nine US Internet Companies in Broad Secret Program'. *The Washington Post*, June 7, 2013.

Greenwald, Glenn, and Ewan MacAskill. 'NSA PRISM Program Taps into User Data of Apple, Google, and Others'. *The Guardian*, June 7, 2013.

Gross, Oren. 'Chaos and Rules: Should Responses to Violent Crises Always Be Constitutional?'. *The Yale Law Journal* 112, no. 5 (2003): 1011–1134.

Gross, Raphael. *Carl Schmitt und die Juden: Eine deutsche Rechtslehre*. Frankfurt am Main: Suhrkamp, 2005.

Kennedy, Ellen. *Constitutional Failure: Carl Schmitt in Weimar*. Durham: Duke University Press, 2004.

Kosseleck, Reinhard. *Futures Past: On the Semantics of Historical Time*. Translated by Keith Tribe. New York: Columbia University Press, 2004.

Mehring, Reinhard. *Carl Schmitt: Aufstieg und Fall: Eine Biographie*. Munich: Beck, 2009.

Poetzsch-Heffter, Fritz. 'Vom Staatsleben unter der Weimarer Verfassung: Erster Bericht, vom 1. Januar 1920 bis zum 31. Dezember 1924'. *Jahrbuch des öffentlichen Rechts* 13 (1925).

Posner, Eric, and Adrian Vermeule. *The Executive Unbound: After the Madisonian Republic.* Oxford: Oxford University Press, 2010.

Scheuermann, William E. 'Emergency Powers and the Rule of Law after 9/11', *The Journal of Political Philosophy* 14, no. 1 (2006): 61–84.

Schmitt, Carl. *Politische Theologie: Vier Kapitel zur Lehre von der Souveränität.* Berlin: Duncker und Humblot, 1996 (1922). Translated as: Carl Schmitt, *Political Theology: Four Chapters on the Concept of Sovereignty.* Translation by Georg Schwab. Chicago: Chicago University Press, 2005.

Schmitt, Carl. 'Die Diktatur des Reichspräsidenten nach Artikel 48 der Weimarer Verfassung'. In Carl Schmitt, *Die Diktatur.* Berlin: Duncker und Humblot, 1994 (1921/1924), 209–257.

Schmitt, Carl. *Verfassungslehre.* Berlin: Duncker und Humblot, 1993 (1928). Translated as: Carl Schmitt, *Constitutional Theory.* Translated by Jeffrey Seitzer, foreword by Ellen Kennedy. Durham: Duke University Press, 2008.

Schmitt, Carl. *Der Hüter der Verfassung.* Berlin: Duncker und Humblot, 1969 (1931).

Schmitt, Carl. *Der Begriff des Politischen: Text von 1932 mit einem Vorwort und drei Corollarien.* Berlin: Duncker und Humblot, 2002 (1932). Translated as: Carl Schmitt, *The Concept of the Political.* Translated by George Schwab. Chicago: Chicago University Press, 2007.

Schmitt, Carl. *Legalität und Legitimität.* Berlin: Duncker und Humblot, 2005 (1932).

Schmitt, Carl. 'Der Missbrauch der Legalität'. In *Tägliche Rundschau,* July 19, 1932.

Schmitt, Carl. 'Die Verfassungsmässigkeit der Bestellung eines Reichskommissars für das Land Preussen'. *Deutsche Juristen-Zeitung* 37, no. 15 (1932): 953–958.

Schmitt, Carl. 'Der Führer schützt das Recht', *Deutsche Juristen-Zeitung* 39, no. 15 (1934): 945–950.

Sontheimer, Kurt. *Antidemokratisches Denken in der Weimarer Republik.* Munich: Deutscher Taschenbuch Verlag, 1994.

Tushnet, Mark. 'Controlling Executive Power in the War on Terrorism'. *Harvard Law Review*118, no. 8 (2005): 2673–2682.

Tushnet, Mark. 'Emergencies and the Idea of Constitutionalism'. In *The Constitution in Wartime: Beyond Alarmism and Complacency,* edited by Mark Tushnet, 39–54. Durham: Duke University Press, 2005.

Weitz, Eric D. *Weimar Germany: Promises and Tragedy.* Princeton: Princeton University Press, 2007.

Wilde, Marc de. 'The State of Emergency in the Weimar Republic: Legal Disputes over Article 48 of the Weimar Constitution'. *The Legal History Review* 78 (2010): 135–158.

Wilde, Marc de. 'Just Trust Us: A Short History of Emergency Powers and Constitutional Change'. *Comparative Legal History* 3, no. 1 (2015): 110–130.

Winkler, Heinrich August. *Weimar, 1918–1933: Die Geschichte der ersten deutschen Demokratie.* Munich: C.H. Beck, 1993.

Chapter 7

Constitutional preambles and the uncertain future

Nomi Claire Lazar

Constitutions impose elements of certainty on an uncertain political future. They aim to constrain and coordinate political action, increasing predictability, diminishing conflict, and enabling strategic behaviour.[1] Like law generally, modern *written* constitutions turn toward control of the future and constitute a break from the past. By means of their written-ness they suggest a decisive stabilization of future political activity. This contrasts with the backward-forward nature of a premodern Roman or British style constitution, where the past is always substantially present and the future understood to evolve. Resting on the solid word, the written constitution implies that uncertainty can be controlled within expected forms of continuity, established at a specific moment in time.

Where written constitutions do draw on the time before promulgation, the place of that time is in a preamble. Most constitutions have one, and many bubble over with talk of the past. But, I shall argue, even these historical accounts aim at future control. For, the promulgation of a constitution is also an event with political consequences and one purpose of preambles is to legitimize this event. Preambles speak to an audience whose approbation is useful to the success of the constitution at a specific moment in political time. A preamble can frame a constitution as a temporal hinge to lurch a state forward in a desired direction. While historical preambles settle the past in a form supportive of future aims, they do this by invoking conceptions of the flow of time that give shape to an expected future. It is partly by means of that temporal shape that preambles create future expectations that mitigate subjective experiences of uncertainty, and, hence, help to construct legitimacy. In other words, the constructed shape of things past strongly implies the shape of things to come: the temporal schema tells us what to expect.

From this perspective, constitutions, and modern written constitutions in particular, are forward looking. But, as I shall argue, the forms of uncertainty written constitutions aim to control may be misidentified, raising spectres for constitutional politics. Substantial scholarly attention has been focused, of late, on states of emergency which seem to confront the written constitution with the ultimate

1 Sanford Levinson, 'Do Constitutions Have A Point? Reflections on "Parchment Barriers" and Preambles', *Social Philosophy and Policy* 28 (2011): 150–178.

uncertainty, even as the Schmittian figure of the sovereign is intended to dispel it. As Marc de Wilde argues in Chapter 6, constitutions may well be able to face this challenge better than Schmitt and his followers assume. But other challenges remain. Schmitt had focused on sovereign power to suspend the constitution, and there may be no such power in a polyarchy. But as a people, their values, goals and constituent membership inevitably shift over time, polyarchical political engagement changes the lived meaning of constitutional provisions, making their future application hard to predict. At the same time, informal contestations over power in constitutionally delineated offices generates a shifting array of constitutional conventions, which supplement or even supervene written provisions. Nonetheless, written constitutions ultimately lack the flexibility of their unwritten forebears, and may face a challenge to their longevity as well. The average lifespan of a constitution is only 17 years. Hence, a written constitution aims to control the future by cementing the barriers and conduits of power, the state symbols, rights and duties which together purport to give the state its character. But as 'the people' and their self-conception, and polyarchical articulations changes, so too, whether formally or conventionally, the constitution does too.

In what follows, I begin with an analysis of the future orientation of constitutions. I argue that only in the presence of continuity can constitutions manage future uncertainty. That is, not only must the constitution be expected to last, but we must have a reasonable expectation that the institutions it describes will continue to function in the manner foreseen. That in turn would necessitate continuity of political climate and of human political behaviour, expectations which – in the former case at least – may be unwarranted.

In the second part I argue that continuity is characteristic of pre-modern constitutions which rely more explicitly on the development and revision of unwritten conventions. That continuity is bi-directional, drawing substantively on past events when looking to the future. By contrast, modern, written constitutions, still aiming for future continuity, purport, at the moment of their proclamation, to establish a radical rupture with past political time. This is not to say that the past is erased. Rather, in a precedent governed constitution, the historical *content* of a past event is what matters, while in a written constitution – normally in a preamble – it is the constructed *shape* of past events which exerts control over the uncertain future. By picking out a series of past events in a preamble, the framers of a constitution create a shape, an arc through time, situating the event of the constitution in that arc. That arc, I will argue, constructed around the event of the constitution, may serve as a rhetorical frame, a conception of the flow of time which implies what the constitution – as a political event – means, implying too the shape of the future it purports to enable. The constitution is thus cast as a pivot which points the direction forward, and this, too, is a means of attempting to control uncertainty. I illustrate this technique of temporal-rhetorical framing using examples from the Hungarian and Chinese constitutions. In their historical and comparative situation, those preambles show with especial clarity how the constructed shape of a past, not just its content, can be deployed in written constitutions in a bid to control an uncertain future. Finally, in the third part, I draw attention to how flawed our expectations of continuity may be, despite the claims of preambles. Constitutions and the rhetoric which frames them may present the illusion of control, but the future holds its secrets.

Constitutions and the uncertain future

What is a constitution for? Eskridge identifies three core understandings of a constitution's purpose in the history of political thought. The Aristotelian approach takes the constitution (unwritten) as the soul of the state, expressing 'the identity and aspirations of the polity'.[2] It dictates what kind of place the state aims to be, what it values, what principles are fundamental. We see this explicitly in the Indian constitution, for example, in the 1973 case *Kesavanada Bharati v. State of Kerala*,[3] where the Indian Supreme Court held that the basic structure of the constitution (and hence, one might argue, of the political society that shapes and is shaped by the constitution) was described in the preamble and not subject to amendment. It is equally apparent in some citizens' devotion to the *idea* of their constitution, even when they are unfamiliar with its contents. The second historical approach is Lockean. Here, the fundamental purpose of the constitution is to delineate the rights in the social contract, and make these enforceable through judicial review.[4] And finally, the Benthamite approach, primarily forward looking, understands the constitution as a tool enabling future benefits for the polity with lower costs.

While Eskridge notes the oppositional political positions these divergent constitutional understandings support,[5] they nonetheless share a core and fundamental feature: whatever else a constitution might do, it manages forms of uncertainty. From an Aristotelian perspective, the constitution establishes what kind of place the state is, what will be tolerated and what anticipated going forward. Fundamental principles help clarify where we are, and help us anticipate where we will be. This gives the spiritual boundaries of the state a principled orientation that points the way forward. From the Lockean perspective, mutual rights guarantees provide a secure framework for individual planning. And along the utilitarian line, constitutions attend both to the necessity of establishing regular, predictable political behaviour and to the importance of flexibility for furthering the public good.

Lockean and Benthamite perspectives underline that, when constitutions set out the rules of the political game, each player has a credible commitment from others, and a mutual understanding of the scope of formal power, its distribution and its

2 William Eskridge, 'The California Proposition 8 Case: What is a Constitution For', *California Law Review* 98 (2010): 1248.
3 *Kesavanada Bharati v. State of Kerala* (1973) 4 S.C.C. 225.
4 Eskridge, 'What is a Constitution For', 1248.
5 Eskridge, 'What is a Constitution For', 1235.

limits. This establishes forms of certainty necessary to future planning. Normally, constitutions also indicate conditions under which those limits and power distributions can be altered to face altered circumstances. Rights come with enumerated limitations. Powers come with conditions of expansion or contraction.[6] Understood from any of these perspectives, constitutions, both modern and pre-modern, written and unwritten, have always been a form of law the purpose of which is to manage an otherwise uncertain future, laying down hedges, as Hobbes called laws,[7] to guide action and make some elements of future action more predictable. All forms of law guide behaviour, aiming to establish some measure of control going forward.

But to serve this purpose a constitution must be expected to last. With frequent constitutional change, the future horizon is limited. And even while the constitution does last, political agents must plan for a future beyond its reach. This then creates future uncertainty which is, at each moment, already operative. Hence, a constitution that would control an uncertain future must be built with longevity in mind, precluding the need for, or even the ease of, frequent change. But this would necessitate two assumptions, two forms of *certainty*, which serve as pillars for *limiting uncertainty*. First, if constitutions enable and constrain the actions of office holders and office seekers through barriers, conduits and incentive structures, we must assume that anticipated types of political behaviour (human political nature) will remain unchanged through time. Humans must be assumed, over the long term, to be motivated by similar aims (for instance, tribalism, seeking power, honour and money) and to behave in an expected range of ways. Anticipation of these motivations guides the design of institutions shaping that behaviour. Second, that the same constitutional rules should govern for decades or more requires we assume core aspects of a constitution's political climate will be stable too, because informal mechanisms of power necessarily interact with formal power and its formal constraint. By political climate I mean the sum of core public values, unwritten political conventions, and socio-political and economic conditions. Political climate aids political actors in determining the outer boundaries of acceptable or expected political behaviour.

These two assumptions – continuity of political climate and continuity of human political behaviour – allow for control of future events within the context

6 This is true even of the UN rights documents, and is evident in most constitutions where emergency provisions sometimes have their own section or else follow the 'rights' catalogue.

7 Thomas Hobbes, 'Of Crime, Excuse, and Extenuations', *Leviathan* (Oxford: Oxford University Press, 1909). 'For the use of laws (which are but rules authorized) is not to bind the people from all voluntary actions, but to direct and keep them in such a motion as not to hurt themselves by their own impetuous desires, rashness, or indiscretion; as hedges are set, not to stop travellers, but to keep them in the way.' It is noteworthy that many pre-modern theorists of law, such as St. Thomas Aquinas also hold forward-looking perspectives on the purpose of (human) law. Aquinas sees law as a means of training-for-virtue (*Summa Theologica* Q 95.1).

of current forms of certainty. One way to understand this is to think of the kinds of uncertainty anticipated by a modern written constitution in terms of expected types and uncertain tokens. We expect *types* of political behaviour (e.g., power-seeking) and the constitution aims to constrain *token* actions of these kinds. We expect *types* of external challenge to occur in the life-course of a state too – e.g., wars, natural disasters, popular unrest, and disease outbreaks, and other forms of emergency. We expect the type, but any specific token is unusual or irregular in its pattern of occurrence. Constitutions deal with uncertain event tokens like these through flexibility mechanisms that may alter power distributions or limits. For example, limitations on habeas corpus when, 'in Cases of Rebellion or Invasion the public Safety may require it', are allowed under Article 1, Section 9 of the US Constitution, and most contemporary written constitutions contain emergency provisions, or authorizations to create them by law.

All constitutions aim to control future uncertainties, but modern written constitutions do this differently in part because of their different relationship to the past. In pre-modern or unwritten constitutions, precedent constitutes an omnipresent past. A substantive history of past events and decisions is constantly present in the form of precedent and convention. That is, the material events and decisions of the past manifest in the present and into the future. Unwritten or pre-modern constitutions weave the past and present together in a way that renders the future always explicitly dependent on the past. Unwritten constitutions provide both a means of slowing the rate of overall change and of catching up with elements of marginal change more rapidly. On the one hand, we know that whatever will be allowed going forward will be shaped by what has come before, and this gives us a hedge, if not a wall. On the other hand, because unwritten constitutions can choose to draw on an array of precedents and principles, they can be flexible enough to accommodate shifts in circumstance without returning to a founding exercise.

By contrast, a written constitution, in the moment of its promulgation, technically erases past precedent and convention, creating a point of rupture. It symbolically, and to a great extent actually, negates the legal past, by annulling the prior constitution, the government and 'peoplehood' it represents and constructs. In the beginning is the word, and the new words are a new beginning.

Yet, whatever is built in the place of an old constitution, aspects of the pre-existing culture, a vastly overlapping iteration of people and territory, political traditions and elements of collective memory will all carry on. We see empirical evidence of this path-dependency where the same or very similar constitutions are actualized in vastly different ways.[8] New constitutions always make use of existing materials, just as new structures in the Ancient and Medieval Worlds were often constructed of stone harvested from ruins nearby.

8 Robert Putnam, *Making Democracy Work: Civic Traditions in Modern Italy* (Princeton: Princeton University Press, 1994).

Ironically, the unstructured presence where there is a new written constitution, in contrast with the substantive structure of past precedent in unwritten constitutions, opens up a rhetorical opportunity. With the substance of previous constitutional events muted, but still resonant, a skilled drafter has her choice of a spread of events and symbols. She may pick out any events to form a sequence of her choice, such that they form a temporal arc framing the event of the new constitution. If the constitution is a pivot point, a purported break in the continuity of the political state, then what that pivot means, what direction it turns a state toward can be constructed by means of situating events in a sequence surrounding the new constitution.

That is, because written constitutions create a rupture in political time, they orient a *constructive* relation to the past. By this I mean that political actors can construct or impose the trajectory from the past, through the rupture point of the constitution's promulgation, and onward, imposing (the perception of) a future direction. The past is constructed here not by means of substantive events in causal relationship, but rather by invoking a conception of the flow of time, anchored in the event of the constitution's promulgation, the rupture between past and future. Written constitutions often specify this rupture explicitly, through distinctively performative phrases: 'Now', or 'hereby' or 'We declare'. As I want now to argue, the rhetorical framing of that rupture point contributes to the control of the future by means of constructing the past.

Time talk in constitutional preambles

By and large, constitutions aim to mitigate uncertainty about the future, both with respect to everyday political action and with respect to external or internal shocks. Written constitutions do so in part by anticipating that future types of events and actions will be like those we see in the present. In an unwritten constitution, the shape of time which structures our perception of the flow of events is left fluid, weaving its way through time as if of its own accord, with the anticipation that change to come will have elements of both continuity and difference. But written constitutions purport to create a break in temporal continuity. Whatever has come before is now useful only insofar as it can be constructed to point the direction forward and written constitutions, unlike other forms of law,[9] have little to say about the past.

9 However, a recent trend in Canadian legislation has been to use law to make statements about the past or express a collective reaction to a past event. For example, a variety of Acts over the last 20–30 years have served to acknowledge events or experiences of groups of Canadians, while another class of laws reacted to specific crimes. (See Kent Roach, 'The Uses and Audiences of Preambles in Legislation', *McGill Law Journal* 47 (2001): 129.) These laws may be understood more as means of confronting the past, a form of national psychotherapy and reconciliation, with little real impact on the future. This is particularly so where criminal laws which respond to a specific crime make dubious claims to a capacity to prevent similar crimes, i.e., through the imposition of harsh penalties. Because lawmakers know such claims are untenable, these laws are, in reality, *backward* looking and symbolic.

Now, it may seem to tell against this claim that constitutional *preambles* are so often full of time talk. I want to illustrate how such temporal rhetoric may be understood as the construction of this pivot, a technique for orientation and for legitimation. About 80 per cent of historical constitutions have a preamble.[10] Most contain reference to the historic moment, the event, of the constitution's promulgation. When preambles turn toward the past, this is, I will argue, only apparently backward looking. Hence, the pervasiveness of history-talk in these preambles poses a challenge and an opportunity for understanding shifting notions of future orientation in the law.

Situating the state in time

Most constitutions have a preamble, and many contain reference to a country's history. Because preambles are, for the most part, non-justiciable,[11] recent scholarship has argued that the importance of preambles is primarily political.[12] Orgad argues that the

> ...preamble's purpose is not only – perhaps not mainly – to guarantee rights or provide legal arguments but to set down the basic structure of the society and its constitutional faith ... They reflect and affect social and political norms. They encourage cohesion or exacerbate divisions, express the constitutional identity, and are called upon to serve as a device of national consolidation or to reconcile past wrongs.[13]

Similarly, in her advice to the Government of Fiji, the eminent comparative constitutionalist Cheryl Saunders pointed out that '[l]egal operation or effect is not ... the only yardstick by which to measure the significance of a constitutional preamble. Even a preamble which has no legal effect at all, because of the generality of its wording or the approach which the courts have taken towards its interpretation, may be highly symbolic and thus have a real influence on national life.'[14] And constitutional scholars Zhang and Yanhuang have argued, in a Platonic vein, that the right preamble for China '... would give the people a solemn and serious

10 Tom Ginsburg et al., '"We the Peoples": The Global Origins of Constitutional Preambles', *George Washington International Law Review* 46 (2014): 109.
11 Levinson, 'Do Constitutions Have A Point?', 166. For use of preambles in legal arguments in the US context, see Brian Leiter et al., 'A Reconsideration of the Relevance and Materiality of the Preamble in Constitutional Interpretation', *Cardozo Law Review* 12 (1990–1991): 117, 120–121 n. 14. See also Liav Orgad, 'The Preamble in Constitutional Interpretation',*International Journal of Constitutional Law* 8 (2010).
12 Levinson, 'Do Constitutions Have A Point?', 166; Roach, 'The Uses and Audiences of Preambles in Legislation', 149.
13 Orgad, 'The Preamble in Constitutional Interpretation', 738.
14 Cheryl Saunders, 'The Constitutional Preamble', *Fiji Constitution Review Commission Research Papers* 2 (1997), 260–268. See also Levinson, 'Do Constitutions Have a Point', 166.

impression, and let the people believe that the [constitution which follows] is a legal duty that the country will earnestly implement.'[15]

Preambles are thus, as Kent Roach has noted, a useful locus for observing the non-legal purposes of law generally.[16] Law may be symbolic, expressive, conciliatory or belligerent and constitutions evoke all these functions. We know that preambles in particular, can play communicative roles, because we have the records of constitutional conventions in which their political and symbolic importance is consistently discussed.[17] Recent scholars have noted their aspirational or inspirational elements, but these functions do not exhaust the roles of preambles in symbolic politics.[18] In addition preambles can sometimes function like road signs that indicate a one-way street. By necessitating a direction in which a state must go, preambles attempt to exert some control over the flow of political events. Because this direction is new or decisively re-established, the event of a constitution's promulgation may be understood as a turning point and through this lens, history talk in constitutional preambles can be understood as a means through which political actors can construct the event of the constitution as that turning point, a point of rupture. This point, properly framed, indicates the new direction

15 Qianfan Zhang and Chunqiu Yanhuang, 'The Controversy on the Preamble to the Constitution and Its Effects', *Blogpost* (2013). https://chinacopyrightandmedia.wordpress.com/2013/06/10/the-controversy-on-the-preamble-to-the-constitution-and-its-effects/ Accessed December 6, 2014. Plato argued for a very similar purpose for constitutional preambles. In Book 4 of *The Laws* he advocates the judicious use of preambles in order to put denizens 'in a more cooperative frame of mind' and hence to increase their 'readiness to learn'. Plato, *The Laws*, trans. Trevor Saunders (New York: Penguin Books, 1970), 723a.

16 Roach, 'The Uses and Audiences of Preambles in Legislation', 132.

17 See, for example, the *Proceedings of the Australian Constitutional Convention*, see especially the debates of Feb. 9 1997 around 468ff (Canberra, Old Constitution House). The debate over the proposed preamble to the European Union constitution was also explicitly political, particularly with reference to the issue of the inclusion of reference to the Church. Srdjan Civijic and Lorenzo Zucca, 'Does the European Constitution need Christian Values', *Oxford Journal of Legal Studies* 24 (2004): 739–748. The Venice Commission also asserted in its decision on the Hungarian constitution that 'The Commission recalls that preambles have above all a political purpose and represent political declarations meant to stress the importance of the fundamental law, its principles, values and guarantees, for the state concerned and its population.' *Opinion on the New Constitution of Hungary*, CDL-AD (2011) 016, 8. Memorably, *The Economist* criticized European pretensions in regard to the proposed preamble to the EU constitution thus: 'Mr Giscard d'Estaing has suggested hopefully that future generations of European schoolchildren might learn the preamble by heart. But this would seem to be in contradiction of Article II-4 of the constitution's Charter of Fundamental Rights, which states clearly that 'no one shall be subjected to torture or to inhuman or degrading treatment or punishment'. Charlemagne, 'God Meets the Lawyers', *The Economist*, December 4, 2003.

18 Orgad, 'The Preamble in Constitutional Interpretation', 738. Levinson argues that sometimes such a move may have the opposite effect. Levinson, 'Do Constitutions Have A Point?', 178.

forward, it underlines and attempts to legitimate a state's new direction, cementing – or at least attempting to cement – control of an otherwise uncertain future.

In historically oriented preambles, the means of constructing this pivot is what we might call a temporal-rhetorical frame. In situating the event of the constitution's promulgation in a temporal arc, historical preambles join past event series to a projected future, changing expectations of a state's trajectory. Together, these temporal arcs create the pivot point, the identification of which serves to help legitimate the constitution by declaring the meaning of the event of the constitution's promulgation. That is to say, the meaning of an event is always partly given by its place in a temporal arc, a conception of the flow of time which suggests not just how the event is related to other events, as, for example, a simple history would, but how those events *must* be related and understood by virtue of time's shape.

What do I mean by time's shape or a conception of the flow of time? This is a narrative tool for organizing events in sequence. While we normally think of the marking and measuring of time as the work of clocks and calendars, people use several means of organizing experience sequentially, relative to the task. Artificial 12- or 24-hour clocks in digital and mechanical-cyclical manifestations help us coordinate our whereabouts, among other tasks. And the rough measure of the earth's passage around the sun, along with artificial months and numbered days provide a means for planning and for plotting events against each other in chronology across countries and cultures. But in addition to such mechanical techniques, we also make sense of events-in-sequence with reference to heuristic structures of the flow of time. These schemata for understanding the sequential relationship of events to one another take a number of forms and grow clearer by example. Progress, which scholars sometimes mistakenly assume is the dominant conception in modernity, portrays events in a linear fashion as forward-moving, whether endlessly or toward some final fruition. We use a progressive conception of the flow of time when, for instance, we assume that living conditions for each generation will be better than those of the previous generation, or when scholars interpret changes in Chinese politics as steps toward democratic reform. Grand historical cycles inform our understanding of events with respect to, for instance, the rise and fall of great powers, or the rise and fall of politicians, or even the course of human lives in the family context. Eschatology invokes a future moment of rupture, after which everything will be different and the world inverted. And primitivism is a conception of the flow of time that interprets events in terms of inevitable decay from some past golden age. Each of these conceptions provides a schemata within which a specific event can be framed, and hence given meaning. If we change the conception of the flow of time within which the event is cast, we can change the perceived meaning of that event. Hence, conceptions of the flow of time are a means of rhetorical framing.

Conceptions of the flow of time can be deployed to lend substantive meaning to specific events within a sequence, dictating what narrative structures are possible in what contexts. How we conceptualize the *shape* of time acts as a semiotic frame, impacting our received understanding of the significance of specific political events or innovations.[19] That is, where an action or event is cast in a sequence, the shape of that sequence is key to understanding what the event means. By recasting a temporal frame, we can recast the meaning of events also. Time-framing thus provides a tool for turning an occurrence into an event, a pivot that jolts the state onto the path of a desired future. Just as the institutions delineated by the constitution provide a means of attempting to control an uncertain future by channelling types of political behaviour, the time-talk in a constitutional preamble speaks not to the past but *uses* the past as a tool to control the future. It uses the past to establish traditional authority, as a means of Weberian legitimation. But it uses the past in another sense too: to point the state in a desired direction.

Below, the preambles to the Hungarian and Chinese constitutions illustrate this technique. It is not my claim that these cases constitute evidence establishing a general rule. That is, I do not mean to suggest that these examples show what time-talk in preambles is *always* about. Rather, they are, precisely, illustrations, showing the possibilities inherent in this technique of asserting rhetorical control over an uncertain future. I choose these illustrations in particular both because they show the cross-cultural elements of this technique and because they show with particular clarity the role of a constructed arc of events, even beyond the substance of those events. Reconstructing the narrative of the past, as individuals may do with respect to their own lives, this rhetoric constructs the meaning of the present moment also.

Hungary's preamble

The rhetoric in the preamble to the Hungarian constitution places the event of the new Basic Law in a millennial cycle of greatness, of steady rise and rapid decline. The work of Hungary's populist Fidesz party, and particularly of its leader, Viktor Orbán, the Basic Law came into force on January 1, 2012.[20] The preamble describes the institution of the Basic Law in terms of Kairos, the moment that must be seized. Hungary has sunk into moral decay and national confusion, after a

19 In this light, it may be tempting to conflate a conception of the flow of time with a theory of history, but this would be mistaken. To say that ideas about the shape of time, and not just history, are important in politics is to underline the fact that it is not just the character of the events themselves and their causal relationship, but the perceived shape of event-series that alters our perception of their significance. The shape of time is perceived by means of events and highly suggestive of their future shape. History, by contrast, is the *content* of these events and their substantive or causal relations to each other, beyond sequence. History, then, could be understood as the animation of time: time concepts could be understood as two dimensional, while history unfolds in three.

20 See for example ''Destroying Democracy': Hungarians Protest Controversial New Constitution', *Spiegel Online*, January 3, 2012; Charles Gati, 'Hungary's Backward Slide', *New York Times*, December 12, 2011.

decline in the 20th century.[21] It can save itself and set out again on another cycle of greatness, and the mechanism of engineering this pivot upward is precisely the event of the constitution's promulgation. The Hungarian preamble looks explicitly and extensively to the past for orientation, but that orientation is aimed at controlling the future. The preamble reads in part:

- 'We are proud that our king Saint Stephen built the Hungarian State on solid ground and made our country a part of Christian Europe one thousand years ago.
- 'We honour the achievements of our historical constitution and we honour the Holy Crown, which embodies the constitutional continuity of Hungary's statehood and the unity of the nation.
- 'We do not recognize the communist constitution of 1949, since it was the basis for tyrannical rule; therefore we proclaim it to be invalid.
- 'We date the restoration of our country's self-determination, lost on the nineteenth day of March 1944, from the second day of May 1990, when the first freely elected body of popular representation was formed. We shall consider this date to be the beginning of our country's new democracy and constitutional order.
- 'We hold that after the decades of the twentieth century which led to a state of moral decay, we have an abiding need for spiritual and intellectual renewal.

As the preamble continues, talk of the past clearly orients Hungary toward the 'right kind' of future. The preamble further reads:

- 'We trust in a jointly-shaped future and the commitment of younger generations. We believe that our children and grandchildren will make Hungary great again with their talent, persistence and moral strength.
- Our Fundamental Law shall be the basis of our legal order: it shall be a covenant among Hungarians past, present and future; a living framework which expresses the nation's will and the form in which we want to live.

21 Preamble, Hungarian Basic Law 2012. One can already see Orbán's specifically rhetorical interest in the narrative of decline and the need for reinvigoration in his first term as President, when he says: 'After the Second World War, slowly we became grey. One country among Eastern Europe's unfortunate, occupied, socialist states. The best proof of how grey we became comes if we quickly look around, then we will see roughly where we managed to sink into the greyness, what kind of buildings, what kind of material culture, and generally what kind of things we were capable of creating in the past period … I think, before accession to the European Union, it would be good to formulate a picture of Hungary in which there is life, in which that life pulsates, which has colors and a particular flavor, before we get stuck with the image of a diligent, hard-working but not especially exciting, small Central European people.' Quoted in Brigid Fowler, 'Nation, State and Europe in Hungarian Politics: the case of the millennial commemorations', *Europe-Asia Studies* 56 (2004): 57–83.

- We, the citizens of Hungary, are ready to found the order of our country upon the common endeavours of the nation.'[22]

The preamble situates the event of the constitution's proclamation not just in a causal chain of events, what has come before as context for the constitution's promulgation, but as a temporal hinge. It casts the event of the constitution's proclamation as the turning point in a pattern of cyclical rise and fall: St. Stephen founds the nation a millennium ago, it rises to greatness. But eventually, forces of corruption and tyranny spark a precipitous decline. The nation is renewed and reborn through the intervention of the constitution's authors, who implicitly cast themselves as alone displaying the courage to save their nation from inevitable demise. The Hungarian nation is able to set off on a new cycle of greatness, through the restoration of core principles and values. This is accomplished through the agency of the constitution drafters who punctuate the cycle and alter the state's course. Thus, the constitution is cast not just as the declaration of a set of institutional rules, principles, values and rights, not just as law, but as a *mechanism of renewal*, the mark that Hungary is, as at the dawn of the previous millennium, on the rise.[23]

We abstract the shape of time from the sequencing of events, and this abstracted shape in turn directs our interpretation of events' substantive meaning. The preamble, by situating the event of the constitution in an expected flow, casts that event as a pivot point, turning the Hungarian state in a new direction. The placement of the event in sequential relationship *after* moral decline and *in temporal parallel* with the start of a previous cycle of founding (that of St. Stephen) focuses the attention of Hungarians in a specific direction, illustrating and ideally determining what is intended to come next.[24]

22 Hungarian Basic Law (2012) Preamble.

23 Orbán's interest in drawing on millennial connections as a source of legitimacy dates back to his first term in office. During that term, at precisely the Hungarian millennium, he pursued numerous fractious policies intended to invoke that temporal coincidence. In particular, Orbán spent substantial political capital to bring the Holy Crown from the National Museum to the parliament. The Crown, which in name and legend, if not in fact, is associated with St. Stephen, Hungary's millennial founder, not only invokes the original source of legitimate power but is sometimes said to be itself an embodiment of the Hungarian nation in whose *name* (in the Crown's name, not the peoples') Hungarian leaders, royal and otherwise rule. Its move to Parliament was a substantial rhetorical move, with overtones of irredentism and Christian nationalism. For Orbán, the millennium, bound to St. Stephen and the Crown, is a key figure in Hungary's identity and its legitimate rule. See Fowler, 'Nation, State, Europe', 57–83.

24 Undoubtedly, some history-talk in constitutional preambles aims at achieving what Pocock has called a 'strategy of return.' John G. A. Pocock, 'Time, Institutions, and Action', *Politics, Language, and Time* (University of Chicago Press, 1989), 252. Such a strategy aims to legitimate radical innovation by recasting it as a restoration of the original. But, the historical material in constitutional preambles is normally constructed to underline the event of the constitution as a pivot toward a future, a future which the

China's preambles

In illustrating temporal framing as a technique for trumpeting control of an uncertain future, it is instructive to compare China's current (1982) constitution, which came into effect under the reformer Deng Xiaoping, with the 1978 version attributable to Mao's successor, Hua Guofeng. This comparison constitutes our second illustrative case.

The preamble to China's 1978 constitution followed a classic Soviet model, ripe with the rhetoric of rupture. The ongoing struggle and the millennial era of socialism take centre stage, framed by a strikingly attenuated national history. China, in its relevant form, only begins with the struggle to throw off feudalism. Then with Mao's victory in 1949, '[t]he founding of the People's Republic of China marked the beginning of the historical period of socialism in our country.'[25] And while they have 'won great victories' and while the 'dictatorship of the proletariat in [China] has been consolidated and strengthened', China must still 'struggle in unity and carry the proletarian revolution through to the end'.[26] The cultural revolution marked a shift to a new era but China must 'persevere in continuing the revolution' and 'persevere in the struggle of the proletariat against the bourgeoisie and in the struggle for the socialist road against the capitalist road.'[27] The struggle against the peoples' enemies is ongoing, though China aims to be 'a great and powerful socialist country with modern agriculture, industry, national defence and science and technology by the end of the century.'[28] The Cultural Revolution is praised, Mao held up as God-like, and the dominant tone is one of continuing struggle, ongoing rupture, showing strong vestiges of Mao's militant leftism.

This is not simply history, a recounting of a causal succession of events leading to the constitution. Rather it situates those events and the constitution in eschatological time. An eschatological conception of the flow of time charts a course from a continuum through a radical and normally violent break that leads to a defined (often millennial) period of sustained justice and peace. To the extent that time is equated with decay, this violent rupture leads to a time-outside-of-time a new era that will be qualitatively, temporally different. It is toward this goal that the 1978 constitution points. And this eschatological framing is explicit here. Within this frame, where China 'is' in the temporal scheme of things is marked explicitly: in the thick of that rupture, in the midst of struggle, with the previous temporal era decisively at an end and, *after* the break which the struggle represents, a new permanent era of communist life to follow *later*. By virtue of the expectations this eschatological flow of time creates, the temporal frame indicates what people can expect next, it tells them where they are and in what direction China is moving.

constitution claims to make more certain. While the two legitimating strategies are not mutually exclusive, they are also importantly distinct.

25 Preamble, Constitution of China (1978).

26 Preamble, Constitution of China (1978).

27 Preamble, Constitution of China (1978).

28 Preamble, Constitution of China (1978).

The framing of the past points the direction toward the future. The conception of the flow of time thus functions as a sort of map, and it is through this map (which conception) and where (when) the preamble places the event of the constitution's promulgation on it that people are led to understand what the constitution means and what the future is promised to hold.

If we turn to Deng, the reformer's, 1982 preamble, we see radical differences, centring not just on substance, but on temporal form. The new preamble situates the event of the constitution in progressive, rather than eschatological time. To frame this decisive shift, the preamble now extends China's history back millennia. It begins: 'China is one of the countries with the longest histories in the world. The people of all nationalities in China have jointly created a splendid culture …'[29] This has several effects, particularly in the wake of the Cultural Revolution which attempted to extinguish that culture. First, it shifts focus from the regime, from the PRC, to China as an entity that exists beyond its current political manifestation. This is a technique similar to the one Augustus Caesar invoked when he shifted the Roman method of event dating from the consular year, characteristic of Rome as a *republic* to the date *ad urbe condita* – from the city's founding.[30] By drawing attention back to a political body which pre-existed the current regime, he constructed a sense of continuity for an underlying political entity from the past, through the present, to the future: in the Roman case, through the new Imperial regime, and in the Chinese case, a still-socialist, but post-radical-revolutionary age. At the same time, a political actor can place herself in a legitimate line and establish her own authority. This is a further form of instrumentalization of the constructed past, framing not only the event of the constitution, but the constitution of the people itself, and therefore the constitution's authority. That is, whether one stands in a legitimate line depends on the point from which the line is drawn. This is temporal-rhetorical construction. This mode of temporal framing situates China's cultural revolution, and indeed the radical policies of the fifteen years prior, as an historical blip, a marginal deviation from what is otherwise a progressive path. 'The Chinese people waged wave upon wave of heroic struggles for national independence and liberation and for democracy and freedom,' and ultimately achieved victory in the formation of the PRC. But progress moves on: following China's achievement, 'effected step by step,' China will now continue to 'follow the socialist road, steadily improve socialist institutions, develop socialist democracy, improve the socialist legal system and work hard and self-reliantly to modernize industry, agriculture, national defence and science and technology *step by step* to turn China into a socialist country with a high level of culture and democracy.'[31] This is no longer a rhetoric of eschatology, with the event of the constitution marking a continuing period of tribulation and upheaval leading to a decisive and final break. Rather, the constitution here is cast as marking a moment

29 Preamble, Constitution of China (1978).
30 Denis Feeney, *Caesar's Calendar* (Berkeley: University of California Press, 2007), 138.
31 Preamble, Constitution of China (1982).

in the gradual progress of China toward a state in which Chinese people may live in a state able to support their fundamental well-being.

The 1982 constitution, as framed in this scheme, is an event that sets China back on the progressive path it has, give or take a Cultural Revolution, purportedly continued for millennia. This creates expectations for what comes next that, in turn, strongly imply the meaning of the constitution as political event. Thus, the preamble to the Chinese constitution, whatever else it might accomplish, is rhetoric which aims to legitimate and to persuade the Chinese people that their future is not uncertain, but steady and secure.

Zhang Youyu, a constitutional scholar who was assistant-secretary of the constitutional drafting committee for the 1982 document is quite explicit about this. As he explained, '[t]he reason why we must have a preamble is because we are in a transitional period, some things that should be provided in the Constitution cannot be written into its text. The basic task of the country during the transitional period and the conditions for implementing the Constitution ... can all not be written into articles, and if they were written into articles, they could not be written as clearly and incisively as if they would have been put into the preamble.'[32] And he later notes the preamble's role in signalling the constitution's 'progressive orientation, principles and policies, etc.'[33] The preamble, by placing the event of the constitution in a new temporal frame, aims to help legitimize the event of its promulgation, it orients citizens in political time, which political agents pre-construct to serve their rhetorical and political aims.

These examples show that, how a political agent relates events in sequence can frame those events in a way that impacts the interpretation of their significance. This is not just the use of history because it is not just the series of events and their causal interconnections that is at issue. Rather, it is the fitting of these events into a shaped sequence, a conception of the flow of time, that attempts to force an interpretation of past events and expectation of future events. Its extension into the future is at least as important with respect to its substantive meaning.

Preambles and the uncertain future: political climate

Written constitutions, including their preambles, are forward looking and aim to delineate expectations for an uncertain future. Unbound by, though often parasitic upon, past law, past precedent and past events, they permit a radical break from the immediate past and open the way to a new future. But, I want now to suggest, despite the rhetoric in preambles, that written constitutions are particularly weak in this regard. For, the freedom of the founding moment, that very freedom which

32 Youya Zhang, *An Essay Collection on Constitutional Governance*, (Beijing: Beijing Mass Publishing House, 1986), 27–28.

33 Youya Zhang, 'Jinyubu yanjiu xin xianfa, shishi xin jianfa [Further Researching and Implementing the New Constitution]', *Zhongguo faxue [China Law Studies]* 1 (1984). Cited in translation in Zhang and Yanhuang, *Controversy* at note 14.

presents the rhetorical opportunity to construct the event of the constitution, ends in the concrete determination of a written constitution's provisions. Written constitutions, while they are always also governed by convention,[34] do not have the flexibility of their pre-modern counterparts, and this may contribute to the fact that constitutions are, on average, short-lived.[35] Preambles in particular illustrate an object lesson with respect to the predictability of political climate.

Earlier, I noted that one of the pillars of certainty, necessary to support a constitution that effectively controls uncertainty, is constancy of political climate. Because the capacity of a constitution to effectively control an uncertain future is dependent on the continuity of this political climate, this is no small matter. Recent constitutional developments show the extent to which this ought not to be taken for granted, and here I refer to the debate over amendments to the Australian Constitutional Preamble, particularly in the context of the 1998 Constitutional Convention.

At that convention, the core issue under consideration was whether Australia ought to become a republic, and under what institutions. Delegates felt that the Crown-suffused preamble ought to be revisited too. Many Australians, inspired by the example of then-recent constitutions, felt that an opportunity was open to make aspirational statements about the character of their country. The debate was contentious, particularly with respect to the inclusion of what were referred to as 'value words,' such as 'democracy', 'the rule of law' and 'equality'. Two prominent constitutional scholars, Greg Craven and George Winterton argued strongly that this would leave Australia open to unintended legislation-by-judicial-interpretation. Craven argued that Australian '... courts traditionally have been fairly narrow in relation to preambles and generally have not been prone to extrapolate vast and vague doctrines out of constitutions in Australia .... [but] courts have so begun to do, with the result that the insertion of vague terms like "equality", "democracy" and "freedom" in a preamble would almost certainly encourage the courts to take those values throughout the Constitution as if they were substantive and controlling values.'[36] Craven went on that while we may like such values, placing them in a preamble would mean that 'they can sit ticking like time bombs until eventually they explode.'[37] Ultimately, it would move responsibility for a range of issues from a democratically elected parliament to the High Court. Craven warned his compatriots: 'You should have absolutely no illusions that even a harmless term like "equality" could effect substantive, varied and unlooked-for changes in a Constitution and have effects on electoral laws, legislation dealing with courts, with

34 See, for instance Joseph Jaconelli, 'The Nature of Constitutional Convention', *Legal Studies* 24 (1999): 24–46; James G. Wilson, 'American Constitutional Conventions', *Buffalo Law Review* 40 (1992), 645–738.

35 Zachary Elkins et al., *The Endurance of National Constitutions* (Cambridge: Cambridge University Press, 2009).

36 Speech of Greg Craven, *Australian Constitutional Convention Proceedings* (Old Constitution House, 1998), 472.

37 Craven, *Australian Constitutional Convention*, 472.

legal aid, local government laws and laws dealing with resource allocation.'[38] Others voiced similar concerns 'we cannot blindly say that yes, the High Court will … never look at the preamble and say that it just means what it says there on the paper, because that is clearly not the case in terms of High Court amendments and interpretation of the Constitution. *We cannot predict what the High Court will do in 50, 60 or 100 years time.*'[39]

Contention over the preamble was, functionally, contention over how certain one could be that the political climate would remain stable through time. Craven and Winterton thought, on the basis of a respectable trend of evidence,[40] that this could not be expected and that unwritten constitutional elements could potentially respond more flexibly to an uncertain political future, by maintaining parliament's democratic power to decide what the constitution meant. With that battle lost, Winterton argued for a provision that would direct the court not to enforce elements in the preamble, echoing provisions in the Irish constitution.[41] In the constitutional referendum which followed in 1999, both the preamble and the republic were soundly defeated.[42] But the preamble has continued to be a subject of lively debate with strong advocates pushing for reconsideration up to the present day.[43]

Winterton's and Craven's concerns were not without foundation. As Orgad has recently argued, the use of preambles in constitutional interpretation has substantially increased in those jurisdictions which had a tradition along these lines, and has spread to jurisdictions with no such tradition.[44] The changing political climate in which constitutional preambles function underlines one way in which the project of using written constitutions to control an uncertain future is

38 Craven, *Australian Constitutional Convention*, 472.

39 Speech of Julian Leeser, *Australian Constitutional Convention Proceedings*, 496–497. My italics.

40 See in particular Orgad, 'The Preamble in Constitutional Interpretation'.

41 George Winterton, 'The 1998 Convention: A Reprise of 1898?', *University of New South Wales Law Review* 21 (1998), 862.

42 In Australia, a constitutional amendment requires popular majorities of both the electorate and of a majority of states, and Australians have traditionally been conservative with their constitution, rejecting all but eight of the forty-four amendments that have been put to a vote in the last 108 years. No state offered a majority in support of either measure, despite strong polling numbers for a republican form of government. This may have been due to dissention among republicans with respect to the form of institutions proposed (a bi-partisan President, for instance). See Scott Bennett, 'Politics of Constitutional Amendment', *Parliamentary Research Paper*, (2002–3). http://www.aph.gov.au/About_Parliament/Parliamentary_Departments/Parliamentary_Library/pubs/rp/rp0203/03rp11

43 See for instance Anne Twomey, 'Constitutional Recognition of Indigenous Australians in a Preamble', *Sydney Law School Report* (2011); Greg Sheridan, 'Constitutional change will divide not unite the nation', *The Australian*, September 20, 2014.

44 Orgad, 'The Preamble in Constitutional Interpretation'. In the Canadian context, see also Peter Oliver, 'A Constitution Similar in Principle to that of the United Kingdom', Research Paper for Department of Justice Canada, (2006). On file with the author.

precarious. But this challenge is just the beginning. Written constitutions are not as stable or reliable as a simplistic view of, for instance, the American model might suggest. While formal amendment normally requires supermajorities and other high hurdles, a working constitution is subject to constitutional conventions that act as powerful pseudo-legal rules, which, nonetheless, change over time. These conventions are widely recognized with respect to unwritten constitutions such as that of the United Kingdom, but legal scholars have recently shown their power as companions of written constitutions too, even in the United States.[45] So, on the one hand there is bottom up, public engagement with the law which aims to change the operation of the constitution through judicial interpretation. On the other, political contestation over informal power around political offices may create unwritten conventions whose character is hard to predict in advance. Politics and law interact to create and subvert these conventions. So above, and from below, the cut and thrust of politics works to reinterpret the meaning of any written constitution, even as the constitution structures those politics too. In light of these shifting influences and the increasingly rapid pace of social and political change in polyarchies, and in light of this constant enterprise of interpretation and reinterpretation, it is perhaps not surprising, and certainly noteworthy that the average lifespan of a written constitution is a mere 17 years.[46] Hence, the solidity and certainty implied by a constitution's 'written-ness' is something of an illusion. Undoubtedly, the stability of a state impacts the stability of its constitution to begin with. But the relationship between constitutional and political stability at least reminds us that a constitution, as a piece of law, is not of itself sufficient to impose certainty on an uncertain future.

Conclusion

The written-ness of a constitution purports to sweep away the legal detritus of the prior era. But any new constitution necessarily builds with the discarded blocks of the past, strategically chosen not necessarily for their substantive content, but for the rhetorical frames they enable. Among the techniques deployed in the service of legitimizing new written constitutions is the temporal-arc technique I have described and illustrated here. By picking out a sequence of events to form this arc, drafters are able to imply the meaning of the constitution as event, and hence

45 William Eskridge Jr, *A Republic of Statutes* (New Haven: Yale University Press, 2010); Jack Balkin and Sanford Levinson, 'The Processes of Constitutional Change', *Fordham Law Review* 75 (2006): 489–533; Stephen M. Griffin, 'Constitutional Change in the United States', Tulane Public Law Research Paper No. 11-03; Cass Sunstein, *A Constitution of Many Minds* (Princeton: Princeton University Press, 2011); Bruce Ackerman, *We the People: Transformations* (Cambridge, MA: Harvard University Press, 2000); David A. Strauss, 'The Irrelevance of Constitutional Amendments', *Harvard Law Review* 114 (2001): 1457–1505; and Wilson, 'American Constitutional Conventions'.

46 Ginzburg, '"We the Peoples": The Global Origins of Constitutional Preambles', 16.

to insinuate control over the uncertain future. What comes next will be those events which follow naturally in the implied sequence, whether progressive, grand cyclic, or eschatological.

Yet, the Australian debate illustrates the extent to which some pillars of certainty supporting constitutional stability may in fact be uncertain, despite the claims of preambles, and the reassuring solidity of a written constitutional document. It may be reasonable to rely on the constancy of human political nature – honour seeking, alliance forming, domination resisting – but not so political climate. The changing behaviour of High Courts is a case in point, showing how similar constitutional provisions and similar human political behaviour are not jointly sufficient to ensure the predictability of constitutional functionality. Must we then dispense with the idea that constitutions are effective tools for managing an uncertain future? The argument here seems to serve as an object lesson in the impossibility of doing so. Yet, this is not an all or nothing affair. As Sanford Levinson has cautioned, the 'narrative of change' though important to a proper understanding of constitutions, should not obfuscate the extent to which hard-wired institutional structures maintain an element of stability.[47] Some aspects of constitutions 'genuinely settle certain important issues' such as procedures for handing over power.[48] For Levinson, this partly explains the triumph of modern written constitutions: they do a better job, he claims, of establishing certainty. But is this necessarily so? After all, power transitions in the United Kingdom are similarly predictable, governed by deeply entrenched conventions.[49] And when political climate changes, it may be easier for constitutional conventions to shift to meet those challenges than for a process of constitutional amendment to be convened and successfully concluded. This is worth investigating empirically. A constitution acknowledged to be somewhat fluid may open up the possibility that, even if the future is always necessarily uncertain, we can feel confident in the capacity of constitutions not to conquer but rather to keep up with this certainty of political change. Rapid change calls into question the stability of both written and unwritten constitutions, particularly if they aim to settle, rather than frame, political contention. In such a world, it is worth actively considering the benefits of a norm of continuity within flexibility, of

47 Levinson, 'Do Constitutions Have a Point', 154.

48 Levinson, 'Do Constitutions Have a Point', 155.

49 With respect to transitions, we can see constitutional conventions adapting to changes in political climate in the United Kingdom's Cabinet Manual. Stuart Wilkes-Heeg explained that transition rules in the Manual were motivated by the following concerns: 'It strikes me that a key driver was this sense of deep concern that if we ended up with a hung Parliament, if it was not clear what would happen next, that there would be a media feeding frenzy, there would be panic, the financial markets would panic and so on. So, the desire was to have a set of procedures in place that would deal with a situation of absolute confusion.' The motivations described here are clearly informed by contemporary political climate, and particularly by considerations of contemporary *speed. Political and Constitutional Reform Committee – Sixth Report*, March 22, 2011, At paragraph 65. http://www.publications.parliament.uk/pa/cm201011/cmselect/cmpolcon/734/73407.htm Accessed December 6, 2014.

constitutional growth and development, whether through an un- or less-written constitution, acknowledging and actively welcoming the substantial role for conventions in those already written. Whether we go so far as to claim, with Madison, that constitutions are, in effect, parchment barriers,[50] or to assert, with Machiavelli, the primacy of informal over formal power,[51] it is certainly true that the ebb and flow of informal power is at least as important as 'indelible ink' in controlling the uncertain future.

Bibliography

Ackerman, Bruce. *We the People: Transformations.* Cambridge, MA: Harvard University Press, 2000.

Anon. God Meets the Lawyers'. *The Economist,* December 4, 2003.

Aquinas, Thomas. *Summa Theologica.* Aquinas Institute, 2012.

Balkin, Jack and Sanford Levinson. 'The Processes of Constitutional Change'. *Fordham Law Review* 75 (2006): 489–533.

Bennett, Scott. 'Politics of Constitutional Amendment'. *Parliamentary Research Paper* (2002–2003).

Civijic, Srdjan and Lorenzo Zucca. 'Does the European Constitution Need Christian Values'. *Oxford Journal of Legal Studies* 24 (2004): 739–748.

Elkins, Zachary et al. *The Endurance of National Constitutions.* Cambridge: Cambridge University Press, 2009.

Eskridge, William. 'The California Proposition 8 Case: What is a Constitution For'. *California Law Review* 98 (2010): 1235–1252.

EskridgeJr, William. *A Republic of Statutes* (New Haven: Yale University Press, 2010).

Feeney, Denis. *Caesar's Calendar.* Berkeley: University of California Press, 2007.

Fowler, Brigid. 'Nation State and Europe in Hungarian Politics' *Europe-Asia Studies* 56 (2004): 57–83.

Gati, Charles. 'Hungary's Backward Slide'. *New York Times,* December 12, 2011.

Ginsburg, Tom, et al. '"We the Peoples": Global Origins of Constitutional Preambles'. *George Washington International Law Review* 46 (2014): 305–340.

Griffin, Stephen M. *Constitutional Change in the United States.* Tulane Public Law Research Paper No. 11–03.

Hobbes, Thomas. *Leviathan.* Oxford: Oxford University Press, 1909.

Jaconelli, Joseph. 'The Nature of Constitutional Convention'. *Legal Studies* 24 (1999): 24–46.

Lazar, Nomi Claire. 'Making Emergencies Safe for Democracy'. *Constellations* 13 (2006): 506–521.

Leiter, Brian, et al., A Reconsideration of the Relevance and Materiality of the Preamble in Constitutional Interpretation'. *Cardozo Law Review* 12 (1990): 117–163.

Levinson, Sanford. 'Do Constitutions Have a Point? Reflections on "Parchment Barriers" and Preambles'. *Philosophy and Policy* 28 (2011): 150–178.

50 James Madison, *The Federalist Papers* 48 (Signet, 2003), 305.

51 Niccoló Machiavelli, 'Discorsi', *Il Principe e altre opere politiche* (Garzanti, 1974): I.34. See also Nomi Claire Lazar 'Making Emergencies Safe for Democracy', *Constellations* 13 (2006): 506–521.

Machiavelli, Niccoló. *Il Principe e altre opere politiche*. Milan: Garzanti, 1974.
Oliver, Peter. *A Constitution Similar in Principle to that of the United Kingdom*. Ottawa: Department of Justice, Canada, 2006.
Orgad, Liav. 'The Preamble in Constitutional Interpretation'. *International Journal of Constitutional Law* 8 (2010): 714–738.
Plato. *The Laws*. New York: Penguin, 1970.
Pocock, John G. A. *Politics, Language, and Time*. Chicago: University of Chicago Press, 1989.
Proceedings of the Australian Constitutional Convention. Canberra: Old Constitution House, 1997.
Publius. *The Federalist Papers*. New York: Signet, 2003.
Putnam, Robert. *Making Democracy Work: Civic Traditions in Modern Italy*. Princeton: Princeton University Press, 1994.
Roach, Kent. 'The Uses and Audiences of Preambles in Legislation'. *McGill Law Journal* 47 (2001): 129–159.
Saunders, Cheryl. 'The Constitutional Preamble'. *Fiji Consittution Review Commission Research Papers* 2 (1997): 260–268.
Sheridan, Greg. 'Consitutional change will not divide the nation'. *The Australian*, September 20, 2014.
Strauss, David A. 'The Irrelevance of Constitutional Amendments'. *Harvard Law Review* 114 (2001): 1457–1505.
Sunstein, Cass. *A Constitution of Many Minds*. Princeton: Princeton University Press, 2011.
Twomey, Anne. 'Constitutional Recognition of Indigenous Australians in a Preamble'. *Sydney Law School Report*, 2011.
Wilson, James G. 'American Constitutional Conventions'. *Buffalo Law Review* 40 (1992): 645–738.
Winterton, George. 'The 1998 Convention: A Reprise of 1898?'. *University of New South Wales Law Review* 21 (1998): 856–867.
Zanh, Qianfan and Chunqiu Yanhuang. *The Controversy on the Preamble to the Constitution and its Effects*. 2013. https://chinacopyrightandmedia.wordpress.com/2013/06/10/the-controversy-on-the-preamble-to-the-constitution-and-its-effects/ (accessed December 6, 2014).
Zhang, Youya. *An Essay Collection on Constitutional Governance*. Beijing: Beijing Mass Publishing House, 1986.

Part 3

Expediency

Chapter 8

Collective memory, constitutional polity and differentiation of modern society

Jiří Přibáň

Life can only be understood backwards; but it must be lived forwards.
(Kierkegaard, Journals IV A 164 (1843)

Introduction

Societies construct their shared symbolic universe and, according to Norbert Elias, constructed social symbols represent 'a fifth dimension' of human existence. These symbols have expressive power of representing modern functionally differentiated society as a morally and culturally integrated unity.

Political and legal theoretical works on this expressive power of government and constitutions, such as Arnold's *The Symbols of Government*[1] and Smend's *Verfassung und Verfassungsrecht*[2] historically appear at the same time like the most important legal theoretical and methodological debates between Kelsen, Schmitt, Heller and others in the first half of the 20th century.[3] This coincidence shows that methodological issues of legal and political theory and their conceptualizations and fictions, such as the basic norm, are closely related to the problem of symbolic communication in the otherwise functionally differentiated systems of modern positive law and politics.

In this chapter, I therefore argue that the production of social symbols is internally processed by functionally differentiated social systems, such as law and politics, and culture does not ultimately integrate modern society into a unity of foundational values and moral principles. The concept of culture refers to the temporal dimension of individual systems and can be functionally and sectorally differentiated into legal cultures, political cultures, economic cultures, scientific cultures etc. Regarding the legal and political systems and their historical

1 Thurman Arnold, *The Symbols of Government* (New Haven,: Yale University Press, 1935)
2 Rudolf Smend, *Verfassung und Verfassungsrecht* (Leipzig: Duncker & Humblot, 1928)
3 For the German legal theoretical and political context, see especially Arthur J. Jacobson and Bernard Schlink (eds), *Weimar: A Jurisprudence of Crisis* (Berkeley CA: University of California Press, 2000).

constitutionalization, the concept of culture, therefore, does not predetermine the existence of constitutional polities and cannot guarantee their normative integration.

I open my argument by a brief introductory section documenting how memories can be constructed, reconstructed and shared as a common culture in modern society and then, in the next section, move on to discuss Halbwachs's classic concept of collective memory as a social construct unlimited by past traditions and shaped by the present society and its normative expectations, beliefs, interests and concerns. Collective memories are constituted by present societal expectations and selective operations of different systems, such as the systems of positive law and politics. Questioning the integrative capacity of shared collective memories in particular and culture in general, I subsequently argue that, unlike traditional societies, modern society does not have its *functionaries* who would keep it integrated as guardians and enforcers of cultural values and moral norms. Despite this sociological truth, modern secular societies evolving into national polities look for their functionaries and guarantee the symbolically sacred status to their political leaders and national heroes. In the next two sections, I therefore analyse this paradox of the sacred nature of modern cultural nationalism and its various attempts at reconciling the sacred ideal of human unity and the profane fact of societal differences. Instead of simply being used as the symbol of unity, culture needs to be reformulated as a specific and differentiated part of modern social communication constituted by parallel processes of remembering and forgetting present in all social systems. The concept of polity subsequently needs to be formulated as the politically and culturally differentiated self-description of society which depends on specific comparisons of historical and territorial differences. The symbolic imagination of nations as 'truly existing', yet ideal polities brought to their modern life from 'historical sleep' needs to be confronted by the sociological fact that any constitutional polity is the internal concept constructed by coupling between the systems of politics and law. The polity's identity as imagined unity does not lead to the ultimate cultural and societal inclusion and integration. In fact, the social systems of positive law and politics constitute the societal symbolic universe by internalizing the temporality of constitutional polity as its collective memory, identity and selfhood of constituent power. I critically conclude that the semantics of historical self-reflection of constitutional polity as the 'real' polity representing the whole society is part of the specific cultural function of memory operating within the systems of law and politics. All references to historical and normative 'foundations' and 'constitutive' moments of such polity use memory as operation selecting between remembrance and forgetting which actually supports and enhances general operations of the systems of positive law and politics. While this specific selection does not make culture an autopoietic system of modern society, it further supplements the internal communication of the systems of positive law and politics and thus makes it possible to speak, for instance, of legal and/or political culture as collective memory.

Politics of shared memories

When the British Prime Minister Neville Chamberlain made the remark about 'a quarrel in a far-away country between people of whom we know nothing' after signing the Munich Agreement in September 1938,[4] he wanted to justify his apparently sensible and pragmatic response to the international crisis not directly affecting the United Kingdom at the time. However, this sentence quickly achieved the symbolic status and continues to be used by British, Czech and other European historians and politicians as an example of extremely poor political judgment and an appeasement nightmare of international politics.

Furthermore, before Christmas 1938, other Britons, knew of people living in Czechoslovakia enough to organize special trains taking Czech children of Jewish origin to the relative safety of the British Isles. The Englishman Nicholas Winton organized a very special mission which rescued nearly 700 children in the 'Czech Kindertransport', many of whom spent the wartime in a Czechoslovak refugee boarding school in South Wales.[5]

Another example of Britons who knew of people living in Czechoslovakia was a film director Humphrey Jennings who used a script written by a Czech poet and novelist Viktor Fischl and reconstructed a tragedy of Lidice in the village of Cwmgiedd in South Wales in 1942. The whole Welsh mining village participated in a film project to commemorate deaths and suffering of their Czech fellow coalminers from a village in Central Bohemia which was destroyed in June 1942 on Hitler's order in reprisal for the assassination of Reinhard Heydrich by a British-trained group of Czech and Slovak soldiers.[6]

In short, political hopelessness of the British ruling elite during the Munich agreement certainly can be contrasted with Winston Churchill's leadership but even more so with solidarity, determination and sheer humanity of ordinary Britons, Czechs, Slovaks and all others standing on the side of freedom and fighting against the Nazi regime. These specific historical events continue to be extremely important and significant for present politics, identity and expressive symbolism beyond both countries. The 'appeasement politics' has become part of normative political jargon while Nicholas Winton was nominated for the Nobel Prize and his statues installed in both the Czech Republic and the United Kingdom after this extraordinary personal history, kept private for many decades by Winton, became known to the public in the 2000s.

Furthermore, these shared memories reveal the general importance of time for every culture and politics and their values, principles and practices. They show that collective memory-building is not limited to the national cultures and political or

4 David Faber, *Munich: The 1938 Appeasement Crisis* (New York: Simon & Schuster, 2008), 375–376.

5 Muriel Emanuel and Vera Gissing, *Nicholas Winton and the Rescued Generation: Save One Life, Save the World* (Elstree: Vallentine Mitchell & Co., 2001).

6 For more details about the film *The Silent Village*, see Ian Aitken (ed), *Encyclopedia of the Documentary Film*. 3-volume set (Oxon: Routledge, 2006), 683.

constitutional systems. National memories easily migrate from one nation to another and shape the value and normative context of international and supranational communities and organizations, such as the United Nations and the European Union.

Collective memories can be constructed, reconstructed and shared as a common culture because of language and social communication. Like peoples, social institutions, ideas, art and technology, concepts and words thus have specific history. They emerge, dominate, change and disappear leaving various traces in historical knowledge and intellectual traditions. Old concepts acquire new meaning or get replaced by new ones. They are used in new contexts and for different social purposes.

In contemporary globalized society with its digital technologies and the mass media, collective memories and their manifold conceptualizations are shared, transformed, fragmented and forwarded at high speed. The binding force of cultural values and principles conceptualized and incorporated in collectively shared memories and their impact on the systems of positive law and politics, therefore, needs to be carefully scrutinized and analysed against the background of some classic concepts of sociological, legal and political theories and philosophies in the following sections of this chapter.

On collective memory in law and politics

Almost a century ago, the French sociologist Maurice Halbwachs analysed collective memories and summarized their constitution of the relationship between the past and present in the following words:

> ... in reality the past does not recur as such ...the past is not preserved but is reconstructed on the basis of the present. ... Collective frameworks are ... the instruments used by the collective memory to reconstruct an image of the past which is in accord, in each epoch, with the predominant thoughts of the society.[7]

Halbwachs's sociological theory of collective memory can be described as a theory of the past stored and interpreted by social institutions. According to this view, the past is a social construct shaped by the present and its normative expectations, beliefs, interests and concerns.[8] As such, collective memory always involves both persistence and change, continuity and novelty, remembering and forgetting.[9]

7 Maurice Halbwachs, *On Collective Memory* (Chicago, IL: The University of Chicago Press, 1992), 39–40.

8 For the international law and politics context, see Keith M. Wilson (ed), *Forging the Collective Memory: Government and International Historians Through Two World Wars* (Oxford, Berghahn Books, 1996).

9 Michael Bernard-Donals, *Forgetful Memory: Representation and Remembrance in the Wake of the Holocaust* (Albany: SUNY Press, 2009).

Memory beats reality[10] and present expectations of historical justice open new possibilities of political and societal transitions. Collective memory is both setting up a framework of values, images and narratives outside the passage of time and inseparable from it.[11] It is captivated by the course of time while giving it general stability and timeless validity. Its societal function is in the present, yet consists in integrating the present and the past into one permanent and meaningful condition of social life.[12] Dealing with the past and collective memory can involve partisan moralism and abuses by self-interested agents and ideologues described as 'activists of memory'.[13]

Like any other social system, law contributes to the codification of collective memories by both supporting and changing its existing images, narratives and values. Legislation and landmark judgments shape self-perception and identity of different polities.[14] Constitution-making usually plays a transitional role by legislating for political changes and normatively consolidating societal evolution.[15]

Apart from legal justice and instruments promoting societal change and evolution while dealing with historical injustices and political failures, specific measures of transitional justice drawing on political compromise and non-legal measures and often giving up on some principles of the rule of law, such as non-retrospectivity of laws, are employed to facilitate political and legal changes.[16] For instance, post-apartheid South Africa set up the Truth and Reconciliation Commission to deal with the past political crimes, injustices and discrimination by their evidencing, collecting, publishing and archiving. Limited access to legal remedies, especially criminal justice measures blocked by the politics of amnesty, was to be compensated by the promise of constituting a new public discourse which would put the past crimes on public trial without potentially disruptive effects of retribution and thus contribute to the post-apartheid politics of democratic inclusion.[17]

Quasi-judicial and administrative truth and reconciliation commissions dealing with the past political crimes and injustices became a typical hallmark of transitional justice in many countries around the world. They were to facilitate political transitions from the authoritarian past to the democratic future and drew on

10 Halbwachs, *On Collective Memory*, 51.
11 Gerd Sebald and Jatin Wagle (eds), *Theorizing Social Memories: Concepts and Contexts* (Oxon: Routledge, 2016).
12 Aleida Assman and Laure Shortt (eds), *Memory and Political Change* (Houndmills, Basingstoke: Palgrave Macmillan, 2012).
13 Tzvetan Todorov, 'Abuses of Memory', *Common Knowledge* 1 (1996) 22.
14 Mark Osiel, *Mass Atrocity, Collective Memory and the Law* (New Brunswick, NJ: Transaction Publishers, 1997).
15 Laurel E. Miller and Louis Aucoin (eds), *Framing the State in Times of Transition: Case Studies in Constitution Making* (Washington DC: United States Institute of Peace Press, 2010).
16 Ruti G. Teitel, *Transitional Justice* (Oxford: Oxford University Press, 2000), 230.
17 Richard Wilson, *The Politics of Truth and Reconciliation in South Africa: Legitimizing the Post-Apartheid State* (Cambridge: Cambridge University Press, 2001).

principles of the public discourse and collective memory archiving and bearing witness to the unjust past.

Another institutional form of dealing with the past political crimes and injustices have been institutes of national memory or remembrance and state-sponsored institutes of the authoritarian and totalitarian past studies spreading in post-communist countries, such as Poland, Slovakia, the Czech Republic and Ukraine.[18] While often profoundly different in their structure and function, these institutes, like truth and reconciliation commissions, typically respond to the past injustices by legal, semi-legal and non-legal means and their purpose is to contribute to the constitution of new collective memory and public discourse. Again, they are not impartial bodies researching and archiving the past but publicly funded institutions with a clear political agenda of making normative distinctions between the past and present. They, therefore, commonly contribute to the conflicts between political parties and present ideological divisions.

Truth commissions and institutes of national remembrance had one important function during political and societal transitions, namely the constitution of collective memory. The history of these commissions and institutes thus illustrates a profound truth about every dealing with the past and its legal as well as non-legal forms. Regarding the legal context of collective memory, the first important statement about law, justice and their temporality is that any legal and political dealing with the past is not driven by some archetypical notion of justice and universal legal principles of polity damaged in the past and revisited by present agents to be repaired and restored. It, rather, is reality of the present which pushes legality and political power to shake up and reconstitute the society's collective memory.

Collective memory constituted by laws, courts and special public bodies, such as truth commissions and institutes of national remembrance, is an outcome of present politics, not past injustices. It is archival in its methodology, yet profoundly selective in its politics. Like the individual mind, society reconstructs, reconstitutes and transfigures its memory under the present political, moral and juridical pressure. Through law and politics, collective memory is not merely reproducing past events, but reshaping them by giving them a new voice and description.

The society's functionaries

Unlike in modern society, collective life goes on along slow habitual folkways in traditional societies. Collective memory as the present reconstitution of the society's past hardly exists because the past is experienced as present in those societies. Social hierarchy mirrors the ability of particular groups to represent the knowledge

18 Georges Mink, 'Institutions of National Memory in Post-Communist Europe: From Transitional Justice to Political Uses of Biographies (1989–2010)' in *History, Memory and Politics in Central and Eastern Europe: Memory Games,* ed. Georges Mink and Laure Neumayer, (Houndmills, Basingstoke: Palgrave Macmillan, 2013), 155–172.

and values prevailing and instituted in the relevant society. These groups enjoy honour and privileges and are elevated to the special status because of this representative function transcending temporal limitations and symbolically unifying the society in its totality beyond the past and present.

In *Divinity and Experience*, Godfrey Lienhardt famously analysed the Dinka people of the Southern Sudan, especially their myths and social structure established on the basis of access to the divine powers. For Lienhardt, divinity signifies the totality of experience of nature and society including the various divine Powers. In the Dinka's origin myth, Divinity and humans used to be a unity as were sky and earth, life and death, sky and earth or father and son. Because humans voluntarily split from this unity, the Dinka seek to draw these poles closer by different rituals and actively engaging with different clan-divinities pertaining to the experiences of agnation.

According to Lienhardt, one particular group of 'the spear-masters'[19] had a central place in the religious ceremonies of the whole community and effectively controlled experience of divine unity of the whole society through symbolic actions and rituals. They prepared the ritual sacrifices and guaranteed the cosmology of shared symbols and, because of this religious and political status, could be regarded as the *functionaries* of the whole society representing its collective bonds of the common origin and constituting its present symbolic totality.

In their myths, the clan of the spear-masters cooperated to defeat a divisive human Power of the oldest son blocking the way for other children by sacrificing an ox. Because of this skill and action, they received a mandate from the divine Power to officiate in overcoming death rituals. For Lienhardt, these cattle sacrifices are not meant to achieve specific practical ends. They, rather, are symbolic events dramatizing universal humans' aim to control their fate by countering divisions, disorder and death. Sacrifices are symbolic dramas bringing the opposite poles, such as father and son, to their unity thus securing perpetuation and continuity of the clan in particular and society in general.

The fact that the society, under the direction of these spear-masters, conducts specific rituals and each of its members focuses on individual tasks means that the religious ritual creates from the individual participants a single coherent body in which human fellowship itself becomes a sacred form. The community constitutes a divinity that cannot be approached individually, but only in the form of the collective ritual. Its spell only works as long as one remains a member of it, so to step outside it or in any way cast doubt on its social order means exposing oneself to mortal danger.

Imagined nations and their functionaries

In modernity, the slowness and temporal stability of traditional and segmented societies disappear and life becomes faster, mobile and a lot more innovative. The

19 Godfrey Lienhardt, *Divinity and Experience: The Religion of the Dinka* (Oxford: Clarendon Press, 1961), 171.

past becomes a matter of present performance[20] and all changes become temporal, yet with permanent effect.

The modern phenomena of faster time and change[21] profoundly affect collective memory. Pre-modern societies are integrated by specific privileged groups and their power to symbolically unify the chaotic reality at the level of the origin myths, such as the spear-masters clan of the Dinka people. Against this segmented differentiation and symbolic integration, modernity means both the loss of unity of collective memory and the ultimate authority of its symbolic representation in culture. Different families, religious groups and social classes constitute different collective memories. The ultimate unity of cosmology is replaced by cultural plurality. Nevertheless, the question of who is the society's functionary and what myths and symbolic 'spears' have to be mastered to perform this representative function persists as an important ideological question full of references to the national culture with its principles and ideals even when it is sociologically obvious that the concepts of culture and nation rely on the comparative methodology and relativistic perspective.

Despite this sociological truth, the modern concept of nation and nationalism continues to regard national solidarity as a sacred gift of historical sense and providence. Nations create their origin myths in their effort to be self-constituted as polities. Unlike pre-modern societies making no distinction between the past and present social experiences, nations, however, profoundly believe in historical time and evolution incorporating the ultimate destiny of collective life and idealized future. Their political and legal self-constitution, therefore, draws on the supremacy of future expectations over historical experiences.[22]

In modernity, belonging does not have to be shared physically, because it can be transmitted via media such as books, newspapers and images as well as in official legal documents like passports and health insurance cards. Nations thus create much more imaginary communities than that of the physically shared Dinka rituals and symbolic universe. The social matrix and cosmology of modern nations is much more complex and legal documents are part of it. Even so, the question still remains as to who in modern national polities wields the spear and is therefore their 'functionary'![23]

20 Karin Tilmans, Frank van Vree and Jay Winter (eds), *Performing the Past: Memory, History, and Identity in Modern Europe* (Amsterdam: Amsterdam University Press, 2010).

21 See, for instance, Hartmut Rosa's chapter in this volume and Hartmut Rosa and William E. Scheuerman (eds), *High-speed Society: Social Acceleration, Power, and Modernity* (University Park PA: University of Pennsylvania State University Press, 2009).

22 Reinhart Koselleck, *Futures Past: On the Semantics of Historical Time* (New York: Columbia University Press, 2004), 255.

23 For a critique of the functionary as a sociological and particularly political category, see, for instance, Helmut Schelsky, *Funktionäre – Gefährden sie das Gemeinwohl?* (Stuttgart: Seewald, 1982).

Looking for these functionaries in the modern era, the Panthéon in Paris, for instance, reveals the republican desire to elevate the most famous sons of the newborn nations to the symbolic heights where human thoughts and deeds meet divine providence. The French Revolution swept away the Church with its dignitaries and privileges, but eventually substituted religion with its own cults. Although Robespierre clamped down hard on the followers of the Cult of Reason, his radical politics of discontinuity introduced the new Cult of the Supreme Being, which had to be celebrated during the Jacobean terror.[24]

The revolutionary leaders were at one moment deified, but at the next vilified and their remains removed from the Panthéon to anonymous graves. Nevertheless, to this day evidence can be seen in the building of the attempts at carrying even such secular affairs as the Revolution, its people and their leaders and thinkers to the very threshold of divine immortality. Ancient myths about the foundation of cities and whole civilizations thus find their new forms in modern political romanticism. People gather around their political leaders and national heroes to show them gratitude and to place themselves at least for a while in the shadow of their splendour and prominence.

When the Scottish philosopher Thomas Carlyle commented that the history of the world is but the biography of great men,[25] it was those very deified heroes and movers of human destiny he had in mind. One of the fundamental paradoxes of modern secular society therefore lies in the fact that it keeps itself alive by establishing new pseudo-religious cults and creating apotheoses for individuals and nations in order to maintain a balance in civilization between the mundane and the sacred – a balance formulated by modern social theory, for instance, as the distinctions of unity and differences, integration and differentiation etc. The next section, therefore, analyses this paradox of societal unity constituted by differences in the context of modern cultural nationalism and its various attempts at reconciling the sacred ideal of human unity and the profane fact of societal differences.

The concept of culture and nation: from social integration to differentiation

The German philosopher Johann Gottfried von Herder introduced the holistic interpretation of national cultures in which values, beliefs, ideas and even sentiments are considered internal aspects of one culture as the centre of gravity of total social life. According to this view, understanding the nation's character requires embracing and identifying with the totality of its ethnic and historical existence.

24 Michael L. Kennedy, *The Jacobin Clubs in the French Revolution, 1793–1795* (Oxford: Berghahn Press, 2000), 161.

25 Thomas Carlyle, *The Works of Thomas Carlyle, Volume 5: On Heroes, Hero-Worship and the Heroic in History* (Cambridge: Cambridge University Press, 2010 digital version; originally published 1897).

Herder's philosophy of cultural nationalism assumes that the natural state of every nation is living according to its national character.[26] The state and its laws are expected to correspond to this 'character' mirrored in the nation's history and culture. Culture, therefore, determines the unique 'nature' of each nation and its contribution to the Romantic notion progress of reason and humanity.

The other side of this holistic interpretation of culture as the society's value and normative cage is Herder's belief in radical differences between national cultures, their infinite variety and plurality. This Romantic paradox of particular cultural nationalisms leading to the universal humanism based on the Enlightenment ideals of cosmopolitanism has important implications for sociological and anthropological methodology because it proves that all forms of social life can and should be analysed from the comparative perspective.[27] The paradox shows that the expressive symbolism of modern culture as the society's self-description through the unity of its values and normative principles still persists and constitutes part of the otherwise differentiated systems of positive law and politics. At the same time, it is only the comparative methodology of social sciences that can describe inter-systemic and intra-systemic legal and political communication including its symbolic cultural aspects.

The Romantic emphasis on cultural uniqueness and differences opens the possibility that various cultures can be contrasted to each other and people can learn from different beliefs, practices, habits, folkways and their comparisons. These comparisons and contrasts involve political power struggles and legal rules and principles and their effects on the modern concepts of nationhood, statehood and democracy. Cultural identity thus remains a common point of reference of political and legal communication while, at the same time, differentiated systems of law and politics constitute their internal semantics referring to either political, or legal culture as sets of practices and conventions specifically self-referring to the political and legal communication.

Because of cultural symbolism, it is possible to keep the image of society as unity which, however, consists of differentiated images of society communicated through different social systems, such as law and politics. Furthermore, cultural symbolism makes it possible to contrast and compare these images of specific communities as one unity to other culturally defined communities as specifically differentiated units evolving in modern society.[28] What can be contrasted and compared remains experienced as different in cultural practices and symbolized in critical self-reflections of different communities.[29]

26 Johann Gottfried von Herder, 'Letters Concerning the Progress of Humanity' in J. G. von Herder, *Philosophical Writings* (Cambridge: Cambridge University Press, 2002), 361.

27 Niklas Luhmann, *Theory of Society, Volume 2* (Stanford, CA: Stanford University Press, 2013), 225.

28 Geoffrey Cubitt (ed.), *Imagining Nations* (Manchester: Manchester University Press, 1998).

29 Klaus Eder, 'Symbolic Power and Cultural Differences: A Power Model of Political Solutions to Cultural Differences' in *Constituting Communities: Political Solutions to*

From this perspective, the concept of polity needs to be taken as the politically and culturally differentiated self-description of society which depends on specific comparisons of historically and territorial differences. Furthermore, focusing on the temporal differentiation of culture, it can be stated that every culture is constituted by parallel processes of *remembering* and *forgetting*. In this respect, Niklas Luhmann comes to the conclusion that 'culture is indeed nothing other than the memory of society, hence the filter of forgetting/remembering and the appropriation of the past to determine the variation framework of the future'.[30]

Constitutional polity as the internal concept constructed by coupling between the systems of politics and law and its identity as imagined unity draw on the general idea of collective existence brought to its modern life from 'historical sleep'. This national awakening and recollection of the glorious past are necessary for the symbolic image of a glorious historical march of the nation as polity towards its unique destiny. The future is certain and bright and nations just need to re-discover their true 'nature' and collective character by employing their collective memories.

Due to its permanent orientation on future expectations, collective memory, nevertheless, is at permanent risk of being lost in modern society. Nations, therefore, constitute their *historiographies* and project them into their political and legal institutions. More importantly, they also use both law and politics to write their *biographies* depicting them as persons with distinct identity.[31]

These historiographies and biographies are selective because their function is to codify collective memories of nations and any other polities. These memories are not primarily interested in the society's past but its *history* as a set of present stories about the past constantly selecting specific events and differentiating between the glorious and inglorious past.[32]

This relationship between historiographies and biographies is typical of constitutional documents and landmark legal cases as well as official textbooks of national histories or programmes and propagandas of different political parties and general ideologies. It remains to be said that this mutual influence of historiographies and biographies is not limited by the framework of national societies and easily stretch to supranational and international polities, such as the EU and the United Nations.

In the following sections, I, therefore, analyse how the sacred/profane distinction and societal paradoxes related to it affect the modern concept of values and their

Cultural Conflict, ed. Per Mouritsen and Knud Erik Jorgensen, (Houndmills, Basingstoke: Palgrave Macmillan, 2008), 31–52.

30 Niklas Luhmann, *Theory of Society, Volume 1* (Stanford, CA: Stanford University Press, 2012), 355.

31 Benedict Anderson, *Imagined Communities: Reflections on the Origin and Spread of Nationalism* (London: Verso, 1983), 204.

32 See, for instance, Patrick H. Hutton, *History as an Art of Memory* (Hannover NH: University Press of New England, 1993).

adoption by the system of positive law and democratic constitutionalism both within and beyond modern national statehood.

The holism of constitutional values and principles

Despite the ultimate humanism of Herder's philosophy reflected, for instance, in the belief that cultural unity achieved through statehood must eventually serve the universal desire for peace, the collective strife for cultural authenticity and perfection necessarily differs among individual nations. Herder's normative expectations that, like individuals, nations as social groups will embrace the same imperative of 'do unto others as you would have them do unto you', still contains the Enlightenment's optimism of the universal peace. Nevertheless, the logical consequence of Herder's cultural nationalism and holistic notion of culture is pluralism of cultural values and their spatial and temporal differentiation in modern society.

The holistic notion of culture as a closed and definite system of values and norms shared by a specific community in their totality is described by Seyla Benhabib as a 'poor man's sociology'.[33] Cultures cannot guarantee integration in modern society and therefore cannot be perceived as undifferentiated and fully integrated wholes. If culture is a system of shared meanings constituting collective identity through permanent references to the past and future, the Herderian Romantic concept of culture cannot survive the sociological findings of how the constitution of different cultures is internally invented and contested and externally open to other cultures due to the porous boundaries. Every culture, consequently, is socially constructed and never coherent in terms of internal values and normatively closed to the outside. It is permanently contested from both within and without.

Instead of the sociologically assumed integrative function, culture's function is that of differentiating and therefore necessarily conceiving of collective identity including collective memory as a system of hybrid and creative continuities and discontinuities. The notion of culture as the fully integrating, consensual and binding system of core societal values and moral norms hardly can explain contestations and clashes of value positions in modern liberal societies described by Max Weber and, after him, Isaiah Berlin and many other social and political theorists and philosophers.

The holistic notion of culture as a reservoir of generally binding values, integrative principles and shared norms still may persist in some theories of law and politics. The hope that liberal reasoning and conclusions eventually prevail over non-liberal and illiberal views as prejudices, such as formulated in Dworkin's legal

33 Seyla Benhabib, 'Cultural Complexity, Moral Interdependence and the Global Dialogical Community' in *Women, Culture and Development: A Study of Human Capabilities,* ed. Martha Nussbaum and Jonathan Glover, (Oxford: Clarendon Press, 1995), 241–244. For Benhabib's general view of culture and critique of cultural holism, see her *The Claims of Culture* (Princeton: Princeton University Press, 2002).

and political holistic philosophy,[34] is but the hope of a particular political culture promoting political and moral, if only 'overlapping' consensus. Rawls and Dworkin's philosophies of political and constitutional principles mainly reveal one sociological fact about all cultures, namely their promotion of particular beliefs to the status of general principles and the failure to live up to their internal ideals. In the case of politically liberal cultures, it especially is the belief that modern societies necessarily evolve towards higher rather than lower forms of collective life and the hope that illiberal ideas are best confronted by the open nature of liberalism.

Dworkin's Hercules probably was the last hero with the status of the Dinka spear-masters. His superior position of the society's functionary was even supported by the powerful and complex myth of 'the Law's Empire'.[35] Nevertheless, the theory of law's systemic integrity of principles and values is nothing but a view described by Dworkin himself as 'religion without God' which employs constitutional arguments as a special kind of the Dinka-like spears and shields connecting us with inevitability and divinity.

Polity of principles versus polity of practices

Legal and political philosophies of the society's basic structure and integrative principle, such as Dworkin's empire of law governed by Hercules the Judge[36] and Rawls's two principles of justice as fairness,[37] share the common belief in one correct answer to political problems and one correct method to deal with them. These philosophies, therefore are part of what the Polish philosopher Leszek Kolakowski called 'the epistemological utopia'.[38]

According to Kolakowski, this utopia is an intrinsic part of our culture searching for the ultimate transcendental grounds and improvement of our thinking and being. Nevertheless, this search is coeval with another important part of the same culture – the sceptical and/or empiricist renouncement of this possibility to reach ultimate truth and certainty regarding the grounds of our thinking and being.

Describing this intellectual dichotomy of modern culture, Kolakowski comments that 'diggers' in quest of our philosophical and social utopias are as important as sceptical 'healers' who keep us vigilant against prejudices of reason and all kinds of wishful thinking.[39] Because of this fragile cultural balance, our societies can survive the utopian dreams of everlasting fraternity and equality without any social and human differences. Modern culture needs a sceptic to point out that equality as ultimately shared identity of all people without differences is self-contradictory and

34 See, for instance, Ronald Dworkin, *Freedom's Law: The Moral Reading of the American Constitution* (Oxford: Oxford University Press, 1996), 80.

35 Ronald Dworkin, *Law's Empire* (Cambridge, Mass: The Belknap Press, 1986).

36 Dworkin, *Law's Empire*, 313ff.

37 John Rawls, *A Theory of Justice* (Cambridge, Mass: Harvard University Press, 1971), 4.

38 Leszek Kolakowski, *Modernity on Endless Trial* (Chicago: The University of Chicago Press, 1990), 133.

39 Kolakowski, *Modernity on Endless Trial*, 136.

only can fuel further and equally dangerous contradictions and revolutionary utopian paradoxes, especially the paradox of abolishing all political hierarchies and differences by a special class of rational/revolutionary elite.

From a very different sociological perspective, Talcott Parsons, critically addressing problems of economic and social crisis of the 1930s, came to address another cultural and intellectual dichotomy of modern society in his lecture *The Professions and Social Structure.*[40] Parsons analysed the role of expert knowledge possessed, nurtured and permanently improved by various professions, such as lawyers, economists and doctors. According to him, it is the high level of expertise, universal practice of their vocation, and primarily non-economic and non-profit orientation towards common values what entitles these professions as specific social groups to their job of facilitating both universalism and specification in social structure and organizations. Due to their specific knowledge, these groups are elevated to the status of a social elite delivering policies and benefit to different social realms by the specific quality of their knowledge.

Analysing this status of the modern society's functionaries and their 'epistemological utopia' myth of the correct method and knowledge of principles and values – the myth of the transcendental structure of society beyond time and space – requires analysing the status of these allegedly universal principles and values.

Ronald Dworkin famously considered legal *principles*' function as *holding* the political community together and representing its normative foundations while the function of legal *policies* consisted in *achieving* communal goals and goods. As Dworkin commented: 'If we care so little for principle that we dress policy in its colors when this suits our purpose, we cheapen principle and diminish its authority.'[41]

Dworkin's identification of principles with authority immediately raises the question of their social status and functionality. As Stanley Fish responds, authority, however, 'does not preside over the debate from a position outside it but is the prize for which the debaters vie.'[42] Constitutional principles, therefore, do not have a superior force of rational arguments. Instead, they are outcomes of competing vocabularies which prevailed in public and professional contestations.

Any rhetoric of principle subsequently should be considered a second-order generalization of general legal rules. It is part of the general political process of transforming the particular into the universal. According to this view, principles are not cognitively and culturally transcendental foundations of modern democratic polities. They operate as mere guidelines helping legal and political practices to cope with conflicts and contingencies emerging in these polities.

Intellectual searches for morally neutral and culturally transcendental principles are doomed to fail because 'Democracy is not a program for transforming men

40 Talcott Parsons, 'The Professions and Social Structure', *Social Forces* 17 (1939): 457–467.

41 Ronald Dworkin, *A Matter of Principle* (Oxford: Clarendon Press, 1985), 6.

42 Stanley Fish, *There's No Such Thing As Free Speech … And It's a Good Thing, Too* (Oxford: Oxford University Press, 1994), 11.

and women into capacious and generous beings but is a device for managing the narrow partialities ... it is not a cooperative venture. Rather, it is a competitive one.'[43]

Legal and constitutional principles and rules have the function of protecting the system of positive law against two specific social risks – violence amounting to the famous picture of the robber's gun and arbitrariness of decision-making, especially in courts. Nevertheless, framing a social conflict as 'a matter of principle' always involves indeterminacy and even 'adhockery'.[44] Principled resolutions and reasons are then social facts – practices which are 'a function of the personal and institutional history that has brought you to a moment of dispute'.[45]

This critique of the philosophical image of polity as a rationally organized community of transcendental principles and universal values demonstrates the impossibility of using culture as the ultimate normative reservoir and guarantor of social integration. However, it also shows that principles operating within the systems of positive law and politics need to be perceived as regulatory programmes enabling these systems to function and not as their normative foundations and preconditions.

As Lon L. Fuller famously commented almost half a century ago, the principles of legality are 'a practical art'[46] and their social function perhaps may be less noble or principled but certainly reasonable and pragmatic in sociological terms, namely 'to subject human conduct to the governance of rules'.[47] This practical art understandably relies on the personal and institutional history and constitutes its polity of rules and principles travelling through the society's time and significantly affecting its collective memory. Polity, statehood and constitution subsequently can be explored and examined in their changing meaning within the differentiating function of culture.

Within the systems of positive law and politics, this recourse to culture as memory of collectively shared practices stabilizes specific systemic operations by reformulating them exactly as integrative principles and foundational values. In this sense, Fuller's description of 'eight ways to fail to make law'[48] is but an analysis of different conditional programmes running in the system of positive law and guaranteeing its functionality. This practical art of legality shows that principles are not 'out there' externally determining the legitimate order of political society but always 'in here' operating within the society's legal system. In this sense, Fuller's title *Morality of Law* has to be interpreted as morality operating within the system of positive law.

43 Stanley Fish, *The Trouble With Principle* (Cambridge, Mass: Harvard University Press, 1999), 306.
44 Fish, *The Trouble With Principle*, 65.
45 Fish, *There's No Such Thing*, 18.
46 Lon L. Fuller, *The Morality of Law: Revised Edition* (New Haven: Yale University Press, 1969), 91.
47 Fuller, *The Morality of Law*, 106.
48 Fuller, *The Morality of Law*, 33ff.

However, specific cultural communication evolving in modern society and affecting its systems of positive law and politics still needs to be analysed to comprehend one specific concept emerging through structural irritation between modern democratic politics and positive law, namely the concept of constituent power and popular will as the allegedly ultimate legitimation formula in constitutional democratic politics.

From the polity of constitutional principles to the symbolic image of constituent power

Niklas Luhmann importantly asked 'why society invents a concept of culture to describe its memory'[49] and came to the conclusion that '[O]nly in modern societies has a sufficiently general concept of culture developed that is suitable for distinguishing social memory from other social functions.'[50] In this respect, Luhmann also acknowledged Talcott Parsons's intellectual intuition that social memory should be distinguished from other social functions and that this function consists of 'latent-pattern maintenance' and such latency is the task of the cultural subsystem.

The general concept of culture as reflection on self-descriptions of modern society and its national or supranational and transnational contextualization, rather than simply drawing on moral and civilizational universalism, opens radically new possibilities of social observation and self-identifications.[51] The concepts of culture and collective identity, therefore, should be considered as specific forms of societal differentiation and comparisons conducted within specific social subsystems, such as law and politics in which, for instance, the semantics of constituent power or constitutional and popular sovereignty as the democratic polity is its specific example. It makes possible to differentiate between democratic and undemocratic political systems, compare different democratic 'cultures' and regimes, analyse their historical evolution etc.

The opening section describing specific Czech experiences and politics of shared memories of World War II persuasively demonstrates that the constitution of collective memory is not limited to nationhood and these memories evolve beyond national imaginary landscapes. However, imagined collective identity of modern nations is specific to democratic politics and these identities, therefore, have to be analysed within the framework of modern democratic procedures, rules, mobilizations and power struggles.

The democratic polity's symbolism draws on the specific self-description of society as the totality of one people/nation. It thus resolves the profound paradox of modern politics in which the social multitude of individuals with their 'inalienable' rights and freedoms is transformed into the social unity of one people exercising

49 Luhmann, *Theory of Society, Volume 1*, 354.
50 Luhmann, *Theory of Society, Volume 1*, 354.
51 Luhmann, *Theory of Society, Volume 2*, 176.

its sovereignty through the state. The people is perceived as constituent power of this state, yet limited by its written constitution at the same time.

No wonder *political constitutions* have become those *mysterious objects of desire* of modern nations in Europe and elsewhere. They became ultimate representations of the people as political nations and thus completely changed the concept of the polity by identifying it with political nationhood. The modern constitutional state was thus originally differentiated from the body of social hierarchies, particularisms and loyalties and constituted a new body politic, yet through increasing modernization as democratization became ever more symbolically representative of the whole society and its sovereign power could be legitimized only by virtue of democratic authority.

The paradox of transformation of the social multitude to the political unity thus meets another paradox – the modern paradox of constitutionalism in which the constitutional democratic state both organizes constituent power by using it as its legitimation formula and makes it limited by constituted power of its institutions operating on the basis of the above discussed constitutional principles and values. The sovereign people is a symbolic concept accommodating both paradoxes and turning them into the collective self-attribution[52] of political decisions and legal norms. However, this semantic capacity of turning the social and historical multitude into one self-constituted and self-constituting polity is possible only *retrospectively* in an act of self-recognition and self-identification of the members of a polity with its commonly shared past and projected future.

In the context of constitutional theory, this ontology of collective selfhood has been elaborated, for instance, by Hans Lindahl who defines the collective self of constituent power of the people as existing 'in the modes of *questionability* and, by way of its acts, of *responsiveness*'.[53] However, the notion of polity as imagined community legitimized by its identity and 'real' values hardly can be treated as a synonym of general society which is functionally differentiated and therefore cannot be founded on some essentialist politics of nationhood, statehood and cultural integration. Polity's self-identification is channelled by collective memory which has the capacity to imagine a specific polity as the totality of society, yet cannot guarantee its unity, political centralization and constitution of ultimate social authority.

Ontology of collective selfhood subsequently has to be replaced by the sociological perspective which would analyse polity as both a concept signifying societal unity through cultural symbolism and power structure processing collectively binding decisions and their legitimation. Collective memories and recognized selfhood of polity founded on shared values and destiny cannot integrate

52 Hans K. Lindahl, 'Constituent Power and Reflexive Identity: Towards an Ontology of Collective Selfhood' in *The Paradox of Constitutionalism: Constituent Power and Constitutional Form*, ed. Martin Loughlin and Neil Walker (Oxford: Oxford University Press. 2007): 9–24, at 19.

53 Lindahl, 'Constituent Power and Reflexive Identity: Towards an Ontology of Collective Selfhood', 21.

functionally differentiated society. Instead, it has to be analysed as an internal construct of the political system which, through the semantics of constitution, finds its legal form and gets communicated within the system of positive law.

Society is not a normative idea even when it can be imagined through the system of either constitutional principles and values, or cultural traditions and collective memory. Society as imagined community channelling its identity through education, history and collective memories is just one of many images evolving and operating through the specific semantics of different social systems, such as politics and law.

Unlike totalitarian and authoritarian regimes drawing on 'real' community with constituent power, constitutional democracy and representative government are part of political and philosophical nominalist tradition. It is a grave mistake to consider popular sovereignty as a 'real' part of the construction of legal and political reality manifesting itself in the ultimate general will of the people. It is equally wrong to treat principles and values constituting this democratic polity as universal and transcendental because, as was demonstrated in the previous section, their operative capacity is limited by the particular and immanent framework of constitutional democratic politics.

The symbolic meaning of both constituent power of the sovereign people and principles or values constituted by the basic normativity of political constitution are internally constructed by the systems of positive law and politics and therefore cannot operate as their external foundations and legitimation formulas.

Conclusion: on culture as memory and the impossibility of foundations in law and politics

The original paradox of constitutionalism and nation state, therefore, is not that of the irresolution between the constituent power of nation as imagined community of shared memory and collective bonds on one side and constituted power of the democratic state and its general principles and values incorporated in the body of constitution on the other side. It, rather, is the paradox of constitutional polity imaged both as unlimited collective will constituent power and limiting legal principles which ultimately demonstrates the impossibility to symbolically integrate the modern functionally differentiated society and hierarchically bridge over structural irritations and differences between the systems of positive law and politics.

Constituent power of the people is retrospectively imagined as the symbolic unity of actually differentiated society and turned into the cultural canon of collective memory. This specific function of culture as collective memory equally symbolizes constitutional principles as ultimate societal values and transcendental foundations even in the modern culturally relativistic intellectual and social environment. However, it is not some pre-politically existing community of 'the people' sharing memories and destiny and making all politics an existential matter of life, death, survival and fight against their enemies. Instead, it is the functionally differentiated systems of positive law and politics which are 'real' constituent powers of the democratic constitutional polity and its collective memory.

Collective memories are thus internal constructs of social systems, such as law and politics, and therefore necessarily differ because each system constitutes its specific internal memory as culture. This is why lawyers and legal scholars speak of different legal cultures. What they actually mean is a subsystem of collectively shared practices, techniques, concepts and interpretations evolving within a particular system of law and making it possible to solve present problems by a recourse to the past legal experiences. Similarly, political culture is nothing but a subsystem of remembered practices and power decisions relevant for present political challenges and future expectations. This subsystem cannot be appropriated by any particular group acting as the society's functionaries.

Historically, democratization of political power coincides with its juridification. Popular sovereignty, therefore, is inseparable from constitutional sovereignty and legality as both a restraining and empowering medium became institutionalized in the democratic constitutional state. Nevertheless, current globalized politics and law persuasively show that this interplay between power (politics) and legality (law) expands beyond the institutional framework of the modern nation state. This process of societal expansion and functional differentiation beyond state institutions also shows the impossibility to symbolically unify and synthesize past experiences and future expectations through the medium of legality and/or political power.

Society is the complex unity of differences which may be symbolized as polity of historically constituted common bonds between human beings as both political and moral agents. However, this symbolization functions only within the functionally differentiated and specifically institutionalized systems of modern law and politics. To conclude, these systems produce specific internal memories described as legal or political cultures, yet this symbolic communication cannot be treated as a precondition or foundation of their general operations within and beyond modern statehood and national or post-national imagination.

Bibliography

Aitken, Ian (ed), *Encyclopedia of the Documentary Film*. 3-Volume Set. Abingdon: Routledge, 2006.

Anderson, Benedict. *Imagined Communities: Reflections on the Origin and Spread of Nationalism*. London: Verso, 1983.

Arnold, Thurman. *The Symbols of Government*. New Haven: Yale University Press, 1935.

Assman, Aleida, and Laure Shortt (eds), *Memory and Political Change*. Houndmills, Basingstoke: Palgrave Macmillan, 2012.

Benhabib, Seyla. 'Cultural Complexity, Moral Interdependence and the Global Dialogical Community'. In *Women, Culture and Development: A Study of Human Capabilities*, edited by Martha Nussbaum and Jonathan Glover, 235–259. Oxford: Clarendon Press, 1995.

Benhabib, Seyla. *The Claims of Culture*. Princeton: Princeton University Press, 2002.

Bernard-Donals, Michael. *Forgetful Memory: Representation and Remembrance in the Wake of the Holocaust*. Albany: SUNY Press, 2009.

Carlyle, Thomas. *The Works of Thomas Carlyle, Volume 5: On Heroes, Hero-Worship and the Heroic in History*. Cambridge: Cambridge University Press, 2010 digital version; originally published 1897.

Cubitt, Geoffrey (ed.). *Imagining Nations*. Manchester: Manchester University Press, 1998.

Dworkin, Ronald. *A Matter of Principle*. Oxford: Clarendon Press, 1985.

Dworkin, Ronald. *Law's Empire*. Cambridge, Mass.: The Belknap Press, 1986.

Dworkin, Ronald. *Freedom's Law: The Moral Reading of the American Constitution*. Oxford: Oxford University Press, 1996.

Eder, Klaus. 'Symbolic Power and Cultural Differences: A Power Model of Political Solutions to Cultural Differences'. In *Constituting Communities: Political Solutions to Cultural Conflict*, edited by Per Mouritsen and Knud Erik Jorgensen, 31–52. Houndmills, Basingstoke: Palgrave Macmillan, 2008.

Emanuel, Muriel, and Vera Gissing. *Nicholas Winton and the Rescued Generation: Save One Life, Save the World*. Elstree: Vallentine Mitchell & Co., 2001.

Faber, David. *Munich: The 1938 Appeasement Crisis*. New York: Simon & Schuster, 2008.

Fish, Stanley. *There's No Such Thing As Free Speech ... And It's a Good Thing, Too*. Oxford: Oxford University Press, 1994.

Fish, Stanley. *The Trouble With Principle*. Cambridge, Mass: Harvard University Press, 1999.

Fuller, Lon L. *The Morality of Law: Revised Edition*. New Haven: Yale University Press, 1969.

Halbwachs, Maurice. *On Collective Memory*. Chicago IL: The University of Chicago Press, 1992.

Hutton, Patrick H. *History as an Art of Memory*. Hannover NH: University Press of New England, 1993.

Jacobson, Arthur J., and Bernard Schlink (eds), *Weimar: A Jurisprudence of Crisis*. Berkeley CA: University of California Press, 2000.

Kennedy, Michael L. *The Jacobin Clubs in the French Revolution, 1793–1795*. Oxford: Berghahn Press, 2000.

Kolakowski, Leszek. *Modernity on Endless Trial*. Chicago: The University of Chicago Press, 1990.

Koselleck, Reinhart. *Futures Past: On the Semantics of Historical Time*. New York: Columbia University Press, 2004.

Lienhardt, Godfrey. *Divinity and Experience: The Religion of the Dinka*. Oxford: Clarendon Press, 1961.

Lindahl, Hans K. 'Constituent Power and Reflexive Identity: Towards an Ontology of Collective Selfhood'. In *The Paradox of Constitutionalism: Constituent Power and Constitutional Form*, edited by Martin Loughlin and Neil Walker, 9–24. Oxford: Oxford University Press, 2007.

Luhmann, Niklas. *Theory of Society, Volume 1*. Stanford, CA: Stanford University Press, 2012.

Luhmann, Niklas. *Theory of Society, Volume 2*. Stanford, CA: Stanford University Press, 2013.

Miller, Laurel E., and Louis Aucoin (eds), *Framing the State in Times of Transition: Case Studies in Constitution Making*. Washington DC: United States Institute of Peace Press, 2010.

Mink, Georges. 'Institutions of National Memory in Post-Communist Europe: From Transitional Justice to Political Uses of Biographies (1989–2010)' In *History, Memory and Politics in Central and Eastern Europe: Memory Games*, edited by Georges Mink and Laure Neumayer, 152–172. Houndmills, Basingstoke: Palgrave Macmillan, 2013.

Osiel, Mark. *Mass Atrocity, Collective Memory and the Law*. New Brunswick NJ: Transaction Publishers, 1997.

Parsons, Talcott. 'The Professions and Social Structure', *Social Forces* 17 (1939), 457–467.

Rawls, John. *A Theory of Justice*. Cambridge, Mass: Harvard University Press, 1971.

Rosa, Hartmut, and William E. Scheuerman (eds), *High-speed Society: Social Acceleration, Power, and Modernity*. University Park PA: University of Pennsylvania State University Press, 2009.

Schelsky, Helmut. *Funktionäre – Gefährden sie das Gemeinwohl?*Stuttgart: Seewald, 1982.

Sebald, Gerd, and Jatin Wagle (eds), *Theorizing Social Memories: Concepts and Contexts*. Oxon: Routledge, 2016.

Smend, Rudolf. *Verfassung und Verfassungsrecht*. Leipzig: Duncker & Humblot, 1928.

Teitel, Ruti G. *Transitional Justice*. Oxford: Oxford University Press, 2000.

Tilmans, Karin, Frank van Vree and Jay Winter (eds), *Performing the Past: Memory, History, and Identity in Modern Europe*. Amsterdam: Amsterdam University Press, 2010.

Todorov, Tzvetan, 'Abuses of Memory', *Common Knowledge* 1 (1996), 6.

von Herder, Johann Gottfried, 'Letters Concerning the Progress of Humanity'. In J. G. von Herder, *Philosophical Writings*. Cambridge: Cambridge University Press, 2002.

Wilson, Keith M. (ed), *Forging the Collective Memory: Government and International Historians Through Two World Wars*. Oxford: Berghahn Books, 1996.

Wilson, Richard. *The Politics of Truth and Reconciliation in South Africa: Legitimizing the Post-Apartheid State*. Cambridge: Cambridge University Press, 2001.

Chapter 9

Informing life: temporal politics of information in the administration of pandemics[1]

Sven Opitz

Pandemic emergencies are irreducibly marked by a close interrelation of temporal and informational politics. The Ebola outbreak of 2014 in West Africa has brought to the fore several examples of such interrelation. The Emergency Committee under the International Health Regulations of the WHO has, for instance, repeatedly highlighted the role of exit screening as a means for preventing the international spread of disease and for gathering data:

> States [with intense Ebola transmission] should maintain and reinforce high-quality exit screening of all persons at international airports, seaport, and major land crossings, for unexplainable febrile illness consistent with potential Ebola infection. ... States should collect data from their exit screening processes, monitor their results, and share these with WHO on a regular basis and in a timely fashion.[2]

In addition, the WHO has also asked states to 'check their ... preparedness through simulation'.[3] The latter term refers to different practices of enactment, ranging from emergency exercises to computational modelling techniques.[4] Simulations envision future courses of the pandemic and provide a testing ground

1 Some of the research for this chapter has been conducted during a Fellowship between October 2013 and March 2014 at the Centre for Advanced Studies of the German Research Foundation (DFG) *Media Cultures of Computer Simulation* (MECS) at Leuphana University. I would like to thank all the members at MECS, my co-fellows, and in particular Sebastian Vehlken for their intellectual generosity.
2 WHO, *Statement on the 3rd Meeting of the IHR Emergency Committee Regarding the 2014 Ebola Outbreak in West Africa*, October 23, 2014.
3 WHO, *Statement on the 2nd Meeting of the IHR Emergency Committee Regarding the 2014 Ebola Outbreak in West Africa*, September 22, 2014.
4 On the key role of computer simulations in governing the Ebola outbreak cf. Kai Kupferschmidt, 'Disease Modelers Project a Rapidly Rising Toll from Ebola', *Science Insider* (2014): accessed June 29, 2016, http://www.sciencemag.org/news/2014/08/disease-modelers-project-rapidly-rising-toll-ebola; on enactment policies in general cf. Stephen J. Collier, 'Enacting Catastrophe: Preparedness, Insurance, Budgetary Planning', *Economy and Society* 37 (2009): 224–50.

for administrative measures that might lower the pathogen's reproductive rate. Despite their fundamental difference, both screening and simulation technologies are thus valued by the WHO for suturing the temporal with the informational. Their use during the Ebola crisis exemplifies how political attempts at *stopping* disease transmission operate through combining the *anticipation* of transmissions and the *generation of data* about actual, probable or potential transmissions.

This accent on employing information technologies for the anticipation of future pandemics characterizes the contemporary regime of global health security, which has emerged since the late 1980s.[5] Epidemiological intelligence is 'directed ahead of the current' in order to contain 'pre-pandemic viruses'.[6] This temporal orientation is very clearly expressed in a programmatic statement by Nathan Wolfe, Professor in Human Biology at Stanford University and founder of the Global Viral Forecasting Initiative: 'we must not only respond to pandemics, but work to predict and prevent them'. For this purpose, Wolfe thinks of information infrastructures in terms of a 'worldwide immune system … that will detect … biological threats before they go global'.[7] Such preventive detection, however, constitutes a particular challenge since it has to perceive novelty at a very early stage and sense its potential for what the WHO Department of Global Capacities Alert and Response calls an 'unexpected, internationally-spreading event'.[8] Preventive detection aims at information about the interconnectedness of life as it is about to unfold. For initiating anticipatory responses to future pandemic outbreaks, the regime of global health security depends on 'apparatuses that continuously monitor phenomena that may give rise to catastrophic events'.[9]

This particular mode of future orientation makes the pandemic an exemplary case of what has been described as our contemporary 'emergency imaginary'.[10] The 'emergency imaginary' envisions a future that harbours disruptive, potentially

5 Andrew Lakoff, 'Epidemic Intelligence: Toward a Genealogy of Global Health Security', in *Contagion: Health, Fear, Sovereignty*, ed. Bruno Magnusson and Zahi Zalloua (Seattle: University of Washington Press, 2012), 44–70.

6 Martin French and Eric Mykhalovskiy, 'Public Health Intelligence and the Detection of Potential Pandemics', *Sociology of Health & Illness* 35 (2013): 174–197, 175; Muriel Figuié, 'Towards a Global Governance of Risks: International Health Organisations and the Surveillance of Emerging Infectious Diseases', *Journal of Risk Research* 17 (2014): 469–483, 480.

7 Nathan Wolfe, 'Epidemic Intelligence', *The Economist*, November 22, 2010, 6; Nathan Wolfe, *The Viral Storm: The Dawn of a New Pandemic Age* (London: Allen Lane, 2011), 200–217.

8 WHO, 'Review of Activities in 2014', *Global Capacities Alert and Response* (2014): accessed May 20, 2015, http://apps.who.int/iris/bitstream/10665/199747/1/WHO_HSE_GCR_2015.7_eng.pdf?ua=1.

9 Lorna Weir and Eric Mykhalovskiy, *Global Public Health Vigilance: Creating a World on Alert* (London: Routledge, 2010), 8.

10 Craig Calhoun, 'A World of Emergencies: Fear, Intervention, and the Limits of Cosmopolitan Order', *Canadian Review of Sociology and Anthropology* 41 (2004): 373–395; Sven Opitz and Ute Tellmann, 'Future Emergencies: Temporal Politics in Law and Economy', *Theory, Culture & Society* (2015): 107–129.

cataclysmic events such as natural disasters, terrorist attacks, financial crisis or large-scale accidents.[11] Due to their high impact, these events have to be addressed with highest priority in the present. Nothing is more urgent then the pending catastrophe. Yet due to their low probability, they are almost impossible to foresee. One has to act in the face of radical uncertainty and expect the unexpected, as the by now proverbial imperative goes. The political rationality of the 'emergency imaginary' thus instantiates a specific folding of the epistemological and the temporal: for becoming actionable with regard to the future, *information about the not yet fully formed* is required. Accordingly, in order to take measures against a pandemic emergency, one has to apprehend catastrophic virulence *in formation.*

This chapter delves into the *aporia* of information at the core of such temporal politics. In a first step, it elaborates how the anticipation of emerging pandemic threats stands in a tensed relation to liberal law.[12] Liberal law traditionally enfolds the epistemological into the temporal in a manner that is diametrically opposed to the political rationality of the 'emergency imaginary'.[13] It primarily seeks to gather evidence from completed facts, not from potential future events. According to its most cherished principles and procedures, it does not apply its force on what might become, but on what has been. Developing the divergent epistemic temporalities of liberal law and emergent life almost as ideal types provides a heuristic framework for the subsequent analysis. As will be demonstrated in a second step, their seemingly strict opposition becomes more nuanced as soon as one focuses on the concrete informational instruments employed to capture the not yet formed in administrative practice.[14] For this purpose, the inquiry concentrates on two very dissimilar political technologies for governing infectious disease: quarantine and computer simulation. Drawing on Gregory Bateson's concept of information, quarantine and computer simulation are examined as devices that generate information about a life that is always already in formation. Juxtaposing one of the most ancient and one of the most advanced technologies in this way allows for a more detailed understanding of the temporal complexities and interferences in the government of pandemics. Focusing on the concrete devices designed to extract information from what is in formation brings to light how

11 Claudia Aradau and Rens van Munster, *Politics of Catastrophe: Genealogies of the Unknown* (London: Routledge, 2011); Marieke de Goede and Samuel Randalls, 'Precaution, Preemption: Arts and Technologies of the Actionable Future', *Environment and Planning D* 27 (2009): 859–878.

12 The qualification of law in terms of *liberal* law serves as a shortcut: it is not meant to refer to a particular political context ('all law in liberal democracies'), but rather is supposed to indicate the set of legal standards and safeguards that the liberal tradition holds dearly, such as the inviolability of constitutional principles, individual protective rights, the separation of powers, guarantees of due process etc.

13 Opitz and Tellmann, 'Future Emergencies', 113–116.

14 For a similar sensibility towards the 'informatic practices', i.e. the 'material practices that call information into being' see Martin French, 'Gaps in the Gaze: Informatic Practice and the Work of Public Health Surveillance', *Surveillance & Society* 12 (2014): 226–243.

heterogeneous temporal orientations are being re-assembled in the domain of administrative practices.

Future matters: the government of emergence and the temporality of law

The historical ontology of microbial life underwent a transformation since the 1980s that has turned it into nothing less than a temporal paradigm of contemporary security. Decisive for this shift is the comprehension of life in terms of emergence. To attribute emergent properties to the living implies that a 'body [is] capable of moving out of phase with itself through a combination of its own recombinatory genetic processes and correlative stimuli from its environment to produce further morphogenesis'.[15] Emergent processes harbour the potential for abrupt, discontinuous change resulting from turbulent environmental interactions at the verge of chaos. The concept of emergence highlights 'the relentless, sometimes catastrophic upheaval of entire co-evolving ecologies' and the possibility of 'sudden field transitions that could never be predicted in linear terms from a single mutation'.[16] Under such circumstances, the future appears not only to be out of control, but as radically unpredictable and potentially disruptive.

The notion of Emerging Infectious Disease (EID) inscribes this set of implications into the centre of public health security.[17] It indicates that the matter of concern is no longer an identifiable actual disease but the event of emergence itself: the very instance in which pathogens enter human populations for the first time (e.g. through zoonosis) or in which newly evolving strains of pathogens appear (e.g. through genetic mutation or reassortment).[18] Due to the emergent properties of disease, one does not know when the next pandemic will occur or where it will originate. Even more, one does not know what it will *be*: what kind of viral strain will emerge, how symptoms might develop, how transmission takes place, or what sort of vaccine might offer protection. In this way, the ontology of emergent life constitutes a 'general crisis environment' in which EIDs reside as very particular 'threat form'.[19] It corresponds with modes of defence that have to

15 Michael Dillon, 'Governing Terror: The State of Emergency of Biopolitical Emergence', *International Political Sociology* 1 (2007): 7–28, 12.

16 Melinda Cooper, 'Pre-empting Emergence. The Biological Turn in the War on Terror', *Theory, Culture & Society* 23 (2006): 113–135, 116.

17 Landmark publication in this respect are Stephen S. Morse, ed., *Emerging Viruess* (Oxford: Oxford University Press, 1993), and Joshua Lederberg, Robert E. Shope and Stanley C. Oaks, ed., *Emerging Infections: Microbial Threats to Health in the United States* (Washington DC: National Academy Press, 1992).

18 Kate E. Jones et al., 'Global Trends in Emerging Infectious Diseases', *Nature* 451 (2008): 990–994.

19 Brian Massumi, 'National Enterprise Emergency: Steps Towards an Ecology of Powers', *Theory Culture & Society* 26 (2009): 153–185, 154; on the notion of vulnerability in current biosecurity cf. Carlo Caduff, 'On the Verge of Death: Vision of Biological Vulnerability', *Annual Review of Anthropology* 43 (2014): 105–121.

address the unknown and not yet determined – the potentially catastrophic event of a future pandemic.

Such modes of intervention into an unpredictable future interfere dramatically with the temporality of law as it has been devised, instantiated and celebrated in the liberal tradition. Drawing on Niklas Luhmann's account of legal temporality, the temporal friction between liberal law and the government of emergence can be ascribed to two very distinct forms of handling a particular time differential: the time differential between present future and future present.[20] Liberal law, on the one hand, supports an indifferent stance toward the future. It stabilizes normative expectations over time, thereby binding the transition into the future present. As Luhmann puts it, law allows for a 'mere continuation of the past and the present in a world full of surprises, full of enemies, full of conflicting interests.'[21] If the future present disappoints the expectations secured by law, one can retroactively insist on them by referring to norms. The future present thus has to turn into a past to become legally relevant. Only in the form of a present past can a peculiar matter become the proper object of legal knowledge. Only after all the evidence about a completed incidence has been established and all voices have been heard can the legal judgment occur. Proceeding slowly with regard to matters of the past is therefore not *per se* a defect in law, but a precondition for accurate legality and for entrusting the legal system with binding the future already in the present.[22]

For the government of emergence, on the other hand, it is the future that makes a difference. The time differential between the present future and the future present becomes the field of intense intervention: by paradoxically taking the unknown future as an object of knowledge, the government of emergence seeks to avert a catastrophic course of events to come. By expecting the unexpected it aims to achieve a future present different from the one imagined as worst. For this purpose, the government of emergence proceeds proactively. In doing so, it

20 On the terminology of 'present futures' and 'future presents' cf. Niklas Luhmann, 'The Future Cannot Begin: Temporal Structures in Modern Society', *Social Research* 43 (1976): 130–152. The most thorough elaboration of legal temporality is to be found in Niklas Luhmann, *Law as a Social System* (Oxford: Oxford University Press, 2004), 141–172 (and *passim*); for a detailed analysis of the temporal interferences between law and security in connection to Luhmann's theory of law see Sven Opitz, *An der Grenze des Rechts: Inklusion/Exklusion im Zeichen der Sicherheit* (Weilerswist: Velbrück, 2012), 269–307.

21 Niklas Luhmann, *Ausdifferenzierung des Rechts. Beiträge zur Rechtssoziologie und Rechtstheorie* (Berlin: Suhrkamp, 1999), 73 (own translation).

22 This aspect of legal temporality is also highlighted by Bruno Latour: 'Common sense finds the slowness of … law … incomprehensible: 'why take so much trouble to judge?', it demands. … What a waste of time! … If the production of doubt in law … [was] criticized in these terms …, judges … would immediately … celebrate the necessity of time, slowness, care, expense, elitism, quality and respect for procedure …; all of us depend vitally on these costly and ponderous institutions, which require … the application of procedures that are exasperatingly meticulous, because these are the only means we have to avoid arbitrariness and superficiality', Bruno Latour, *The Making of Law: An Ethnography of the Counseil D'État* (Cambridge: Polity Press, 2010), 220–221.

pushes the distinction between normative and cognitive expectations to the limit.[23] Cognitive expectations seek to learn from events to happen in a future present. But the government of emergence does not have the time for such procedure. It rather seeks to learn from facts before they actualize. It wants to apprehend catastrophic possibilities and act on them preemptively. There is thus an affinity between the state of emergence and the state of emergency. In a world of emergent, unpredictable threats the irregularity of emergency is the normal premise of action. Under such conditions, politics cannot allow itself to be bound by rules but must counter catastrophic threats by exceptional means. If anything, the exception becomes the rule.

This schematic account suggests two fundamentally different rationalities of action with incompatible temporalities (see Table 9.1). In the literature, they are often cast in terms of a contrast between the prerogative action of a sovereign in a state of exception and those constitutional safeguards designed to keep executive bodies in check.[24] Especially some of the ad hoc quarantine measures taken during the SARS crisis more than a decade ago might support such a clear-cut view.[25] In a different way, the early classification of the 2009 H1N1 virus ('swine flu') as a pandemic corresponds as well with the temporal rationality of governing emergent life. In retrospect, the response to H1N1 is often seen as a prime example for the misallocation of resources due to an exaggerated threat perception. But such a retrospective assessment does not affect a governmental rationality that demands orientation toward a radically unknown future. In 2009 the WHO, in other

Table 9.1 Conflicting temporalities of liberal law and of governing emergent life

Temporality of Liberal Law	*Temporality of Governing Emergent Life*
Indifference towards the future	The future makes a difference
Normative expectations	Expecting the unexpected
Knowledge about past events	Apprehension of future events
Retroactive action: jurisdiction	Proactive action: preemption
Slow process	Fast action
Rule	Exception

23 This distinction is elaborated in Niklas Luhmann, *Social Systems* (Stanford: Stanford University Press, 1995), 319–325.

24 With a strong focus on the temporal pressures exerted on the chronometrics of the liberal institutions since the early 20th century, William Scheuerman, *Liberal Democracy and the Social Acceleration of Time* (Baltimore: Johns Hopkins University Press, 2004). See also Marc de Wilde's chapter in this volume that critically discusses Carl Schmitt's concept of the sovereign exception with regard to its temporal underpinnings.

25 Estair van Wagner, 'The Practice of Biosecurity in Canada: Public Health Legal Preparedness and Toronto's SARS Crisis', *Environment and Planning A* 40 (2008): 1647–1663.

words, followed the imperative not to take the time waiting for the pandemic to actually occur but to act swiftly on the potentiality of disease.

Most interesting for the current argument on the relation between law and life, however, are features of the International Health Regulations (IHR) that also exhibit the tension summarized in Table 9.1. The IHR entrusts the Director-General of the WHO with the power to decide whether 'an event constitutes a public health emergency of international concern' (IHR, Article 12). The notion of the 'event' is of particular significance here. Due to its rather open meaning, the term establishes an 'all-risks approach' toward the future.[26] In the ambit of the IHR an 'event' is not limited to a specific and known disease with a quantifiable virulence but it applies to any 'occurrence that creates a potential for disease' (IHR, Article 1). As a consequence, it covers all 'incidents involving natural, accidental or deliberate release of chemical, biological or radiological materials' (IHR, Appendix 2). While the decisional leeway in matters of emergency is thus kept possibly large, human rights provisions remain comparably weak. The IHR only oblige the authorities to choose the 'least intrusive and invasive' measures available (IHR, Article 23). They do not grant substantial basic rights or due process protections with regard to compulsory measures (e.g. vaccination). One can therefore conclude that the temporal rationality of governing emergent life has found its way into the main legal document in global health security. Within the IHR it provokes the inflection of some of the most venerable liberal legal principles.

To a certain extend, the case of the IHR has already complicated the account of the two antagonistic temporalities of liberal law and the government of emergent life. Instead of assuming a fixed opposition of external forces – the executive branch *versus* the judicative branch, the political system *versus* the system of law, the sovereign exception *versus* the legal state etc. – it points to the articulation of conflicting rationalities *within* a regulatory apparatus. Such hybrid arrangements prevail especially at the mundane level of administrative technologies.[27] Due to its operative requirements, the administration of emergent life functions as a kind of 'translation zone' where competing concerns about security and legality are to be aligned. In analysing administrative technologies such as quarantine and simulation, the schematic opposition presented in Table 9.1 is therefore not taken as an

26 David P. Fidler and Lawrence O. Gostin, 'The New International Health Regulations: A Historic Development for International Law and Public Health', *Journal of Law, Medicine & Ethics* 34 (2006): 85–94, 86.

27 This assumption is supported by a recent study that shows how federal administrative bodies in Australia 'moved away from the spectre of catastrophe' during the H1N1 pandemic. In line with the argument presented here, the authors draw the conclusion that sociology 'needs to extend beyond identifying the distinct rationales of security informing public health and attend the immanent unfolding of securitisation in the day-to-day work of disease governance', Emily Waller, Mark Davis and Niamh Stephenson, 'Australia's Pandemic Influenza "Protect" Phase: Emerging Out of the Fog of Pandemic', *Critical Public Health* ahead-of-print (2014): 1–15, 12–13.

empirical given, but rather to be used as a heuristic foil for exposing the interferences of the different logics. It may help to elaborate how normative and preemptive elements are being re-assembled for acting on the time differential between present future and future present. In order to trace such hybrid arrangements, the following sections conceive of administrative technologies as information technologies that generate data for the purpose of anticipating and preventing future pandemics.

Administering time differentials: information technologies with Gregory Bateson

Whereas computer simulation fits our digital imaginary of information technologies, it may come as a surprise to subsume quarantine under the same category. Yet as Keller Easterling underlines with regard to Gregory Bateson's famous notion of information as 'a difference that makes a difference', the digital imaginary is too narrow for developing a proper concept of information:

> Anything – human or non-human, digital or non-digital – could be a carrier of information. … Bateson … saw information as an ordinary currency for exchanges between humans and non-humans. … Objects do not need to be enhanced by digital technologies … To the degree that they 'make a difference' in the world, they create influences, intentions, and relationships that constitute information. The information manifests, not in text or code, but in activity.[28]

The category of information is, in other words, not tied to a particular type of digital or analogue media. What matters is the inherently temporal conversion of one difference into another. To use one of Bateson's favourite examples, the stick of the blind person constitutes an information technology in so far as it detects an obstacle (first difference), which is then transformed into the alteration of the body's movement (second difference).[29] Accordingly, quarantine and simulation are devices of in-formation in so far as they produce differences, which then make a particular difference in administrative activities. Yet in this processing of differences, they are confronted with a particular challenge since they aim at putting into form one of the most mutable and mobile matters: the '*global biological* as a single, integrated system containing emergent risks'.[30]

Bateson's concept of information basically circumscribes a mechanism of ordering and sorting: 'Order is seen as a matter of sorting and dividing. But the

28 Keller Easterling, *Extrastatecraft: The Power of Infrastructure Space* (London/New York: Verso, 2014), 85.
29 Gregory Bateson, *Steps to an Ecology of Mind* (Chicago: University of Chicago Press, 2000), 465 and *passim*.
30 Bruce Braun, 'Biopolitics and the Molecularization of Life', *Cultural Geographies* 14 (2007): 6–28.

essential notion in all sorting is that some difference shall cause some other difference at a later time.'[31] Beyond this background, one might bestow the full political meaning on the cybernetic term of the 'governor' when dealing with the administrative technologies of quarantine and simulation. As information technologies they register particular differences and feed them (back) into circuits of control. The notion of 'informing life' marks the threshold at which life is endowed with a form that matters in further administrational ordering practices – a process to which Bateson refers to in terms of 'transforms of difference' travelling along organizational pathways, channels and conduits.[32]

As outlined above, the paradoxical governmental injunction to expect the unexpected and to tackle the radically unknown in the field of Emerging Infectious Disease implies a particular informational problem. The imperative to generate information about a future pandemic, which is per definition conceived of as an entity not fully formed, constitutes a fundamental challenge. To be sure, already in Bateson's seemingly trivial example, the interval of information – the transmission *and* transformation of a difference – is directed at the future: the blind man's stick is designed to prevent the collisions of bodies by feeding a tactile datum into the corporeal self-steering of the blind man. But in the case of EIDs things are temporally more complex. Information has to be drawn from a future that has not materialized in the stable form comparable to an object detectable through a stick. Nevertheless, the future has to take *some* form in the present in order to act on it. The future has to make a difference in the present of those administrative practices that aim at a different future present.

For understanding this process, one has to attend to the two intimately related operations of *sensing* and *coding* at work in every informational interval. Each information technology depends on a sensory apparatus that is receptive to particular differences. To avoid overburdening the blind man's stick, we can also think of an ordinary sieve: it differentiates matter only with regard to differences in size or density, and not, for example, in smell.[33] This raises the question about how technologies such as quarantine or simulation extract in-formative differences from evolving life: how do they generate differences for instance between potentially contagious and non-contagious bodies, potentially critical or non-critical situations, potentially effective and non-effective measures? At the same time, each information technology operates through code and coding. It not only detects differences but also translates them into other differences, an operation which is necessarily carried out according to particular criteria. The code designates the

31 Bateson, *Steps to an Ecology of Mind*, xxxi.
32 Bateson, *Steps to an Ecology of Mind*, 318.
33 More broadly understood, the operation of sieving can be applied beyond the realm of the grainy: 'norms and laws may sieve (accepting certain behaviors rejecting others), as may price and infrastructure. … More generally, sieves are essential to information processing', Paul Kockelman, 'The Anthropology of an Equation: Sieves, Spam Filters, Agentive Algorithms, and Ontologies of Transformation', *HAU: Journal of Ethnographic Theory* 3 (2013): 33–61, 35, 37.

'rules of transformation' at work in the interval of differences.[34] This raises the question about how administrative techniques such as quarantine or simulation process information: how do they transform the differences they perceive into the differences that matter in the administration of disease? Or to draw both operational aspects together: how is a life in formation sensed and coded in order to meet the informational challenge at the core of governing EIDs?

Quarantine as an art of waiting: on the forensics of possibility

As is well established in the historical literature on public health, the measure of quarantine was developed in the Italian city-states of the 14th century, where port authorities issued isolation periods for ships before they were allowed to dock.[35] Interestingly, quarantine had almost disappeared in the second half of the 20th century, but had a strong comeback during the SARS crisis of 2002–03. Since then quarantine has turned into a crucial component of the contemporary security dispositif designed to tackle the threat of EID.[36] If biosecurity 'today names a set of political responses within globalization that take the unpredictability of molecular life ... as their justification', then quarantine, although far from being uncontroversial, is seen as one such response to the problem of controlling the dynamism inherent in life.[37]

Against the backdrop of its pre-modern genealogy, we usually identify quarantine with measures of isolation. The overlap between the two is indeed obvious: the quarantined person is being separated and segregated from others in order to interrupt contacts that may transmit disease. Yet to understand quarantine properly, one has to notice how it differs from isolation. The IHR define isolation as the 'separation of ill or contaminated persons or affected baggage, containers, conveyances, goods or postal parcels' (IHR, Article 1). Hence, isolation is a mode of social sorting that takes into account differences of actual bodily states. The form of information processing follows a relatively simple code: the measure of isolation is taken because a person is presently ill, or it is not taken because a person is not ill. The temporality of this measure, in principle, follows the structure of a

34 Bateson, *Steps to an Ecology of Mind*, 130. Code is 'executable' in the sense that it 'performs indicated tasks according to the encoded instructions', Adrian Mackenzie and Theo Vurdubakis, ' Code and Coding in Crisis: Signification, Performativity and Excess', *Theory, Culture & Society* 28 (2011): 3–23, 6.

35 For a brief overview cf. Andrea A. Conti, Gian F. Gensini and Magdi H. Yacoub, 'The Concept of Quarantine in History: From Plague to SARS', *Journal of Infection* 49 (2004): 257–261; for a more in-depth historical account of quarantine and especially the political and economic disputes it raised cf. Mark Harrison, *Contagion: How Commerce has Spread Disease* (New Haven: Yale University Press, 2012).

36 Sven Opitz, 'Regulating Epidemic Space: The *Nomos* of Global Circulation', *Journal of International Relations and Development* 19 (2015): 263–284.

37 Braun, 'Biopolitics and the Molecularization of Life', 15; see also Nick Bingham and Steve Hinchliffe, 'Securing Life: The Emerging Practices of Biosecurity', *Environment and Planning A* 40 (2008), 1534–1551.

'conditional program', which Luhmann sees predominantly at work in law.[38] Its characteristic is an if/then-sequence: *if fact X is given, then decision Y is to follow.*

Quarantine differs from isolation by taking a proactive stance. It aims at 'the separation from others of *suspect persons* who are *not ill* or of *suspect baggage*, containers, conveyances or goods in such a manner as *to prevent* the *possible* spread of infections or contamination' (IHR, Article 1, italics added). This legal definition indicates that it would be misleading to reduce quarantine to the spatial aspect of enclosure. Rather, it conjoins the measure of containment with a temporal calculus for generating and processing information. Quarantine reckons precisely with the temporal lag that exists between infection and the visibility of symptoms. It addresses the indeterminacy of a body during the incubation period: spurred by the problem of the 'healthy carrier', it acts on a body's potential of being a vector of contagion.[39] Quarantine is therefore not so much about predicting what a body can become, but about waiting for a determinable status to emerge. It uses time to in-form life by letting life in-form itself. It does not lack a certain irony, then, that one of the most ancient administrative technologies employed in governing infectious disease actually operates in 'real-time'.[40] Quarantine takes exactly the time an infectious disease takes to manifest itself for generating a difference (ill/healthy) that will then make a difference (isolation-hospitalization/release).

At the same time, quarantine is itself haunted by the problem of indeterminacy that it wants to solve. At least some of the concerns raised against quarantine stem from the fact that it starts with seemingly 'indifferent' bodies. Or more precisely, bodies to be quarantined are not coded as ill or healthy, they do not have any informational value with reference to this distinction – they could be both. But at least if quarantine is not applied indiscriminately, bodies do not enter quarantine totally uninformed either. They are instead coded as suspicious or non-suspicious of carrying a disease. This, however, harbours the fundamental problem about how to identify a suspect body that does *not* show symptoms of disease: how to distinguish a body that *might* make a difference? The IHR gives a hint for solving this problem practically by referring to the 'tracing of contacts of suspected or

38 Luhmann, *Law as a Social System*, 196–203.

39 For a cultural analysis of the 'healthy carrier' and its societal implications cf. Priscilla Wald, *Contagious: Cultures, Carriers, and the Outbreak Narrative* (Durham: Duke University Press, 2008), 68–113. 'The healthy carrier', Wald writes in regard to its first appearance in the early 20th century, 'dramatized the biological underpinnings of all social interactions and their potential danger in an interconnected world.' This general observation is not limited to the historical situation investigated by Wald. The difficulties of identifying healthy carriers give rise to atmospheres of suspicion, in which invisible threats tend to multiply and amplify each other – especially in the age of EID.

40 Lindsay Thomas has highlighted that 'real time'– despite its promise of a 'transparent simultaneity' – is always already 'mediated time' and that the current real-time technologies of tracking global disease all have their intervals of 'lagging behind', Lindsay Thomas, 'Pandemics of the Future: Disease Surveillance in Real Time', *Surveillance & Society* 12 (2014), 287–300, 292.

affected persons' (IHR, Article 18). As a study of the procedure established by the Singapore Ministry of Health during the SARS outbreak in 2003 details, the

> components of contact tracing included the following: obtaining all patient movements during the symptomatic stage; identifying the persons who had contact with the patient during these movements; and instituting follow-up action on the contacts for a 10-day period.[41]

Starting from a map of movements, contact lists were to be created by contact-tracing centres and a quarantine-board had to decide on the basis of these lists about whom to quarantine. According to this quasi-paradigmatic procedure, it is the physical contact that generates the very suspicion that makes a difference whether to quarantine or not. The physical contact turns a person into 'suspect person' as well as baggage into 'suspect baggage' or containers into 'suspect containers'. Quarantine thus implies a thoroughly post-liberal concept of suspicion based on spatial proximity. Instead of referring to evidence for a voluntarily committed deed, the suspicion relates to a potential bodily state derived from physical contacts. The restriction of the freedom to move is not justified with reference to personal responsibility for specific acts, but happens solely on grounds of a bodily intercourse which might make a difference in the future. It is exactly this possibility that is to be detected through quarantine.

The temporality immanent to quarantine combines elements from the two temporal modes schematically outlined above. Albeit quarantine is driven by the orientation towards the future, it is not a technology of pre-emption in the full sense. As Brian Massumi underlines, 'pre-emption is when the futurity of unspecified threat is affectively held in the present in a perpetual state of potential emergence(y) so that a movement of actualization may be triggered.'[42] Faced with the task of picturing the ultimate preemptive measure vis-à-vis EID, one would have to think of an equivalent to what geo-engineering is to climate change: an intervention that is 'incitatory' as it becomes 'immersed in the conditions of emergence of a threat'.[43] The scenario of a genetically modified pathogen designed to intervene into the future evolution of disease would probably be a good candidate in this respect. Such a thought experiment shows that quarantine functions differently. It acts on the not yet determinable, but it does not trigger

41 Peng L. Ooi, Sonny Lim and Suok Kai, 'Use of Quarantine in the Control of SARS in Singapore', *American Journal of Infection Control* 33 (2005): 252–257, 252. See also Martin Cetron et al., 'Isolation and Quarantine: Containment Strategies for SARS 2003', in *Learning from SARS: Preparing for the Next Disease Outbreak* (Washington DC: The Washington Academies Press, 2004), ed. Stacey Knobler et al., 71–83.

42 Brian Massumi, 'Potential Politics and the Primacy of Preemption', *Theory and Event* 10 (2007): marginalia 1–34, 23.

43 Ben Anderson, 'Preemption, Precaution, Preparedness: Anticipatory Action and Future Geographies', *Progress in Human Geography* 34 (2010): 777–798, 790.

the actualization of disease.[44] Unlike preemptive action, quarantine does neither accelerate the course of events nor intervene into the emergence of disease in order to avert it. Quarantine is much more passive. It constitutes a patient art of waiting for disease to reveal itself under locally controlled conditions.

For informing about disease in this way, quarantine folds a cognitive mechanism into a quasi-jurdidical temporal structure. It combines features of a test and a trial: Quarantine takes its time for an investigation that moves from a suspicion to a finding, which is not so much a verdict but a result. Although the suspicion grows out of a list of physical contacts, it is not limited to the past in the same way a criminal suspicion is. It is a suspicion about what might be *and* what might become at the same time. Relying on this suspicion, quarantine's *telos* is a concrete future present where a body will reveal whether disease has already been there or not. The symptoms that a quarantined body develops mark the end of the quarantine and the ultimate proof of its preventive necessity. Quarantine thus executes a particular combination of pro- and retroactivity: quarantine apprehends a possible future in order to let the future happen in a spatially secured setting. The forensics of possibility feeds into the control of its actualization.

Simulating virulence: the multiplication of present futures

Although simulation models have become a well-researched object in the philosophy of science, their impact as information technologies in administrative practice – what might also be called their particular 'social' or 'political life' – has been explored to a much lesser extent.[45] Such neglect is remarkable given the current ubiquity of simulation methods. As Gabriele Gramelsberger and Erika Mansnerus point out in one of the very few studies available, computer simulation especially is about to become one of the main instruments for informing policy options.[46] This might be most obvious in the field of climate policy, but it is also

44 To be sure, historically quarantine has always been criticized for serving as a dangerous hotbed in which healthy persons contracted disease in the first place by being contained together with the ill, cf. Harrison, *Contagion*, especially Chapter 4. However, such cases were considered to be a regrettable, but unintended side effect to be avoided. Whereas pre-emption would actualize disease, quarantine aims at preventing further infection through determining the actuality of disease.

45 Seminal works in the philosophy of science are Eric Winsberg, *Science in the Age of Computer Simulation* (Chicago: Chicago University Press, 2010) and Paul Humphreys, *Extending Ourselves: Computational Science, Empiricism and Scientific Method* (Oxford: Oxford University Press, 2007). The notion of the 'social life of methods' circumscribes a pragmatist shift from the application of a method towards the impact of its practical usage, cf. the contributions to Evelyn Ruppert, John Law and Mike Savage, ed., *The Social Life of Methods*, Special Issue of *Theory, Culture and Society* 30 (2011).

46 Gabriele Gramelsberger and Erika Mansnerus, 'The Inner World of Models and Its Epistemic Diversity: Infectious Disease and Climate Modelling', in *Ways of Thinking, Ways of Seeing: Mathematical and Other Modeling in Engineering and Technology*, ed. Chris Bissell and Chris Dillon (Berlin/Heidelberg: Springer, 2012), 167–196; see also Erika Mansnerus, 'Using Model-Based Evidence in the Governance of Pandemics' in

the case with the simulation of pandemics: 'Computer-based modeling and simulation techniques are finding increasing use in infectious disease epidemiology as a source of evidence for optimizing vaccination schedules or planning mitigation strategies for pandemic outbreaks.'[47] The fact that the WHO has recently asked states to test and calibrate their response capacities for a potential Ebola outbreak through simulation is indicative of this trend.[48] Against this backdrop, deeper investigations into the socio-logics of pandemic simulations seem more than apposite.

Applying the terminology used so far, computer simulations can be characterized as a meta-information technology. They provide information about processes of in-formation: They seek to determine how administrative practices (such as, for instance, quarantine) that inform life in a particular way make a difference in dealing with the pandemic. This meta-status, however, does not imply that simulations do not take part in the continual 'transforms of differences' (Bateson) characteristic of all information technologies. Computer simulations of pandemics are a far cry from simply reflecting the work of other administrative technologies employed in governing EIDs. Quite the contrary, they themselves put disease into a particular form in order to act on its future unfolding. This means, above all, that they are fully charged with the temporal *aporia* of informing a life not yet fully formed. They themselves make a particular difference in handling the time differential between present future and future present, in combining the retrospective with the prospective, and in aligning the normative with the exceptional.

For specifying the particular form of information generated by pandemic models for administrative purposes, one has to take into account the epistemology of computer simulation. In its most basic sense, a simulation amounts to an imitation of a process by another process in order to generate knowledge about the first process.[49] Science in the age of computer simulation does not learn about the world from the world, but from the model of the world. The crucial point, then, is how the relation between the world and the model is being conceived of. Concerning this fundamental question, it has been convincingly argued that it is highly implausible to understand computer simulations within a 'representationalist' framework.[50] They do not fabricate a point-to-point correlate of the world, but

Pandemics and Emerging Infectious Disease: The Sociological Agenda, ed. Robert Dingwall, Lily M. Hoffman and Karen Staniland (Malden and Oxford: Wiley, 2013), 110–121.

47 Gramelsberger and Mansnerus, 'The Inner World of Models', 172.

48 WHO, *2nd Meeting of the IHR Emergency Committee Regarding the 2014 Ebola Outbreak*

49 This basic notion can be found in Stephan Hartmann, 'The World as a Process: Simulations in the Natural and Social Sciences' in *Simulation and Modelling in the Social Sciences from the Philosophy of Science Point of View*, ed. Klaus G. Triotzsch, Ulrich Mueller and Rainer Hegselmann (Kluwer: Dordrecht, 1996), 77–100.

50 Claus Pias, 'On the Epistemology of Computer Simulation', *Zeitschrift für Medien- und Kulturforschung* 2 (2011): 29–54; Erich Hörl, 'Knowledge in the Age of Simulation – Metatechnical Reflections' in *Simulation: Presentation Technique and Cognitive*

form a hybrid space in which theory and experiment, hypothetic and realization intermingle. Instead of reproducing an outer reality, simulations create an artificial environment within the world. They constitute 'experimental systems' working with approximations, uncertainties and indeterminacies. Rather than reflecting, they 'diffract' the world.[51] Computer simulations are, in other words, 'epistemo-technics' that have moved beyond the correlationism of modern epistemology.[52]

This rather abstract argument can be illustrated with the basic reproductive number R_0 that plays an important role in epidemiological simulation models. Roughly put, R_0 aims to capture the average of the number of infections that one infected person generates. It can be broken down into three factors: *first*, the number of contacts a person has per unit of time; *second*, the probability of an infection per contact; and *third*, the time-span in which a person is infectious. A seemingly simple co-efficient such as R_0 not only requires massive population and mobility data for modelling contacts. It also relies on substantial information about a particular disease: how large, for instance, is a probability of infection if it depends on environmental factors, such as climate and hygiene, or on different degrees of susceptibility within a population contingent on age, gender or income? In regard to such questions simulations irreducibly have to rely on estimations and wisdom of hindsight. They do not expose the one objective truth but constitutively retain moments of conjecture within their operations. Numbers are determined approximately and parameters are recalibrated over several simulation runs, with the effect that the simulation generates its own data. What has been demonstrated for simulations in general therefore applies in particular to pandemic models designed to inform administrative processes: 'performance dissociates from accuracy' and 'adequacy replaces proof'.[53]

But what kind of difference can pandemic models make on such shaky grounds in relation to the future? First and foremost, it follows from this peculiar epistemology that pandemic models constitute a mode of perceiving the future that is not a prediction in the proper sense. A prediction aims at the accurate representation of *the* future present. Against such a benchmark, pandemic simulations would necessarily seem deficient. They do not mirror a dynamic of contagion exactly as it will take place at a clearly circumscribed interval in time. By standards of prediction, they would appear as 'purely fictional' in the sense of being diametrically opposed to reality.

Method, ed. Andrea Gleiniger and Georg Vrachliotis (Basel: Birkhauser 2008), 93–105. These accounts from contemporary media theory imply that computer simulations belong to a 'non-representational' cultural paradigm as famously described in Nigel Thrift, *Non-Representational Theory: Space, Politics, Affect* (London: Routledge, 2007).

51 Karen Barad uses the physical notion of 'diffraction' to move beyond the epistemological relation of reflection with its implication of identitarian sameness, Karen Barad, *Meeting the Universe Halfway: Quantum Physics and the Entanglement of Matter and Meaning* (Durham: Duke University Press 2007), 71–96.

52 Hörl, 'Knowledge in the Age of Simulation', 103.

53 Pias, 'On the Epistemology of Computer Simulation', 34–35.

Yet, de facto they provide a different kind of information. Instead of predicting *the* future present they 'pre-mediate' ***multiple*** futures as present futures.[54] This is why simulations cannot be meaningfully captured as either real or unreal – as it would be the case within a representationalist framework. They rather generate a 'doubling of reality'.[55] That is, they form an additional layer of reality that is supposed to inform administrative practice. Simulations approximate possible developments of a pandemic in order to probe the impact of particular policy choices: how do transmission patterns and reproduction rates change if schools are being closed? If air traffic is being restricted? If public gatherings are inhibited? If quarantine is applied? If vaccines are available for 5% of the population? Etc. The pre-mediation thus explores different versions of a future pandemic.[56] It produces a spectrum of present futures contingent on administrative measures and tests how they might make a difference. What primarily matters, then, is the differential texture of the contagious dynamics created through simulation. The differentials of the differences – the difference as such, so to speak – make the difference.

For fully understanding how pandemic simulations function as information technologies, one has to attend to the peculiar form that disease takes by being simulated: virtual disease. Gilles Deleuze famously used the notion of the virtual in distinction to the actual.[57] Both the actual and the virtual are real. Interestingly, the virtual can even be more intensely real without being actual. This is clearly the case with virtual disease as it gains precedence in the anticipatory regime of contemporary health security. Hence, with the simulation of pandemics different orders of reality start running in parallel. Simulation is introduced into administrative practice to explore the contingency of disease. By virtually probing the effects of different administrative measures it presents versions of infectious disease that are neither necessary nor impossible. This space of contingency serves as an administrative interface that translates virtual into actual interventions: The simulation demonstrates through its pre-mediatory procedures how differences might make differences in order to trigger actual differences. Perceiving the future of virtual disease in this way translates into acting on the future.

54 Richard Grusin, 'Premediation', *Criticism* 46 (2004): 17–39. Premediation characterizes a particular mode of anticipation that stands in close relation to the emergency imaginary: It is fuelled by a 'desire for a world in which the immediacy of the catastrophe, the immediacy of disaster, should not happen again – because it would always already have been premediated', ibid., 21.

55 On the concept of 'doubling of reality' Realitätsverdopplung, cf. Elena Esposito, *Die Fiktion der wahrscheinlichen Realität* (Frankfurt a.M.: Suhrkamp, 2007).

56 Alexander R. Galloway captures this aspect in his reflections on the computer: 'in order to be in a relation with the world informatically, one must erase the world, subjecting it to various forms of manipulation, preemption, modeling and synthetic transformation.... The promise is not one of revealing something as it is, but in simulating a thing so effectively that 'what it is' becomes less and less necessary to speak about.' Galloway, *The Interface Effect* (Cambridge: Polity, 2012), 13.

57 Gilles Deleuze, *Bergsonism* (Cambridge: Zone Books, 1991), 96–99.

One might wonder if this virtual mechanism of informing future life is not the paradigmatic case of the temporality of governing emergence outlined above. In fact, simulations are frequently mentioned as a key technology for securing catastrophic futures beyond probability.[58] The anticipatory aspect undoubtedly prevails in the administrative use of computer simulation: the reaction to an event is tested before the event occurs or becomes catastrophic.[59] At the same time, however, the proactive element still remains tied to the retroactive, the preemptive impact folds back into modes of regulation, and the venture into the unexpected gives rise to normative expectations.

To begin with, the future invoked through computer simulation is neither the affectively charged future enacted in live exercises nor the imaginative future devised in scenario planning. Computer simulations do not primarily seek to create a dramatic atmosphere of vulnerability or an experience of inhabiting the catastrophe. They simply aim at computing versions of higher or lower virulence. Compared with scenario techniques, they are to a lesser degree speculative. To be sure, the phenomena emerging through computer simulation are not 'programmed in advance', as Lindsay Thomas correctly notes with regard to the agent-based simulation EpiCast. But such emergence is dependent on large amounts of historical data – and not on venturesome imaginations.[60] This does, again, not imply that their results are somehow determined. Yet they are also not purely arbitrary since they are bound to facts and figures derived from the past. Data about given facts – such as demographic data, contact patterns or transportation data – 'provides the conditions from which certain phenomena emerge'.[61]

Looking at the political consequences initiated by the information generated through simulation, the distinction between the apprehensive and the normative appears deeply entangled. The results of simulation are to make a difference legally: they are supposed to inform programmes of 'legal preparedness'.[62] The goal of legal preparedness is to install protocols and authorizations that facilitate administrative responses to public health incidents to be expected in the future. Simulations thus pre-mediate the relative efficiency of different policy interventions in order to include some of them into legal preparedness schemes to become

58 See for instance Louise Amoore, *The Politics of Possibility: Risk and Security Beyond Probability* (Durham: Duke University Press, 2013), 11; Aradau and van Munster, *Politics of Catastrophe*, 9, 45.

59 Cf. Limor Samimian-Darash, 'Governing Future Potential Biothreats: Toward an Anthropology of Uncertainty', *Current Anthropology* 54 (2013): 1–22, 8.

60 Thomas, 'Pandemics of the Future', 295.

61 Ibid. As Paul Edwards details at the very first page of his path breaking study on climate models, the relation is intricate: '*without models, there are no data* … but … the models we use to project the future of climate are *not* pure theories, ungrounded in observation. Instead, they are filled with data – data that bind the models to measurable realities', Paul N. Edwards, *A Vast Machine: Computer Models, Climate Data, and the Politics of Global Warning* (Cambridge: MIT Press, 2010), xiiv.

62 Anthony D. Moulton et al., 'What is Public Health Legal Preparedness?', *Journal of Law, Medicine & Ethics* 31 (2003): 672–683.

operative in a catastrophic future present. This implies that the multiplication of present futures achieved by simulation techniques generates a spectrum of what is to be expected from administrative measures. It seeks to initiate a learning process that is supposed to feed into norm generation. It installs a cognitive structure for learning not from actual but from virtual disease events whose informational value is then to be folded into legal code.

In a certain sense, computer simulation can therefore itself be seen as a regulative device. Since its use constitutively involves several runs, it has an in-built tendency towards what Michel Foucault has characterized as 'normalization': computer simulation does not prescribe an abstract norm – which would amount to a practice of 'normation' – but produces an informational normative milieu out of a series of virtual disease events.[63] The differential distribution of virtual disease events corresponds with 'curves of normality' to be reckoned with. The simulation of pandemics inevitably differentiates preferable policy options from less preferable ones by arranging them in relation to each other. Such an informational proto-normative milieu is always already part of a social cybernetics. In administrative practice simulation is supposed to function as a 'governor' that installs a recursive structure: Virtual actions on the future are to be translated into actual actions, which – in turn – feed back into the data used for simulating virtual actions on the future *and so on and so forth*. The 'doubled reality' becomes part of an auto-regulative loop in which governors are being governed. As is always the case with cybernetic feedback-loops, it eventually gets impossible to determine who governs whom. Simulations virtually in-form series of disease events contingent on differential administrative measures for in-forming the government of emergent life whose actions actually might make a difference.

Concluding remarks: mapping hybrid temporalities

The epistemology of emerging disease constitutes a paradigm of security that places the threat of pandemics at the centre of our current imaginary of emergencies. The challenge of anticipating the 'emergency of emergence' harbours a tension between two temporal rationalities that differ especially with respect to their future orientation: the retroactive temporality of law, which is designed to secure expectations, and the proactive temporality of governing emergent life, which has to expect the unexpected. Both temporalities, in other words, differ in the way in which they handle the time differential between present future and future present. This chapter, however, has proposed not to consider their heterogeneous and contradictory quality as empirically given but rather to use the

63 Michel Foucault, *Security, Territory, Population: Lectures at the Collège de France 1977–1978* (Basingstoke: Palgrave, 2007): 'the norm is an interplay of differential normalities … the normal comes first, and the norm is deduced from it', 57; for a further elaboration of this aspect cf. Dianna Taylor, 'Normativity and Normalization', *Foucault Studies* 7 (2009): 45–63.

distinction as a heuristic device. Instead of delineating social temporalities in a highly generalized way, it has turned to the level of comparatively concrete administrative technologies. The basic aim was to examine the way in which they embody and recombine specific temporal features.

Following the work of Gregory Bateson, the technologies of quarantine and computer simulation were analysed as 'information technologies'. It was explored how they unfold the specific *aporia* of information at the core of governing Emerging Infectious Disease: the requirement that information about the not yet fully formed is urgently needed for coping with the catastrophe of a potential future pandemic. It could be demonstrated that quarantine constitutes a technology of waiting based on a particular type of non-liberal suspicion. Quarantine operates in 'real time' as a forensics of a possible actuality: It uses the time a disease takes to develop symptoms in order to determine the status of initially indeterminate bodies. In contrast, computer simulation serves as a technology not for determining an actual state of affairs but for multiplying present futures. It fabricates variations of the potential virulence of virtual disease in order to test the impact of different administrative measures. In this sense, computer simulation serves as a meta-information technology. Processing series of virtual disease events, it produces its own quasi-normative expectations that feed back into the government of actual disease.

Juxtaposing one of the most ancient and one of the most advanced technologies deployed in the government of contagion may have appeared hazardous at first sight. Even if the selection of other technologies would have been possible, it is exactly this stark contrast that brings to the fore the temporal complexities to be found in the contemporary regime of public health security. Beyond the actual findings with regard to quarantine and simulation, hence, this chapter holds a broader methodological lesson. Whereas sociological approaches have highlighted the distinct temporalities of different social fields (such as politics, law, science or economy), the investigation presented here renders visible the temporal diversity to be found in one of these fields by showing how normative, cognitive and apprehensive orientations toward the future are re-assembled and incorporated in administrative technologies. This chapter therefore opens a wider research agenda that delves into the multiple and hybrid temporalities operative in governmental practice.

Bibliography

Amoore, Louise. *The Politics of Possibility: Risk and Security Beyond Probability*. Durham: Duke University Press, 2013.

Anderson, Ben. 'Preemption, Precaution, Preparedness: Anticipatory Action and Future Geographies'. *Progress in Human Geography* 34(2010): 777–798.

Aradau, Claudia and van Munster, Rens. *Politics of Catastrophe: Genealogies of the Unknown*. London: Routledge, 2011.

Barad, Karen. *Meeting the Universe Halfway: Quantum Physics and the Entanglement of Matter and Meaning*, Durham: Duke University Press 2007.

Bateson, Gregory. *Steps to an Ecology of Mind*. Chicago: University of Chicago Press, 2000.
Bingham, Nick and Steve Hinchliffe. 'Securing Life: The Emerging Practices of Biosecurity'. *Environment and Planning A* 40 (2008): 1534–1551.
Braun, Bruce. 'Biopolitics and the Molecularization of Life'. *Cultural Geographies* 14 (2007): 6–28.
Caduff, Carlo. 'On the Verge of Death: Vision of Biological Vulnerability'. *Annual Review of Anthropology* 43 (2014): 105–121.
Calhoun, Craig. 'A World of Emergencies: Fear, Intervention, and the Limits of Cosmopolitan Order'. *Canadian Review of Sociology and Anthropology* 41 (2004): 373–395.
Cetron, Martin, Ram Koppake, Susan Maloney and Patricia Simone. 'Isolation and Quarantine: Containment Strategies for SARS 2003'. In *Learning from SARS: Preparing for the Next Disease Outbreak*, edited by Stacey Knobler, Adel Mahmoud, Stanley Lemon, Alison Mack, Laura Sivitz and Katherine Oberholtzer, 71–83. Washington DC: The Washington Academies Press, 2004.
Collier, Stephen J. 'Enacting Catastrophe: Preparedness, Insurance, Budgetary Planning'. *Economy and Society* 37 (2009): 224–250.
Conti, Andrea A., Gian F. Gensini and Magdi H. Yacoub. 'The Concept of Quarantine in History: From Plague to SARS'. *Journal of Infection* 49 (2004): 257–261.
Cooper, Melinda. 'Pre-empting Emergence. The Biological Turn in the War on Terror'. *Theory, Culture & Society* 23 (2006): 113–135.
Deleuze, Gilles. *Bergsonism*. Cambridge: Zone Books, 1991.
Dillon, Michael. 'Governing Terror: The State of Emergency of Biopolitical Emergence'. *International Political Sociology* 1 (2007): 7–28.
Easterling, Keller. *Extrastatecraft: The Power of Infrastructure Space*. London and New York: Verso, 2014.
Edwards, Paul N. *A Vast Machine: Computer Models, Climate Data, and the Politics of Global Warning*. Cambridge: MIT Press, 2010.
Esposito, Elena. *Die Fiktion der wahrscheinlichen Realität*. Berlin: Suhrkamp, 2007.
Fidler, David P. and Lawrence O. Gostin. 'The New International Health Regulations: A Historic Development for International Law and Public Health'. *Journal of Law, Medicine & Ethics* 34 (2006): 85–94.
Figuié, Muriel. 'Towards a Global Governance of Risks: International Health Organisations and the Surveillance of Emerging Infectious Diseases'. *Journal of Risk Research* 17 (2014): 469–483.
Foucault, Michel. *Security, Territory, Population: Lectures at the Collège de France 1977–1978*. Basingstoke: Palgrave, 2007.
French, Martin. 'Gaps in the Gaze: Informatic Practice and the Work of Public Health Surveillance'. *Surveillance & Society* 12 (2014): 226–243.
French, Martin and Eric Mykhalovskiy. 'Public Health Intelligence and the Detection of Potential Pandemics'. *Sociology of Health & Illness*, 35 (2013): 174–197.
Galloway, Alexander R. *The Interface Effect*. Cambridge: Polity, 2012.
de Goede, Marieke and Samuel Randalls. 'Precaution, Preemption: Arts and Technologies of the Actionable Future'. *Environment and Planning D* 27 (2009): 859–878.
Gramelsberger, Gabriele and Erika, Mansnerus. 'The Inner World of Models and Its Epistemic Diversity: Infectious Disease and Climate Modelling'. In *Ways of Thinking, Ways of Seeing: Mathematical and Other Modeling in Engineering and Technology*, edited by Chris Bissell and Chris Dillon, 167–196. Berlin and Heidelberg: Springer, 2012.
Grusin, Richard. 'Premediation'. *Criticism* 46 (2004): 17–39.

Harrison, Mark. *Contagion: How Commerce has Spread Disease.* New Haven: Yale University Press, 2012.
Hartmann, Stephan. 'The World as a Process: Simulations in the Natural and Social Sciences'. In *Simulation and Modelling in the Social Sciences from the Philosophy of Science Point of View*, edited by Rainer Hegselmann, Ulrich Mueller and Klaus G. Triotzsch, 77–100. Kluwer: Dordrecht, 1996.
Hörl, Erich. 'Knowledge in the Age of Simulation – Metatechnical Reflections'. In *Simulation: Presentation Technique and Cognitive Method*, edited by Andrea Gleiniger and Georg Vrachliotis, 93–105. Basel: Birkhauser, 2008.
Humphreys, Paul. *Extending Ourselves: Computational Science, Empiricism and Scientific Method.* Oxford: Oxford University Press, 2007.
Jones, Kate, Nikkita G. Patel, Marc A. Levy, Adam Storeygard, Deborah Balk, John L. Gittleman and Peter Daszak. 'Global Trends in Emerging Infecioust Diseases'. *Nature* 451 (2008): 990–994.
Kockelman, Paul. 'The Anthropology of an Equation: Sieves, Spam Filters, Agentive Algorithms, and Ontologies of Transformation'. *HAU: Journal of Ethnographic Theory* 3 (2013): 33–61.
Kupferschmidt, Kai. 'Disease Modelers Project a Rapidly Rising Toll from Ebola'. *Science Insider*, August 31, 2014.
Lakoff, Andrew. 'Epidemic Intelligence: Toward a Genealogy of Global Health Security'. In *Contagion: Health, Fear, Sovereignty*, edited by Bruno Magnusson and Zahi Zalloua, 44–70. Seattle: University of Washington Press, 2012.
Latour, Bruno. *Reassembling the Social.* Oxford: Oxford University Press, 2005.
Latour, Bruno. *The Making of Law: An Ethnography of the Counseil D'État.* Cambridge: Politiy Press, 2010.
Lederberg, Joshua, Robert E. Shope and Stanley C. Oaks, ed. *Emerging Infections: Microbial Threats to Health in the United States.* Washington DC: National Academy Press, 1992.
Luhmann, Niklas. *Ausdifferenzierung des Rechts. Beiträge zur Rechtssoziologie und Rechtstheorie.* Berlin: Suhrkamp, 1999.
Luhmann, Niklas. *Law as a Social System.* Oxford: Oxford University Press, 2004.
Luhmann, Niklas. *Social Systems.* Stanford: Stanford University Press, 1995.
Luhmann, Niklas. 'The Future Cannot Begin: Temporal Structures in Modern Society'. *Social Research* 43 (1976): 130–152.
Mackenzie, Adrian and Theo Vurdubakis. 'Code and Coding in Crisis: Signification, Performativity and Excess'. *Theory, Culture & Society* 28 (2011): 3–23.
Mansnerus, Erika. 'Using Model-Based Evidence in the Governance of Pandemics'. In *Pandemics and Emerging Infectious Disease: The Sociological Agenda*, edited by Robert Dingwall, Lily M. Hoffman and Karen Staniland, 110–121. Malden and Oxford: Wiley 2013, 110–121.
Massumi, Brian. 'National Enterprise Emergency: Steps Towards an Ecology of Powers'. *Theory Culture & Society* 26 (2009): 153–185.
Massumi, Brian. 'Potential Politics and the Primacy of Preemption'. *Theory and Event* 10 (2007): marginalia 1–34.
Morse, Stephen S., ed. *Emerging Viruses.* Oxford: University Press, 1993.
Moulton, Anthony D., Richard N. Gottfried, Richard A. Goodman, Anne M. Murphey and Raymond D. Rawson. 'What is Public Health Legal Preparedness?'. *Journal of Law, Medicine & Ethics* 31 (2003): 672–683.

Ooi, Peng L., Sonny Lim and Suok Kai. 'Use of Quarantine in the Control of SARS in Singapore'. *American Journal of Infection Control* 33 (2005): 252–257.

Opitz, Sven. *An der Grenze des Rechts: Inklusion/Exklusion im Zeichen der Sicherheit.* Weilerswist: Vehlbrück, 2012.

Opitz, Sven. 'Regulating Epidemic Space: The Nomos of Global Circulation'. *Journal of International Relations and Development* 19 (2016): 263–284.

Opitz, Sven and Ute Tellmann. 'Future Emergencies: Temporal Politics in Law and Economy'. *Theory, Culture & Society* 32 (2015): 107–129.

Pias, Claus. 'On the Epistemology of Computer Simulation'. *Zeitschrift für Medien- und Kulturforschung* 2 (2011): 29–54.

Ruppert, Evelyn, John Law and Mike Savage, ed. *The Social Life of Methods*, Special Issue of *Theory, Culture and Society* 30 (2011).

Samimian-Darash, Limor. 'Governing Future Potential Biothreats: Toward an Anthropology of Uncertainty'. *Current Anthropology* 54 (2013): 1–22.

Scheuerman, William. *Liberal Democracy and the Social Acceleration of Time.* Baltimore: Johns Hopkins University Press, 2004.

Taylor, Dianna. 'Normativity and Normalization'. *Foucault Studies* 7 (2009): 45–63.

Thomas, Lindsay. 'Pandemics of the Future: Disease Surveillance in Real Time'. *Surveillance & Society* 12 (2014): 287–300.

Thrift, Nigel. *Non-Representational Theory: Space, Politics, Affect.* London: Routledge, 2007.

van Wagner, Estair. 'The Practice of Biosecurity in Canada: Public Health Legal Preparedness and Toronto's SARS Crisis'. *Environment and Planning A* 40 (2008): 1647–1663.

Wald, Priscilla. *Contagious: Cultures, Carriers, and the Outbreak Narrative.* Durham: Duke University Press, 2008.

Waller, Emily, Mark Davis and Niamh Stephenson, Australia's Pandemic Influenza "Protect" Phase: Emerging Out of the Fog of Pandemic'. *Critical Public Health* ahead-of-print (2014): 1–15.

Weir, Lorna and Eric Mykhalovskiy, *Global Public Health Vigilance: Creating a World on Alert.* London: Routledge, 2010.

WHO, *Statement on the 3rd Meeting of the IHR Emergency Committee Regarding the 2014 Ebola Outbreak in West Africa*, October 23 2014.

WHO, *Statement on the 2nd Meeting of the IHR Emergency Committee Regarding the 2014 Ebola Outbreak in West Africa*, September 22 2014.

Winsberg, Eric. *Science in the Age of Computer Simulation.* Chicago: Chicago University Press, 2010.

Wolfe, Nathan. *The Viral Storm: The Dawn of a New Pandemic Age.* London: Allen Lane, 2011.

Chapter 10

Immediacy, *potentia* and constraining emergency powers

Bas Schotel

Introduction

One of the fundamental challenges for public law is how to enable authorities to take effective measures in times of emergency and by the same token put legal constraints on those same emergency powers. It seems that the enabling and constraining functions of law are reverse proportionate: the more emergency powers are effective the less effective are the constraints. Experts of public law have pointed out various causes for the problem of putting effective legal constraints on emergency powers.[1] In his contribution to this volume on law and time, Marc de Wilde singles out an additional cause, namely the temporal assumption underlying emergencies. Often emergencies are presented as an unprecedented future justifying very comprehensive emergency powers and giving some of these powers an almost permanent character in the normal legal order. Taking cue from this temporal dimension, I will explore how the tendency of emergency powers becoming permanent is reinforced by another temporal dimension, namely immediacy. Immediacy refers to the capacity of authorities to perform actions *without intermediary* and *immediately*. When authorities perform directly factual actions – do physical things – they act immediately. *Potentia* represents the capacity to perform factual actions.

The paper will start by a brief schematic explanation of how public law enables and constrains public power in times of normality, i.e. when emergency powers do not apply.[2] The enabling and constraining functions are linked to law's normal temporal categories of *ex ante* and *ex post*. Emergencies tend to elude these temporal categories, catering to more permanent emergency powers. This chapter will then discuss the nature of factual actions, *potentia* and immediacy. It will become clear how already in times of normality, factual actions and *potentia* defy law's normal constraints and temporal categories. The final section explores how the combination of *potentia* and emergency produces a logic of permanent immediacy, which in turn makes it difficult to put legal constraints on emergency powers.

1 See below footnotes 3–7.
2 I hereafter use 'law' as to mean 'public law', unless explicitly stated otherwise.

Emergency powers, legal constraints and time

The starting point for this chapter is one of the perennial challenges of public law: the tension between the effective exercise of public power, democratic legitimacy and individual legal protection. On the one hand, the public expects its government to have the means to effectively pursue legitimate public goals (e.g. security, health). On the other hand, precisely taking measures that are effective may hamper individual legal protection. The law mirrors this tension by both enabling and constraining public authorities. So the law grants powers to public authorities enabling them to take measures. By the same token, the law constrains the authorities as they can only act within limits of these powers. In terms of time, this legal mechanism operates *ex ante* or forward looking. Apart from an *ex ante* constraint, public law also enables and constrains the exercise of public power *ex post* or backward looking. So when officials exercise their powers (granted *ex ante*) their actions are subject to judicial review. Judicial review is both a constraint and enabler of executive action as it determines what actions are legally permitted. Though temporally separated the *ex ante* and *ex post* mechanisms continuously inform each other: the *ex ante* powers inform the decision *ex post* and actors rely on *ex post* decisions to determine the scope of their *ex ante* powers. The challenge for law is that too much enabling compromises the constraining function, and vice versa. Similarly, when *ex ante* powers become too comprehensive and broad they compromise the *ex post* constraints. In other words, the challenge for public law is how to keep the enabling and constraining function in check. Likewise from a temporal perspective, the *ex ante* and *ex post* mechanisms must be kept in balance.

This perennial tension between effectiveness (law's enabling function) and legal protection (law's constraining function) is magnified in the context of emergency powers. If the competences granted to the authorities for dealing with emergencies are defined too restrictively and exhaustively, executive authorities may lack the power to take effective measures. By contrast, if competences are formulated too open ended then judicial protection and democratic checks by parliament may come under pressure. Accordingly, legal scholars often call for using existing (or introducing new) constitutional possibilities to put limits on such wide discretion in terms of time, space and subject matter. By the same token, scholars disagree about the desirability and even possibility of regulating emergency powers. At one end of the spectrum emergency powers are just an extension of the 'normal' regime. In other words, they simply highlight the fundamental tensions already present under 'normal' conditions: the state of exception is always everywhere.[3] At the other end of the spectrum, emergency powers do pose a categorically different problem for the normal legal order. They point to the limits of the normal

3 Ontologically: Giorgio Agamben, *State of Exception* (trans. K. Attell) (Chicago: The University of Chicago Press, 2005); in administrative law: Adrian Vermeule, 'Our Schmittian Administrative Law', *Harvard Law Review* 122 (2009), 1095–1149; practically Eric Posner and Adrian Vermeule, *The Executive Unbound: After the Madisonian Republic* (Oxford: Oxford University Press, 2010).

constitutional order that is otherwise sufficiently capable of dealing with the constitutional challenge under normal conditions. Accordingly, it means that some matters are ultimately beyond the reach of the law.[4] Alternatively the constitutional regime itself must be re-designed in order to bring truly exceptional emergency powers under the normality of the law.[5] Or, the traditional checks and balances should be applied more vigorously albeit *ex post* (primarily through judicial review).[6] Another suggestion combines traditional checks and constitutional re-design and calls for a legalized regime of emergency powers that might be relatively easily mobilized but each time with limited scope. The upshot of this proposal is that emergencies are still governed by law without emergency powers becoming permanent and perverting the ordinary constitutional regime.[7] Still, these attempts to legally capture emergency powers cannot fundamentally address the tension between effective emergency measures and effective legal constraints. Moreover, often elements of the emergency powers tend to endure even if strictly speaking the emergency situation ceases to exist.

One reason why it is so difficult to put effective legal constraints on emergency powers has been pointed out by Marc de Wilde in his contribution. He argues that often emergency powers are created against the backdrop of a highly problematic temporal assumption that emergencies are inherently unprecedented.[8] Emergency powers are called for to cope with events that may threaten the nation but that have not occurred before. In concrete terms, the next terrorist attack is not like just any other future event. Neither do we know *when* a horrible event will occur, nor do we know *what* danger to expect which will cause the next emergency. Emergency has become a matter of radical uncertainty: an unknown-unknown.[9] In terms of legal constraints, unprecedented future eludes the temporal categories of normal law *ex ante* and *ex post*. Since the emergency is unprecedented it cannot be provided for *ex ante*. Similarly, the emergency measures escape *ex post* judicial check because there are simply no standards for evaluating the actions of the authorities for lack of precedence. And if authorities were to be held accountable *ex post* they may be reluctant to take effective measures next time when confronted with an unprecedented emergency. In a way, the law's normal legal

4 E.g. Owen Gross, 'Chaos and Rules: Should Responses to Violent Crises Always Be Constitutional?' *The Yale Law Journal* 112 (2003), 1011–1134.

5 E.g. Bruce Ackerman, 'The Emergency Constitution', *The Yale Law Journal* 113 (2004), 1029–1091.

6 E.g. David Dyzenhaus, *The Constitution of Law: Legality in a Time of Emergency* (Cambridge: Cambridge University Press, 2006).

7 Henk Kummeling, 'Recht in nood', in *Crises, rampen en recht*, ed. E. R. Muller et al., Handelingen Nederlandse Juristen-Vereniging 144 (2014), 291–298.

8 Marc De Wilde, 'Uncertain Futures and the Problem of Constraining Emergency Powers: Temporal Dimensions of Carl Schmitt's Theory of the State of Exception', in this volume.

9 For an in depth study on the uses and meaning of unprecedented future and the notion of 'unknown-unknowns', see Claudia Aradau and Rens van Munster, *Politics of Catastrophe. Genealogies of the Unknown* (Abingdon/New York: Routledge, 2011).

constraints and temporal categories are put out of order. The perverse upshot of this logic is that it paves the way for making the absence of effective legal constraints on executive power a permanent feature of public law.

The perversion of law's normal temporal categories and the permanence of emergency powers is powerfully illustrated by Karin Loewy's discussion of the 1999 Israeli Supreme Court decision on the illegality of torture.[10] The Supreme Court held that torture is illegal, even in times of emergency. As a result, security agents who tortured suspects are criminally liable. So at the face of it, the Supreme Court resisted the perversion of law's normal constraints and temporal categories. Yet, the Court also said that under particular conditions the agents could invoke the necessity defence. By the same token, according to the Court it was up to the Attorney General to 'establish Guidelines regarding circumstances in which investigators shall not stand trial if they claim to have acted from necessity.'[11] The combination of an *ex ante* prohibition on torture and the availability of an *ex post* necessity defence is in keeping with law's normal constraints and temporal categories. By contrast, the Guidelines stipulating detailed procedures for investigators if they want to successfully invoke the necessity defence amount to an *ex ante* legalization of torture. Thus, in the end under pressure of the logic of emergency, the normal temporal *ex post* and *ex ante* categories are compressed making exceptional emergency measures – that are normally illegal – permanently legal.

In the next two sections I will argue that the perverse temporal effects on the law's capacity to constrain emergency powers are reinforced by the use of factual actions and *potentia*.

Factual actions, *potentia*[12] and time

When legal scholars discuss emergency powers, they rarely distinguish between the types of the powers involved. However, from the perspective of law's constraining function it matters to distinguish between measures that consist of issuing directives and measures that constitute factual actions. For example, in the context of

10 Karin Loevy, *Emergencies in Public Law. The Legal Politics of Containment* (Cambridge: Cambridge University Press, 2016), 234–243.

11 Ibid., 237.

12 The following discussion is a summarized version of a part of a broader inquiry into the connection between factual actions, potentia and potentia. Bas Schotel, '*Potentia* and Public Law. Legal protection and the buildup of *factual* public power' (forthcoming). That paper draws for the notion of *potentia* on Michael Oakeshott, 'The Character of a Modern European State', in *Lectures in the History of Political Thought*, Michael Oakeshott (Exeter: Imprint Academic, 2006), 369–371; Michael Oakeshott, 'On the Character of a Modern European State',' in *On Human Conduct*, Michael Oakeshott (Oxford: Clarendon, 1975), 194–195 (not calling it *potentia*); Martin Loughlin, *Foundations of Public Law* (Oxford: Oxford University Press, 2010), 164–171, 407–434; (indirectly) Christopher Hood and Helen Margetts, *The Tools of Government in the Digital Age* (Palgrave Macmillan, 2007) References have been omitted in this summarized version. The notion of immediacy is not discussed in that paper.

an emergency, authorities may impose a curfew prohibiting citizens from entering certain public spaces. This measure is a form of issuing norms or decrees. Simultaneously, in order to effectively implement the curfew and to prevent people to enter certain public areas officials may take factual actions, e.g. building road blocks, patrolling, detaining citizens, etc. In our example, the factual measures are of a rather coercive nature. To be sure many factual actions taken in the context of an emergency need not be coercive as such, e.g. building extra IT protection, installing secure communication lines, gathering information, recruiting new intelligence employees, training security personnel, building new safe-houses, etc.

For want of a better word in English,[13] factual action means an action (or deliberate inaction) that has a tangible effect in physical reality. For example, building a road, placing a surveillance camera, teaching children, driving a bus, putting someone in a prison. The difference between factual action and *potentia* is that the latter is the *capacity* or *power* to perform such factual actions.[14] Probably, the most important form of *potentia* or factual capacity is the corps of loyal, trained, equipped officials (civil and military), as well as tactical and strategic assets (real estate, logistic, information technology and communication infrastructure, and natural resources). I distinguish factual power from the power to issue directives. The latter includes instances whereby authorities set, confirm or apply norms and decisions. So it covers laws, regulations, standards, judgments, decisions, instructions, orders, etc. Typically, under public law doctrine such acts are characterized as legal acts.

From a practical and even theoretical perspective the distinction between factual actions and issuing directives is not watertight. Any form of issuing directives involves factual actions, and any factual action implies a legal or normative background that either authorizes or at least makes epistemic sense of the factual action.[15] Yet, the distinction is meaningful from the perspective of legal constraints on executive power. For example, a typical legal *ex ante* constraint such as competence works relatively effectively when constraining the public power to issue directives. For the effectiveness of a directive depends largely on its perceived authority, legality being an important element in this respect. To ensure the effectiveness of their directives, officials may need the legitimacy bonus that comes with showing respect for the rule of law, e.g. the principle of legality. Precisely because the power of a directive relies partially on its capacity to be obeyed, it matters whether or not the authorities were competent to issue the directive. As a

13 In French administrative law: acte matériel. In German administrative law: Tathandlung.

14 *Potentia* means not only the capacity to do things but also the capacity not to do it. For purposes of this chapter I concentrate on situations where the *potentia* will be exercised and how *potentia* that is too strong makes it difficult to put legal constraints on factual actions.

15 So understanding a phenomenon as a form of 'agency' already presupposes a whole normative background of attributing intentions and actions to agents.

result, a directive that is issued ultra vires is more likely to be simply discarded by norm subjects. Or to say the same from the perspective of legal protection, norm subjects can mount effective legal challenges against the power to issue directives, by simply disobeying in the name of the law ('you are not authorized to issue this directive, so I will not obey it. If you have a problem with it, sue me'). By contrast, when it comes to factual actions, it is more difficult for competence to constrain public authorities when they have simply the 'physical ability to act directly'. For sure, when performing factual actions, officials may have an interest in showing they respect the rule of law in order to avoid resistance and obstruction by subjects. But what if in certain domains the factual power is so strong and well organized that resistance and obstruction are very unlikely? Under such conditions officials can afford to act purely factually without the authority of the law. As a result basic rule of law principles such as legality and proportionality have little constraining force.[16]

In short, when the exercise of emergency powers consists of factual action it is more difficult for the law to constrain *ex ante*, especially when the capacity to perform such factual actions is significant. For sure, there is still the *ex post* check of, for example, judicial review. However, in a fundamental way factual actions escape even *ex post* judicial constraints. The very nature of factual actions in a way defies law's normal temporal categories of the *ex ante* and *ex post* constraints. Factual actions are a matter of immediacy. Immediacy has two meanings here: without intermediary and immediately. Factual actions take place *without the intermediary* of non-officials. Rather than governing through issuing legal directives to citizens, officials intervene directly and simply do the things themselves. And factual actions take place *immediately*, i.e. in the presence without delays. Precisely this immediacy in tangible reality makes factual actions elude the *ex ante* and *ex post* constraints.

Legal scholars have paid little to no attention to how factual actions pose a fundamental challenge for legal protection.[17] Even a legal scholar such as Carl Schmitt, who was very much preoccupied with the concrete and factual, only spends a few words on the matter. Still, these very brief snippets do get to the core of the problem. So when Schmitt seeks to show that under the Weimar constitution the *Reichspräsident* can suspend virtually all articles of the constitution under the state of exception, he spends some time on the legal nature of executive measures.[18] In this respect he states that such executive measures may include

16 To be sure even when powerless in constraining factual actions, the rule of law can still function in such circumstances as a critical standard for voicing indignation and disapproval (similar to human rights in international politics), but it loses its juridical function.

17 Elsewhere, I trace the historical reasons for this lack of attention in Schotel, '*Potentia*'.

18 Carl Schmitt, 'Die Diktatur des Reichspräsidenten nach Art. 48 der Weimarer Verfassung', *Veröffentlichungen der Vereinigung deutscher Staatsrechtslehrer* (1924), reprinted in *Die Diktatur. Von den Anfängen des modernen Souveränitätsgedanken bis zum proletarischen Klassenkampf*, Carl Schmitt, 6th ed. (Berlin: Duncker & Humblot, 1994).

factual actions.[19] And in a similar discussion some years later he explicitly points out the force of such *factual* emergency measures (e.g. armed intervention and shooting people). Though the ordinary legislator (the democratically elected parliament) may invalidate the emergency measures, the factual measures are a *fait accompli*.[20] More importantly, the factual measures themselves cannot be invalidated or their legal force cannot be cancelled.[21] In effect, one of the strongest constraints on legal acts is the mechanism of validation and invalidation, which corresponds with law's normal temporal categories of *ex ante* and *ex post*. When it comes to factual actions legal validity of the legal act authorizing the factual action may be important, but what really matters is the ability to physically do it, i.e. *potentia*. In terms of time, law's normal temporal categories reflect on acts in the future or in the past, while *potentia* makes it possible to act in the immediacy.

Potentia, emergency and permanent immediacy

By their very nature factual actions and *potentia* elude law's normal constraints and its temporal *ex ante* and *ex post* categories. This insight may provide an additional explanation for why law has difficulties constraining emergency powers. Factual actions and *potentia* reinforce the permanency of emergency powers. The starting point is the need for effective measures. In normal times effective government requires not only measures consisting of legal directives but also measures that constitute factual actions. Allegedly, the need for factual actions is even greater in times of emergency. Precisely their immediacy is what make factual actions particularly effective.

In order to actually take factual action immediately, authorities must have the capacity to perform factual actions, i.e. *potentia*. Authorities must be battle ready, if not they will be too late. The question is how much *potentia* is needed when and for how long. Here, the logic of *potentia* meets the temporal assumption that emergencies are unprecedented. Since we do not know what new emergency to expect there is in theory no limitation to the *potentia* needed. So we could never be too much prepared. Also since the emergencies are a matter of an unprecedented future and we never know when the next emergency will occur, there cannot be any time limits on *potentia*. In short, this temporal logic associated with emergencies paves the way for an unlimited *potentia*.

Furthermore, the need for immediacy associated with factual actions and *potentia* reinforces the permanence of emergency powers. This may be illustrated if one thinks through the brief discussion of the Israeli Supreme Court case on the torture. The Court established a general prohibition on torture but would accept

19 'unmittelbare Aktion', '*vi armata*', 'bloss faktische Vorgehen', 'rein tatsächliche Massnahmen' all at Schmitt, 'Diktatur des Reichspräsidenten', 246.

20 'vollendete Tatsachen schaffen' Carl Schmitt, *Legalität und Legitimität* (1932) 8th ed. (Berlin: Duncker & Humblot, 2012), 67.

21 So the shooting of people cannot be 'ausser Kraft gesetzt werden', Schmitt, *Legalität*, 67.

necessity as a defence in individual cases provided the investigators followed the detailed Guidelines issued by the AG. If we look at this arrangement from a European human rights law perspective the problem of immediacy and *potentia* becomes clear. In the famous GDR Border Guard cases the ECtHR looked at the issue of the killings by GDR border guards of people trying to illegally cross the border from East to Western Berlin.[22] German criminal courts condemned the senior officials who designed the shoot to kill policy and the border guards who did the killings. The ECtHR held that these criminal condemnations did not constitute a violation of the ECHR. Interesting, for purposes of this contribution is that the Court treated the senior officials who designed the policy and the border guards in separate cases. The Court found rather easily that the criminal liability of the policy makers was compatible with the ECHR. Yet the question whether the border guards could use the shoot to kill policy as a defence was more complicated. For example a dissenting judge found that they could have relied on this policy.[23] According to his view the senior officials could be held liable while the individual rank and file could be excused. The Court ruled differently and found that the criminal liability of the border guards was also compatible with the ECHR: there was no retroactive application of criminal laws.

Now, both the European Court's majority decision and the dissenting opinion run counter to the Israeli solution. The Israeli Court exempts both policy makers who design the infrastructure that violates the prohibition on torture (in this case the AG[24]) and the agents committing the actual torture. In the European human rights setting the designer of the policy and/or the agents should be held liable if the prohibition on torture is taken seriously. Yet, precisely the concept of immediacy explains the alleged expediency of the Israeli solution. If the individual agents would be held liable then the government would lack the efficacy of having its own agents directly doing the interrogations with torture. In other words, the authorities would lack immediacy in terms of acting *without intermediary*. If the designers of the policy would be held liable then, there would not be an infrastructure in place that makes the interrogations with torture possible when you need it. So, the authorities would lack immediacy in terms of acting *immediately*. The upshot is a kind of permanent immediacy.

A key feature of this permanent immediacy is the amount of *potentia* built up by the authorities. The challenge from the perspective of law is that there are hardly any legal mechanisms available that put constraints on the build-up of *potentia*. The most important constraint is the right of budget. It is the legal right of parliament to vote the budget and thereby determining the allocation of resources to the government. Yet the exercise of the right of budget is a matter of political

22 K.- H.W. v. Germany, 2001 Eur. Ct. H.R. (Mar. 22), hereafter *K.- H.W. v. Germany* (case of the border guards); Krenz et al. v. Germany, 2001 Eur. Ct. H.R. (Mar. 22) (case of the policy makers).

23 Judge Cabral Barreto, para. 1 of partly dissenting opinion under *K.- H.W. v. Germany*.

24 If the AG has immunity then the department under which the office of the AG falls should be held liable.

democracy, not juridical constraints. Moreover, in the context of emergencies the normal democratic constraints resulting from differences in political platforms and factions vanish with the tendency to 'rally behind the flag'.[25]

Finally, *potentia* is very difficult to unwind. There are legal mechanisms in place that can effectively constrain emergency powers that pertain to issuing legal directives. They basically limit those competences in time. This can be done on forehand, sunset clauses. Or by making it easy to withdraw the competences later on. In fact, the emergency power to issue legal directives can be removed in a split second. And even when for example the parliamentary or legislative procedures for ending emergency powers do not offer sufficient constraint, courts can easily cast doubt on legal validity of legal directives issued on the basis of alleged emergency powers, even if it is contested whether the courts are competent to do so. Again, the power to issue legal directives is a matter of legal authority which can be contested and constrained by making legal counter claims. By contrast, when already available *potentia* cannot be easily withdrawn, precisely because *potentia* is a matter of human resources and equipment. Unlike legal competence, you cannot make people and infrastructure disappear with just words. The examples of provisional infrastructure (e.g. camps) becoming permanent are innumerable. But also it is very difficult to de-mobilize large groups of people that have been trained and employed for certain tasks (e.g. armies). So even when times of normality have returned, emergency powers have been withdrawn and officials have discarded the rhetoric of emergency, *potentia* as a permanent power of immediacy remains.

Conclusions

This chapter started from one of the fundamental challenges for public law: how to enable governmental authorities to act effectively and by the same token put legal constraints on them. The connection between effective measures and effective legal constraints seems reverse proportionate: the more governmental powers are effective the less effective are the legal constraints. This challenge is present in times of normality but becomes most evident in times of emergency. The chapter claims that this challenge is reinforced by a temporal dimension that has received little attention by legal scholars, namely immediacy.

In the context of emergency powers, the difficulty of putting effective legal constraints on governmental powers is partially caused by the temporal assumptions underlying emergency powers. Increasingly authorities call for emergency powers in order to cope with events that may threaten the nation but that have not occurred before, i.e. an unprecedented future. The notion of unprecedented future constitutes a challenge for effective legal constraints because it defies the

25 Marc De Wilde, 'Uncertain Futures',, with reference in fn 3 to Mark Tushnet, 'Controlling Executive Power in the War on Terrorism' *Harvard Law Review* 118 (2005), 2678.

normal temporal *ex ante* and *ex post* categories of law. When an emergency is presented as unprecedented it paves the way for a *carte blanche* authorization compromising the possible constraining effect of *ex ante* powers. By the same token, the emergency measures elude *ex post* judicial checks because there are no concrete standards for evaluating the actions of the authorities for lack of precedents. Holding the authorities accountable *ex post* allegedly would make them reluctant to take effective measures next time when confronted with an unprecedented emergency. Apart from the temporal category of unprecedented future, emergency powers also have the tendency of compressing law's normal *ex ante* and *ex post* temporal categories into a single temporal category of permanency. This was illustrated by the Israeli Supreme Court ruling on torture.

In this chapter I have argued that the fundamental challenge of putting legal constraints on emergency powers is reinforced by the temporal category of immediacy. To be effective, not only must authorities issue special or exceptional legal directives (e.g. special laws, regulations, decrees, orders, decisions, etc.). They must also perform physical or factual actions (e.g. surveillance, arresting suspects). These physical acts must be carried out in the immediate presence and often they are to be carried out without intermediary, i.e. by the officials themselves. But in order to act immediately authorities need to have on forehand the capacity to perform the factual actions. Only when they have the capacity to perform factual actions, i.e. *potentia*, can they act immediately when needed.

Combined with the logic of permanency and unprecedented future, the need for *potentia* creates a paradoxical temporal category of permanent immediacy. In order to respond effectively and immediately to any unprecedented emergency authorities allegedly need a theoretically unlimited *potentia*. *Potentia* and the temporal category of immediacy pose an additional challenge for public law's capacity to constrain emergency powers for three reasons. Firstly, public law has more difficulties constraining the exercise of *potentia* than constraining the exercise of legal authority. For it is easier to mount effective legal challenges against measures that consist of legal directives than against measures that consist of physical actions. Secondly, the most important constraint on the build-up of *potentia* is the parliamentary right to budget. Yet, precisely in the context of emergencies the tendency 'to rally behind the flag' significantly compromises the constraining effect of the right of budget. Finally, emergency powers that consist of issuing legal directives can be easily countered and withdrawn by legal interventions. By contrast, when already available *potentia* cannot be unwound by simply issuing a new statute or legal order: unlike legal competence, you cannot make people and infrastructure disappear physically by just changing the law.

This is not the place to discuss how lawyers may increase public law's capacity to constrain emergency powers in light of *potentia*[26] and the temporal category of immediacy. Yet, bearing in mind the theme of this volume, I believe the notion of

26 Elsewhere I provide concrete suggestions how to organize legal constraints on the buildup of potentia, Schotel, '*Potentia*'.

immediacy and *potentia* may point legal scholars to at least three areas of further inquiry. Firstly, we may want to get a more thorough understanding of the distinction between measures that consist of issuing legal directives and measures that consist of physical actions. With a view to legal protection, scholars should examine afresh to what extent the doctrinal categories of public law and especially administrative law capture this distinction. Secondly, scholars may explore the various ways public law can (and cannot) constrain the build-up of *potentia*. In this respect, they may draw on areas of public law where there is quite some experience in constraining the build-up of factual capacity such as environmental law and competition law – albeit factual capacity of private actors, and not public authorities. Finally, the temporal category of immediacy may have close links with the legal institution of the writ of execution under administrative law. The privilege of the writ of execution for public authorities is a key feature of administrative law in general and crucial in the context of emergency powers. Yet, legal scholarship seems to take this legal institution for granted: there is little legal scholarship examining the doctrinal, historical and normative aspects associated with the administration's writ of execution. In short, the temporal category of immediacy may help us better understand basic features of public law that have been either overlooked or taken for granted, in both times of emergency and normality.

Bibliography

Ackerman, Bruce. 'The Emergency Constitution'. *The Yale Law Journal* 113 (2004), 1029–1091.

Agamben, Giorgio. *State of Exception* (trans. K. Attell). Chicago: The University of Chicago Press, 2005.

Aradau, Claudia and Rens van Munster. *Politics of Catastrophe. Genealogies of the Unknown.* Abingdon and New York: Routledge, 2011.

Dyzenhaus, David. *The Constitution of Law: Legality in a Time of Emergency.* Cambridge: Cambridge University Press, 2006.

Gross, Owen. 'Chaos and Rules: Should Responses to Violent Crises Always Be Constitutional?'. *The Yale Law Journal* 112 (2003), 1011–1134.

Hood, Christopher and Helen Margetts. *The Tools of Government in the Digital Age* Basingstoke: Palgrave Macmillan, 2007.

Kummeling, Henk. 'Recht in nood'. In *Crises, rampen en recht*, edited by E. R. Muller et al., Handelingen Nederlandse Juristen-Vereniging 144 (2014), 291–298.

Loevy, Karin. *Emergencies in Public Law. The Legal Politics of Containment.* Cambridge: Cambridge University Press, 2016.

Loughlin, Martin. *Foundations of Public Law.* Oxford: Oxford University Press, 2010.

Oakeshott, Michael. 'The Character of a Modern European State'. In *Lectures in the History of Political Thought*, M. Oakeshott. Exeter: Imprint Academic, 2006.

Oakeshott, Michael. 'On the Character of a Modern European State'. In *On Human Conduct*, M. Oakeshott. Oxford: Clarendon, 1975.

Posner, Eric and Adrian Vermeule. *The Executive Unbound: After the Madisonian Republic* Oxford: Oxford University Press, 2010.

Schmitt, Carl. 'Die Diktatur des Reichspräsidenten nach Art. 48 der Weimarer Verfassung'. *Veröffentlichungen der Vereinigung deutscher Staatsrechtslehrer* (1924), reprinted in *Die Diktatur. Von den Anfängen des modernen Souveränitätsgedanken bis zum proletarischen Klassenkampf*, Carl Schmitt. 6th ed. Berlin: Duncker & Humblot, 1994.

Schmitt, Carl. *Legalität und Legitimität* (1932) 8th ed. Berlin: Duncker & Humblot, 2012.

Schotel, Bas. 'Potentia and Public Law. Legal Protection and the Buildup of Factual Public Power' (forthcoming).

Tushnet, Mark. 'Controlling Executive Power in the War on Terrorism'. *Harvard Law Review* 118 (2005), 2673–2682.

Vermeule, Adrian. 'Our Schmittian Administrative Law'. *Harvard Law Review* 122 (2009), 1095–1149.

Index

Ackerman, Bruce 123n51
ad hoc legislation 33
Améry, Jean 22–3
amnesty 66, 153
anti-discrimination legislation 42
appeasement politics 151
Arendt, Hannah 21n18, 23–4, 42n54, 59, 63, 68
Arnold, Thurman 149
Australia: constitutional amendment 142, 142n42; Constitutional Convention (1998) 141; Constitutional Preamble 141–2; republican movement 141, 142, 142n2
authority: of judiciary 102–4; and time 88–9
authority-paradox 104n71

Barroso, José Manuel 109n6
Bateson, Gregory 172, 177–8
Bauman, Zygmunt 22
Bell, Coral 16
Benhabib, Seyla 160
Benjamin, Walter 111n11
Berlin, Isaiah 160
Bloch, Ernst 50
Brad, Karen 184n51
Brandt, Willy 17
Brown vs. Board of Education 34, 49
Brüning, Henrich 120
burnout 80–1
Bush, George W. 109n5

Caesar Augustus 139
Camus, Albert 26, 28
Canada: symbolic laws 131n9
Carlyle, Thomas 157
Chamberlain, Neville 151
change: resistance to 34–8, 43–6; and time 89, 89n7
China see People's Republic of China
Chirac, Jacques 17
Churchill, Winston 151
civil law actions: over historical injustice 17
code/coding 178–9, 179n34
collective identity 164
collective memory 150; codification 159; culture as 166–7; as internal constructs of social systems 167; in law and politics 152–4; politics of shared memories 151–2
complementarity 29–30, 31
computer simulations 171–2, 177, 182–7
constituent power 164–6
constitution-making 40–1, 153
constitutional conventions 127, 133, 143
constitutional law 84; distinguished from constitution itself 117–18; and emergency powers 115–19
constitutional preambles: function of 126; historically oriented preambles 134–5; Hungarian constitution 135–7; political and symbolic significance 132–4; situating the state in time 132–5; time talk in 131–2; and the uncertain future 140–3
constitutional principles 160–3
constitutional values 160–1
constitutionalism: paradox of 165
constitutions: Aristotelian perspective 128; Benthamite perspective 128–9; Lockean perspective 128–9; promulgation of 126, 127, 130; protection of substance 117–18; purpose 128–31; and the uncertain future 128–31; unwritten/pre-modern 126, 127, 130; written

constitutions 126–7, 130–1, 140–3; see also specific state constitutions, e.g. Hungarian Basic Law
constructive interpretation 39
contingency awareness 96
Convention on the Non-Applicability of Statutory Limitations to Crimes against Humanity and War Crimes (UN, 1968) 54
Corrias, Luigi 6n26, 8, 49n92
Craven, Greg 141, 142
crimes against humanity: concept 21; imprescriptibility 54, 57; monstrosity of 23–4
criminal justice: politics and 15–16
criminal law: role in security 7; see also international criminal law
criminal proceedings: crimes against humanity 24; over historical injustice 15–16, 17
cultural holism 160
cultural identity 158
cultural nationalism 157–60
culture: as collective memory 166–7; concept of 149–50, 160–1, 164; holistic concept 157–8, 160–1
Czech Republic 151
Czechoslovakia 151, 164

De Baets, Antoon 60–2, 63
de Wilde, Marc 9–10, 127, 192
de-synchronization: inter-social 82–4; intra-social 81–2; macro-level 79–80; micro-level 80–1; problem of 79; and social acceleration 79–84, 91–2, 96
Deleuze, Gilles 185
Demjanjuk, John 60
democracy: and pace of lawmaking 82–4
democratic polities: symbolism and constituent power 164–6
Democratic Republic of the Congo: human rights violations 24
Deng Xiaoping 138, 139
depression 80–1
Derrida, Jacques 58–60
Dinka people 155, 156, 161
distributive justice: and formal equality 3; and mutual recognition 65–6
Dworkin, Ronald 39, 160–1, 162
dynamic stabilization: social acceleration and 74–7, 92–3
Dyzenhaus, David 110

Easterling, Keller 177
Ebola: 2014 outbreak 171–2, 183
effective-history 40
Ehrenberg, Alain 80
Eigenzeit: of law 97–9
Elias, Norbert 149
emergence: government of 173–7
emergencies: as inherently unpredictable 109–10, 110, 113, 122, 123–4
emergency imaginary 171–2
emergency laws: speed of legislating 84; v. emergency measures 120, 121
emergency measures: directives v. factual actions 195–7, 202; legal nature of 197–8; v. emergency laws 120, 121
emergency powers: and ex ante legal constraints 122, 123–4; factual actions, potentia and time 195–8; failure to constrain uses of 107–10, 194–5, 197; legal constraints and time 193–5; permanence of 195, 198–200; right to sovereign discretion 114; Schmitt's theory of 109–10, 122–4; and substance of constitution 116–19; as threat to constitution 123, 124; types 195–8; in Weimar Republic 112, 120
Emerging Infectious Diseases (EIDs) 173, 178, 179, 181
empirical feasibility of law 50
environmental law 79–80
epistemological utopia 161, 162
Eskridge, William 128
eternal law 84–5
European Charter of Human Rights 34, 49
European Convention on Human Rights 27, 54
European Convention on the Non-Applicability of Statutory Limitations to Crimes against Humanity and War Crimes 54
European Court of Human Rights (ECHR) 29, 199
European Union: constitution 133n17
executive regulations 84
expediency 10–11; as central value of law 3; justice and legal certainty 5–7; and long-term finality 65

faith: politics of 44–5
Federal Republic of Germany: constitution 27
finality: and judgment 63–6

financial crisis (2008) 82, 83, 92, 107, 109, 109n6, 122
financial regulation 81–2
finitude: and judgment 67–8
Fischl, Viktor 151
Fish, Stanley 162–3
folkways 36–8, 36n17, 49, 154–5
forgiveness 58–9, 67–8
formal equality: and distributive justice 3, 4
Foucault, Michel 187
Francot, Lyana 6n24, 9, 82n13
French Revolution 157
friend/enemy distinction 116
Fuller, Lon L. 163
functionaries: in imagined nations 155–7; in traditional societies 154–5

Gadamer, Hans-Georg 39–40, 41
Galloway, Alexander 185n56
Garapon, Antoine 7–8
Gegenwartsschrümpfung 93–4
genocide: concept 21; imprescriptibility 54; legal definition 56; in Rwanda 24
Germany: constitution 27
German Democratic Republic (GDR): Border Guard cases 199
globalization 22, 27
Gramelsberger, Gabriele 182
Gross, Oren 110
Guantánamo Bay 107n1, 108

H1N1 virus ('swine flu') 175, 176n27
Halbwachs, Maurice 152–3
Hamlet 1
Hartog, François 16
'healthy carriers' 180, 180n39
Hegel, Georg W. F. 26
Heraclites 38
Hessbruegge, Jan Arno 60
Heydrich, Reinhard 151
historical injustice 4; civil law suits 17; criminal proceedings 15–16, 17, 24; reparations 17; truth and reconciliation commissions 17, 24–5, 153
historical justice: experience of the irreparable 23–4; living with the past 27–8; and moral inversion of time 22–3; reconciliation with political condition 24–5; tragedy as tool for taming evil 25–7
historicity: evolution of 16; new order of 17–22, 27
history: discontinuous view of 18–20; liquidation of 21–2; monstrous events 20–1
Hitler, Adolf 151
Hobbes, Thomas 129, 129n7
Holocaust 15, 17, 18, 57–8
hope 50
Hua Guofeng 138
human rights violations: Democratic Republic of the Congo 24; right to truth about 62, 62n42
Hungarian Basic Law 133n17, 135–7

imagined nations: functionaries of 155–7
immediacy: nature of 192; and permanence of emergency powers 198–200; politics of 6
imprescriptibility: of international crimes 53, 55; law of 54–6; temporal dimension 60–3; and the unforgiveable 56–60
India: constitution 128
information: Bateson's concept 177–8
information technologies 177–9
institutes of national remembrance 154
instrumentalism 5–6
International Court of Justice (ICJ) 28, 55
international crimes: core crimes 53, 54, 55; imprescriptibility of 53, 55
International Criminal Court (ICC): establishment and aim 28, 56, 63; Rome Statute 54–5; trial over Ituri conflict 24
international criminal justice 22
international criminal law: as law against inhumanity 55–6
International Health Regulations (IHR) 171, 176, 179, 180
Israel: illegality of torture 195, 198–9

Jankélevitch, Vladimir 56–9
Jaspers, Karl 21n18, 25
Jellinek, Georg 37, 42
Jennings, Humphrey 151
judgment: and finality 63–6; and finitude 67–8
judicial review 193, 197
judiciary: demand for fast administration of justice 100–1; political pressure on 6
Jünger, Ernst 33
justice 7–8; distributive nature 3; and expediency and legal certainty 5–7; as formal equality 3, 4; moment of 22–8; multifaceted nature 62; as spiritual power 30–1; temporal dimension 4

Kelsen, Hans 46, 114, 115, 149
Kennedy, Ellen 114n25
Kesavanada Bharati v. State of Kerala 128
Khan, Liaquat Ali 101, 102
Kolakowski, Leszek 161
Kontingenzbewusstsein 96
Koskenniemi, Martti 63
Kosseleck, Reinhart 111n12
Krabbe, Hugo 114

labour law 81
Latour, Bruno 35–6, 174n22
law: empirical feasibility 50; ex ante and ex post 192, 193; function of 98–9; as functional decelerator 77–8; as instrument of social change 41–6; normative coherence 48; political coherence 49; radical temporality of 38–41, 42; as re-synchronizer 78–82; slowness as fundamental quality 35–8, 101–2; untimeliness of 33–4
lawmaking: pace of 82–6; temporality of different methods 102
Lazar, Nomi Claire 10, 15n1, 16n2, 17n4, 28
Leeuwarder Manifest 101n62
legal certainty 8–10; as central value of law 3; and finality 65; and foreseeability 4–5; justice and expediency 5–7, 62
legal cultures 167
legal forms: and legal change 46–50
legal interpretation: hermeneutic theories 39–40; originalism 39n41, 40; system-theoretical perspective 40–1
legal norms 46
legal policies 162
legal positivism 115, 116
legal principles 162–3
legal slowness 98; as fundamental quality of law 35–8; and relationship between law and society 100–4
legal system: internal differentiation 99, 99n53
legal temporality 38–41, 42, 174
Levinson, Sanford 144
liberal law 172, 172n12, 174, 175
Lienhardt, Godfrey 155
Lindahl, Hans 165
linear time 90
Lisbon Treaty 85
Loewy, Karin 195
Lübbe, Hermann 93
Luhmann, Niklas: on culture 159, 164; on democratic political system 75; on Eigenzeit of law 10–11, 97–8; on internal differentiation of legal system 102; on law as autonomous system 47–8; on legal temporality 174; on scarcity of time 93–4
Lyotard, Jean-François 49

MacCormick, Neil 39
Machiavelli, Niccoló 145
Madison, James 145
Mansnerus, Erika 182
Mao Zedong 138
Marquard, Odo 35, 43–4, 48
Martens Clause 61
Massumi, Brian 181
memory: politics of 62; see also collective memory
memory trials 60
metaphysical guilt 25
modernity 111n12
modificatory legislation 34, 42–3
Mommers, Sophie 6n24, 33n2
monstrous events 20–1
Munich Agreement 151
mutual recognition 65–6

natality 68
national remembrance: institutes of 154
national solidarity 156
nationalism 156
natural law 85
Nazism: and modern German Constitution 27
non-discrimination principle 27
normative coherence of law 48
Nuremberg trials 28, 29

Oakeshott, Michael 38, 42, 44–6, 49
Opitz, Sven 10–11
Orbán, Viktor 135, 136n21, 137n23
The Oresteia (Aeschylus) 26
Orgad, Liav 132, 142

pandemics: temporal politics of information 171–3
pardon 66, 67
Parsons, Talcott 162, 164
People's Republic of China: 1978 constitution 138–9; 1982 constitution

138, 139–40; Cultural Revolution 139, 140
The Plague (Camus) 26
Plato 133n15
political congruence of law 49
politics: criminal justice and 15–16
politics of faith 44–5
politics of immediacy 6
politics of memory 62
politics of scepticism 45
polity: concept of 150, 159; as imagined community 165; principles v. practices 161–4
popular sovereignty 166
positive law 5, 5n23, 85, 163–4
Posner, Eric 110
potentia 192, 196, 196n14, 198–200, 201–2
preambles: treaties 55–6; see also constitutional preambles
the present: shrinking of 93
Přibáň, Jiří 10, 40–1, 49, 50
procedural justice 60
progress 17, 19
public health security 171–2, 173–4
purposiveness of law see expediency

quarantine 172, 179–82

Radbruch, Gustav 3–4, 5, 62–3, 65
radical change: resistance to 43–6
radical temporality of law 38–41, 42
Rasul v. Bush 107n1
Rawls, John 161
'real-time' 180, 180n40
reconciliation: historical injustices 24–5; political origins of 68
Renan, Ernest 19
reparations: for historical injustice 17
restorative justice 4
Ricoeur, Paul 19, 64–6, 67
Roman calendar 139
Rome Statute 54–5
Rosa, Hartmut 8–9, 89, 90–6
Rousso, Henri 18, 19
Rule of Law: aim 48–9; Oakeshott's view of 45

SARS crisis 175, 179, 181
Saunders, Cheryl 132
scepticism: politics of 45
Schmitt, Carl 149; anti-positivist approach 121; on doctrine of inviolability 119–20; experience of revolutionary violence 112; friend/enemy distinction 115–16; on legal nature of emergency measures 120, 121, 197–8; on 'motorized legislator' 85; and National Socialism/Nazis 109–10, 116–17, 116n29; on nature of emergencies 113; on protection of constitution 116–19; on 'state of exception' 113, 114; theory of emergency powers 109–10, 122–4; and Weimar Republic 111–12, 120–1, 121n50
Schotel, Bas 11
security: criminal law as instrument of 7; see also public health security
show trials 63
simulation models 171–2, 177, 182–7
Smend, Rudolf 149
Snowden, Edward, 107n2
social acceleration: and authority of judiciary 102–4; and de-synchronization 79–84, 91–2, 96; and dynamic stabilization 74–7, 92–3; in late modern times 89–97; law as functional decelerator 77–8; law as re-synchronizer 78–82; pace of life 91, 92; social and cultural change 91, 92; systems theoretical perspective on 94–5; technical acceleration 91, 92
social change: acceleration of 91, 92; manifestations of 93
society: as imagined community 165–6
South Africa: Truth and Reconciliation Commission 17, 25, 153
sovereignty: popular sovereignty 166; and state of exception 114–15
state of exception: distinguished from state of necessity 113; and sovereignty 114–15; and suspension of laws 109
state of necessity 113
state of time-emergency 91
state sovereignty 22
Statute of the International Court of Justice 55
statutes of limitation 22, 53
Sumner, William Graham 34, 36–8, 42, 49
symbolic legislation 42, 42n55, 131n9

temporal-rhetorical construction 139
terrorism: 9/11 attacks 22, 123; perspectives on 20; as unprecedented threat;109m 109n5; war on terrorism 1–2, 4, 7, 107

terrorism suspects: detention 108; and emergency powers 109, 123; interrogation 107, 107n1, 123; torture 123
Thomas, Lindsay 180n40, 186
time: as articulation between space and world system 17, 28–30; and change 89, 89n7; conception of the flow of time 134–5, 135n19, 139; linear time 90; moral inversion of 22–3; shape of 134–5, 135n19; as specific moment 16, 22–8; as specific to modern era 16, 17–22; ways of understanding 16–17
torture 7, 123, 195, 198–9
traditional societies: functionaries in 154–5
tragedy: and taming of evil 25–7
treaties: preambles 55–6
truth and reconciliation commissions 17, 24–5, 153–4
Tushnet, Mark 110

United Kingdom: constitutional conventions 143, 144, 144n49
United States: constitution 130, 143; torture of terrorism suspects 7, 123
'unknown unknowns' 4

van Klink, Bart 8
van Roermund, Bert 67–8
Veraart, Wouter 62–3n45
veritas filia temporis 30
Vermeule, Adrian 110
von Herder, Johann Gottfried 157–8, 160
von Hindenburg, Paul 120
von Papen, Franz 121

Wald, Priscilla 180n39
war on terrorism 1–2, 4, 7, 107
Weber, Max 76, 77, 160
Weil, Simone 25
Weimar Republic 111–12, 117, 120–1, 121n50, 122–3
Weitz, Eric 111–12
Westphalian system 22, 28
Wilkes-Heeg, Stuart 144n49
Winterton, George 141, 142
Winton, Nicholas 151
Wistrich, Andrew J. 102
Witteveen, Willem 33, 33n1
World Health Organization (WHO): Department of Global Capacities Alert and Response 171; Emergency Committee 171; International Health Regulations (IHR) 171, 176, 179, 180
World War I 111, 122
World War II: shared memories of 151, 164

Yanhuang, Chunqui 132–3

Zeitnotstand 91
Zhang Qianfan 132–3
Zhang Youya 140

For Product Safety Concerns and Information please contact our EU representative GPSR@taylorandfrancis.com Taylor & Francis Verlag GmbH, Kaufingerstraße 24, 80331 München, Germany